Henry III

Matthew Lewis is an author and historian with particular interest in the medieval period. His books include a history of the Wars of the Roses, a biography of Richard, 3rd Duke of York, and two novels of historical fiction telling the life of King Richard III and the aftermath of the Battle of Bosworth. He also writes a history blog, sharing thoughts and snippets. He can be found on Twitter @MattLewisAuthor.

Henry III

The Son of Magna Carta

Matthew Lewis

AMBERLEY

First published 2016
This edition published 2018

Amberley Publishing
The Hill, Stroud
Gloucestershire, GL5 4EP

www.amberley-books.com

British Library Cataloguing in Publication Data.
A catalogue record for this book is available from the British Library.

ISBN 978 1 4456 8653 0 (print)
ISBN 978 1 4456 5358 7 (ebook)

Typesetting and Origination by Amberley Publishing.
Printed in the UK.

Contents

Introduction

King Henry III of England is a monarch who slips from the notice of history. Many famous events took place during his reign, but few would know that he was sitting on the throne at the time they occurred. He is overshadowed by events before his rule, great problems and even greater personalities during his kingship, and by the force of will that was his son and successor.

There are, however, intriguing reasons for looking deeper into the rule and personality of this elusive man. If he is remembered, it is as a poor king. Perhaps not the nasty man his father, King John, had been, but a feeble, weak-willed man who lurched from problem to disaster, with only the briefest flashes of competence that were always undone by the return of ineptitude. There are precious few moments of glory for a biographer to seize on and extol, and an equally absent sense of a vicious tyranny from which the country needed to be saved, thus leaving us without an obvious hero or villain.

Yet somewhere the sense persists that there must be more to this man and his story. He came to a throne under a level of threat that was unprecedented since his great-great-great-grandfather William the Conqueror's invasion, and he was propelled to it just weeks after his ninth birthday. His father had left a mess and an heir in no position to straighten things out. By his death at the age of sixty-five, Henry had been king of England for fifty-six years, a record not surpassed for over 600 years. How is it that a man who accomplished this apparently simple yet deeply unlikely feat is remembered only as a failure?

Henry lived and ruled through a time of genuinely cataclysmic change for England. With Henry being the first child king since Anglo-Saxon times, we will examine how this fundamental fact left indelible marks on the man that he became. Giant personalities amongst his peers, including such legendary figures as William Marshal and Simon de Montfort, impacted his reign and altered the political landscape of the Angevin Empire and of England as the two became irrevocably fractured from each other. These men, too, must have affected the king as they shaped his rule.

That this period is dominated by figures other than the king points to a weakness in his character, but the fact remains that he inherited a kingdom beyond his control, ruled it for over half a century, and handed over a crown ripe for the expansion his son, Edward I, craved. Can this really have been an accident, or did Henry possess qualities overlooked for centuries? Examples of Henry's deep devotion to the Church and passion for building still surround visitors to England today. Westminster Abbey, which draws tourists from around the world, is Henry's Gothic masterpiece, built from the ground up to his specification. Did Henry's notion of Christian piety, the Church and his position within it define his rule by restraining him, or create a legacy that can be visited 800 years later?

In many ways Henry III is an enigma. The greatest mystery of all is how he has been so forgotten amongst the great events of his own reign. By delving into contemporary chronicles and state papers, we will reveal a man who may have been let down by history.

Prologue

At Chinon Castle on 6 July 1189, King Henry II of England lay dying. He had ruled the vast Angevin Empire for thirty-five years as the founder of the Plantagenet dynasty, but by the end his sprawling domains and troublesome family were slipping out of his control. He had imprisoned his own wife, seen his oldest son die whilst in open rebellion and lost his third son to a riding accident. His second son, Richard, was in league with the King of France and rebelling against his father's tight grip on power. Only his youngest legitimate son, John, whom Henry had favoured above all others, remained loyal.

Richard had, with the assistance of Philip Augustus, King of France, been attacking and defeating his father. When Henry had been forced to offer his son the kiss of peace as part of an almost total surrender, the king was supposedly heard to whisper in his son's ear, 'God grant that I die not until I have avenged myself on thee.' In his prime, Henry had been likened to a lion in stature, aspect and ferocity, but now, aged fifty-six, he was carried to Chinon to lick his wounds. It was plain that he was dying, perhaps from a perforated ulcer, and it was equally clear that Richard would be the next king of the Angevin dominion.

Henry was the son of Empress Matilda and, through her, a grandson of Henry I and a great-grandson of William the Conqueror. His other maternal great-grandfather was Edward the Exile, son of the Anglo-Saxon warrior king Edmund Ironside. In him flowed the blood of the Normans and Anglo-Saxons. From his father he acquired the duchy of Anjou and with his marriage to Eleanor of Aquitaine he came to rule over more of what is modern France than the King of France did, and could claim authority over a strip of Europe that ranged from Northumbria in the north to the Mediterranean coast of France in the south.

All that Henry had asked for in return for his capitulation was a complete list of those who had rebelled against him. The lion finally gave up the fight when he saw the name of his beloved John at the very top of that list. The son Henry had wanted to succeed him had publicly sided with Richard when it became clear his father was losing. As the old king let go of his grip on life he was kept company by William Marshal, a man whose loyalty to the crown (perhaps rather than the wearer thereof) was already clear but whose finest moment was yet to come, and by Geoffrey, Archbishop of York, one of his illegitimate children. Gerald of Wales recorded the king's final words as 'Shame, shame on a conquered king', though another source offers more prophetic words, recording Henry telling Geoffrey, the only one of his children at his deathbed, 'You are my true son, the others, they are the bastards.'

Richard became king and is remembered as the Lionheart, a fearless warrior and able crusader but a man who spent less than a year of his decade as king within England. His capture on return from crusade all but bankrupted the country, and Philip Augustus began to flex the long-dormant muscles of France to recover territory he believed was his. Although remembered for a long time as a hero, Richard has begun to be seen as a terrible king whose negligence must in part be blamed for the troubles that followed his premature death at the siege of Châlus-Chabrol in 1199, aged forty-one and childless.

John had been prodding his brother's kingdom in his absence and now saw his chance for power. His main rival was Arthur of Brittany, son of his older brother Geoffrey, but John had him imprisoned and probably killed to remove the threat. King John struggled to impose order on a kingdom that was short of funds, an empire that was crumbling and barons who saw in the chaos the kind of opportunities that had fuelled The Anarchy, ended only half a century earlier by John's father.

King John proved an energetic administrator in his efforts to replenish the treasury but his personality grated on the country and on his barons in particular. John was wont to exercise his magisterial authority for his own gain – financial and physical. He extracted money at an unprecedented level whilst taking the wives and daughters of his barons to his bed, offending honour and financial interest in a combination and with a frequency that became intolerable. The rest is all too well known as civil war erupted once more and John was forced to put his name to Magna Carta. As quickly as he sealed it, John abandoned the imposed clauses, and had he held on to power the Great Charter might well have been forgotten by history. The revered place that it holds around the world today as a cornerstone of England's development and the basis of the Constitution of the United States of America is not due to John or the barons who imposed the settlement on him; Magna Carta owes its place in history to those who followed John.

If the personalities of Henry II, Richard I and King John led England to the brink of disaster, the return from that precipice in order to ensure the future of the nation is the story of the long rule of Henry III. The son of Magna Carta would have his work cut out for him, and the journey would be far from smooth. Henry was his father's son, but his father had lost an empire and almost the last kingdom within it. His every strength and weakness, every triumph and character flaw, would define the future of a kingdom that was all but lost even before he became king.

1

Henry of Winchester

Henry was born at Winchester Castle on 1 October 1207, the oldest son of King John and his second wife, Isabella of Angoulême. He was John's first legitimate child and therefore heir to the crown of England, though virtually all of the Angevin Empire amassed by his grandfather King Henry II, for whom he was probably named, had been lost. Henry was born into a Continental Angevin, family with strong connections to Normandy, who now had little left beyond England's shores. He was born into crisis.

John had been king for eight years by the time his son was born and he was struggling. His brother Richard had left him an empty treasury and a portfolio of territories largely neglected by their king, though he had used some competent men to try and compensate for his lengthy absences. John had been using every trick in a medieval king's repertoire in order to replenish the bare treasury and tighten his grip on the sprawling Angevin lands. In 1200, John had kept the see of Lincoln vacant for two years, enabling him to collect £2,000 of the bishopric's revenue before a replacement was appointed.

On 13 July 1205 Hubert Walter, the Archbishop of Canterbury, had died. John appears to have planned to keep this position vacant for as long as possible so that he could acquire the substantial income of England's premier see. The monks of Canterbury had other ideas and elected their sub-prior Reginald, only for John to apply sufficient pressure to cause them to set his election aside. The king ensured that his choice, John de Gray, Bishop of Norwich, was elected next when it became clear that he was not going to be able to keep the see empty. Pope Innocent III, a reformer with a strong conviction of the Church's supremacy over temporal rulers, set the election aside and proposed his own choice, Stephen Langton. Canterbury's monks were satisfied with the choice, but John resisted the imposition of papal authority in a matter for which he claimed sole jurisdiction.

Stephen Langton, who had been created a cardinal in 1206, was finally installed by the Pope on 17 June 1207. The king's furious reaction, fuelled by his indignation at the Pope meddling in affairs he considered his own, was to seize the assets of the archbishopric and refuse Langton entry into England. Such tensions between Church and Crown were not new: John's father Henry II had famously clashed with Thomas Becket, and John seemed to be following in his father's footsteps, doubtless driven hard by the infamous Plantagenet temper.

Six months after Henry of Winchester was born, England was placed under an interdict by Innocent. (The effect of an interdict was the withdrawal of religious service to the community.) With the exception of care of the dying and certain feasts, religious life was halted. Bells fell silent across the country, and the impact on the medieval mind of the removal of religious participation cannot be underestimated. The point of the stricture was to force obedience by frightening a populace who would surely fear for their immortal souls. However, it was not the populace who were at odds with the papacy.

Evidence and details about Henry's childhood, like most of his era, is frustratingly sparse. He did not travel with his father, whose itinerant court was rarely settled in one place, and probably spent his younger years with his mother. At the age of four or five, in the year 1212, he was placed under the care of Peter des Roches, Bishop of Winchester, another figure who was to prove vastly important to Henry's early years. To some extent this removal from John's frantic rule and constant motion must have offered Henry some security and, as he grew old enough to understand such things, shielded him from the worst of the opposition to John.

By 1215, Henry had four legitimate siblings. Richard was born on 5 January 1209, just fifteen months after Henry, followed by Joan on 22 July 1210. After a break of four years Isabella was born in 1214 and the family was completed by the arrival of Eleanor in 1215. By the time of Eleanor's birth John's rule was in dire straits and rapidly hurtling toward a defining moment in English history – and in the life of young Henry of Winchester.

In October 1209 Stephen Langton, the exiled Archbishop of Canterbury, excommunicated King John. In addition to the interdict still in place across his kingdom, John was now personally excluded from the community of the Church. All of the bishops of England were ordered by Pope Innocent III to leave the country, and with only one exception, Peter des Roches, Bishop of Winchester, they obeyed and vacated the kingdom. As his authority began to disintegrate, John fell out with one of his favourites, William de Braose, a major landholder in the Welsh Marches, Wales and Ireland. Arthur of Brittany had been in William's custody when he had disappeared and was presumed murdered. The precise cause of John's rift with William is unclear, and although there were debts John claimed he was owed, his persecution of William went beyond a reasonable effort to recover money.

After fleeing to Ireland, William tried to rebel with the aid of the Welsh prince Llywelyn the Great but in 1210 he was forced to flee to France where he died the following year. His wife Maud and oldest son William had been captured and imprisoned by John, who sought the extortionate sum of £40,000 for their release. Unwilling, or more likely unable, to pay, they languished in a cell until they died. According to legend, they were starved to death; when the cell was opened, their bodies were found slumped together, Maud's teeth marks visible on her son's cheek where she had tried to eat him in order to stay alive after his death. This episode marked a watershed in John's reign as his barons had their king's malice laid bare before them.

William Marshal had displayed some sympathy for de Braose, offering him a safe haven for a while, but in 1210 he returned to the king's fold and joined John's expedition to Wales against de Braose. In spite of this, Marshal attracted John's suspicion and the king demanded that he answer for harbouring de Braose. When Marshal offered to undergo trial by combat, none could be found willing to face the famous knight, even though he was now in his sixties, such was his reputation and the esteem in which he was held. This episode caused William Marshal to effectively retire to his Irish estates; baronial trust for the king evaporated.

King John worked harder and harder to extract funds. His aim was to attempt to reconquer Normandy and other territories lost to Philip Augustus – the intention was not without merit. Many English barons were still Norman in their sympathies and outlook, and most had lost land and titles as the Angevin Empire had disintegrated. A campaign to regain these lost lands and incomes would serve not only to bolster John's position but also to offer a chance of honour across the Channel, a distraction from domestic problems that John by now surely knew was not only desirable but perhaps essential.

In 1212, Innocent issued a papal bull that more formerly excommunicated John and declared him dethroned, meaning that his barons were at liberty to select another to put in John's place. All of John's subjects were absolved of their loyalty to him, yet the papacy's efforts to drag England to heel had so far all but backfired. The country had been under interdict for four years by this point and it must simply have become a fact of life. Moreover, the prohibition of appointments to religious offices meant that as more and more fell vacant and their revenue reverted to the Crown, John grew richer from the sanctions. He had tried to keep sees vacant for as long as possible before as a form of income generation, but now the Pope was doing it for him across the whole country. This increased income allowed John to plan his attempt to cross the Channel.

Innocent's latest measure did, however, allow some of the more disaffected or ambitious barons to legitimately try their luck. There was a barons' plot led by Robert Fitzwalter and Eustace de Vesci in early 1212 to murder John and drive his children from the kingdom. It is likely that some English barons eyed the throne themselves, though Philip Augustus was perhaps the most natural person to offer the realm to. Young Henry of Winchester was placed under heavy protection, and the plots were enough to drag William Marshal out of his retirement on his Irish estates and back to John's side. The attempt ultimately failed, but Henry was now being affected by his father's increasing unpopularity.

By July 1212 John had assembled a force with the intention of invading Poitou, but a fresh uprising in Wales, led by Llywelyn the Great, frustrated his plans and forced him to divert the men he had gathered to subdue the incipient threat rather than sail to France. At the beginning of the campaigning season in 1213 it was clear that Philip Augustus intended to reverse John's plans and invade England himself. Doubtless thrown into a panic, John took a monumental and desperate step that would turn around his fortunes and define England for decades to come.

On 15 May 1213, John met with Pandulf, a papal legate, and formally submitted England to papal authority, to be held thereon as a fiefdom of the papacy. John's letter to Rome, recorded in the *Brut Chronicle*, confesses 'forasmuch as we have grieved and offended God and our mother church of Rome, and forasmuch as we have need to the mercy of our lord Jesus Christ', he could not offer enough to the Church unless he took the ultimate step. John continued:

> We offer and freely grant to God, and to the apostles Saint Peter and Saint Paul, and to our mother church of Rome, and to our Holy father the Pope, Innocent the third, and to all the Popes that cometh after him, all the realm and patronages of churches of England and of Ireland, with all the appurtenances, for remission of our sins, and help of our kin's souls, and of all Christian souls, so that from this time afterward, we will receive and hold of our mother church of Rome, as fee farm, doing fealty to our holy father the Pope, Innocent the third, and to all the Popes that cometh after him, in manner abovesaid.

The effect of this submission was, as John wrote, to 'bind us, and all that cometh after us, and our heirs forevermore, without any gainsaying, to the Pope'. It was a drastic and apparently desperate step, but it also instantly transformed John's precarious position: he and England were immediately under the care and protection of the Pope. In that moment, England was converted from international pariah to the most cherished nation of one of the most powerful popes ever to rule in Rome. England would pay Rome a tribute of 1,000 marks per year, and John was required to allow the return of Robert Fitzwalter and Eustace de Vesci. In return, Philip Augustus was forbidden from launching his invasion by the Pope.

In early 1214, John was on the offensive again. This time he crossed the Channel and met with some early successes in alliance with the German Emperor Otto, the dukes of Lorraine and Brabant, and the counts of Flanders and Boulogne. The advances were cut short, though, on 27 July 1214 when Philip Augustus met the combined army, the English portion of which was commanded by William Longespée, Earl of Salisbury and John's half-brother, one of his father's illegitimate children. At the Battle of Bouvines, Philip won a comprehensive victory that has come to be seen as a pivotal moment in the development of France as a nation. It was so complete a destruction of his enemies' causes that Otto was ejected from his throne, William Longespée, the Duke of Lorraine and the counts of Boulogne and Flanders were captured, and King John was forced to agree a five-year truce in September. Atop that, he had to explain the loss of the tax income – with nothing to show for it – to his already disgruntled barons.

In January 1215 the barons, armed and in uncompromising mood, met with John. They demanded a Charter of Liberties that was based on a Coronation Charter issued by Henry I over one hundred years earlier. The reasons for harking back to this particular document are clear. Henry I, son of William the Conqueror, had taken the throne after the death of his brother, William Rufus. The arrival of the Norman kings had thrown the kingdom into turmoil, and Henry I, who married Matilda of Scotland, the daughter of Edward the Exile and a princess of the House of Wessex, shortly after his accession, showed himself far more conciliatory than his father or brother had been. This may have been a symptom of Henry's initially weak position or perhaps a genuine belief that Anglo-Saxons and Normans could not remain forever at odds, but by 1215 Henry's charter was to serve another purpose, that of bridling a king against his will.

Henry I's Charter of Liberties had pledged that 'if any of my barons, earls, or others who hold of me shall have died, his heir shall not buy back his land', with similar protections for widows and for those wishing to arrange marriages for their female kin. Henry swore to 'restore to you the law of King Edward', meaning the Confessor, and promised that his justice would not be for sale: 'If any of my barons or men commit a crime, he shall not bind himself to a payment at the king's mercy as he has been doing in the time of my father or my brother; but he shall make amends according to the extent of his crime as he would have done before the time of my father in the time of my other predecessors.' Henry I had promised to set aside the very crimes that John's barons now accused him of.

John resisted and raised the stakes further by taking the cross on 4 March 1215, pledging himself to go on crusade. This may have been an attempt to scare the barons and further ingratiate himself with the Pope, but the fact that John felt the need to take such a step shows just how precarious he knew his own position was becoming. Within two months, John was seated at Runnymede, applying his seal to the Great Charter his barons had forced upon him. Almost immediately, John tore up Magna Carta and applied to Innocent III to be released from the oaths forced on him by the barons. Innocent, seeing a challenge to and diminution of his own authority in his new fiefdom, readily agreed and condemned those who had sought to shackle their king. The papal bull issued on 24 August 1215 confirmed that John had been forced to seal a document Innocent called 'illegal, unjust, harmful to royal rights and shameful to the English people', confirming that it was 'null, and void of all validity for ever'.

In response, the *Brut Chronicle* records that the barons 'ordained amongst them the best speakers and wisest men, and sent them over the sea to King Philip of France, and prayed him that he would send Louis his son into England, to be King of England and have the crown'. Prince Louis was married to Blanche of Castile, the daughter of Henry II's daughter Eleanor and therefore niece to John. It is telling that he was viewed as a reasonable, even preferable, alternative to John, whose own heir Henry of Winchester was still just eight years old. The barons had lost patience and decided that the only answer to their complaints was to remove John, and with France resurgent, they invited the king's son to help them do their dirty work.

On 22 May 1216, Prince Louis of France landed at Sandwich in Kent. John's half-brother, William Longespée, defected to the baronial rebels; their weight of numbers posed a severe threat to John. As the king moved to Corfe Castle, his son Henry was installed at Devizes Castle, and the rebels, led by Prince Louis, stormed across the country in a blaze of success. John responded with his trademark energy and enthusiasm, uprooting his court, gathering all of his treasure and marching to put out fires wherever they sprang up. He moved through the Welsh Marches and cut east across England. Louis had taken London, meeting little opposition as he spread his influence. In July, Pope Innocent III died and was replaced by the elderly Honorius III, who committed to the pursuit of the Crusade that Innocent had wanted.

Whilst taking a shortcut across the Wash on 12 October, John lost his baggage train including much of his treasure, his holy relics and perhaps even his crown. The stresses of the last months and even years had taken their toll on John and he was stricken by the enemy of all frequent campaigners: dysentery. He struggled on to Newark, carried upon a litter as he became unable to ride or walk. By the time he reached Newark Castle he must have known that his time was up and that he was beyond physical salvation. The king wrote a will that betrayed his preoccupations and, during the night of 18 October 1216, he slipped into the arms of death as his kingdom slid from Angevin control.

2

The Marshal

The aftermath of John's death was to prove a watershed moment in English history. William Marshal, who had served Henry II, Henry the Young King, Richard I and John, had proved an unrivalled servant to the Angevin kings, even managing to walk the fine line of obedient dissent where he deemed it necessary. Although for a time he had fallen out of favour with John, it was in the king's hour of direst need that Marshal returned to his side to be welcomed with open, and probably grateful, arms. An elderly man of around seventy, Marshal nevertheless bore with him the weight of a reputation hard won and well-crafted on the tourney circuit of Europe. A biography of William Marshal entitled *L' Historie de Guillaume le Marechal* (*The History*) was penned shortly after his death and recounts the great feats of his life. The author, Jean, had access to William's closest friend and may well have been an eyewitness to some of the events of his later life. *The History* represents the first biography of a member of the knightly class and offers a distinctly secular view of the late twelfth and early thirteenth centuries, in contrast to the more prevalent ecclesiastical commentaries of the monastic chroniclers. Although it is often romantic and clearly aimed at the promotion of William's reputation, the facts are generally accurate. The speeches attributed to the personalities at many points, although not captured verbatim, probably represent the gist of what was said, perhaps with a little tweaking applied to improve the original orations. It is thanks to *The History* that we have so much detail of its subject's finest hour, a light that shone out from one of England's darkest nights.

The *Brut Chronicle* recounts a story that whilst on his travels John was staying at Swineshead Abbey when a monk delivered a poisoned cup to the king. He supposedly placed a toad within a goblet and pricked it many times, causing the foul poison within it to spread around the sides of the cup. The monk then filled it with ale and took it to the king, taking a long draught himself before passing it to John. The monk immediately took himself off to the infirmary, where he died; John fell ill, leading to his eventual death at Newark. As unlikely as this tale is, it perhaps indicates the mood within the country, that John was the problem rather the solution, even with his new-found friendship with the papacy. King John's is the oldest will of a king to remain extant today, still resting in the library at Worcester Cathedral. Although copies of his father's will and those of the Anglo-Saxons Alfred and Eadred remain, John's is the oldest original. Its most striking feature is its size. The document is small, no larger than a modern postcard, and folded into a tiny parcel. The reason for this size is given within the short text of the will.

I, John, by the grace of God king of England, lord of Ireland, duke of Normandy and Aquitaine, count of Anjou, hindered by grave infirmity and not being able at this time of my infirmity to itemize all my things so that I may make a testament, commit the arbitration and administration of my testament to the trust and to the legitimate administration of my faithful men whose names are written below, without whose counsel, even in good health, I would have by no means arranged my testament in their presence, so that what they will faithfully arrange and determine concerning my things as much as in making satisfaction to God and to holy Church for damages and injuries done to them as in sending succour to the land of Jerusalem and in providing support to my sons towards obtaining and defending their inheritance and in making reward to those who have served us faithfully and in making distribution to the poor and to religious houses for the salvation of my soul, be right and sure. I ask, furthermore, that whoever shall give them counsel and assistance in the arranging of my testament shall receive the grace and favour of God. Whoever shall infringe their arrangement and disposition, may he incur the curse and indignation of almighty God and the blessed Mary and all the saints.

In the first place, therefore, I desire that my body be buried in the church of St Mary and St Wulfstan at Worcester. I appoint, moreover, the following arbiters and administrators: the lord Guala, by the grace of God, cardinal-priest of the title of St Martin and legate of the apostolic see; the lord Peter bishop of Winchester; the lord Richard bishop of Chichester; the lord Silvester bishop of Worcester; Brother Aimery de St-Maur; William Marshal earl of Pembroke; Ranulf earl of Chester; William earl Ferrers; William Brewer; Walter de Lacy and John of Monmouth; Savaric de Mauléon; Falkes de Bréauté.

Still using titles he had long since lost, John points to his own infirmity as the reason for the hurried and brief will. It must be remembered, too, that any inventory might have looked a little scant after much of the crown jewels and an unknown quantity of treasure had sunk into the Wash. The comment does suggest, though, that this is a singular occurrence and that under more favourable circumstances the will would have been more substantial. Time, however, was not on John's side – though his will offers a glimpse of just who still was.

The papal legate, unsurprisingly, leads the list of those to whom John entrusts his wishes. Peter des Roches, Bishop of Winchester, was a powerful and loyal associate, and the bishops of Chichester and Worcester had also remained loyal; Aimery de Saint-Maur was the Master of the Knights Templar in England. The names of these spiritual men are followed by laymen, with William Marshal, Earl of Pembroke, listed first. Ranulf de Blondeville, Earl of Chester, was one of the most powerful magnates in England and represented the type of rare baron cut from the Anglo-Norman, post-Conquest mould who was, like Marshal, innately loyal to the Angevin regime as long as reward and patronage continued to flow his way. William Ferrers, Earl of Derby, had also stuck to John's cause throughout the troubles. William Brewer had been a prominent administrator within John's government, holding a number of offices as sheriff in southern counties, and Walter de Lacy and John of Monmouth were barons who had not deserted John's cause. Savaric de Mauléon and Falkes de Bréauté were soldiers, mercenaries of French and Norman origin who had been key to John's military efforts.

These thirteen men were the only ones John was able to name as his executors but, crucially, they were some of the biggest political figures in the country. Although John's personality and style of kingship had driven away many, those he had managed to keep about him were powerful men of influence, and it was upon them that John rested his only hope for the future of his sons. The will deals, in essence, with only three matters. John's concern that reparations be made to the Church and succour given to the poor may ring sharply with the avaricious and cruel man remembered by history but was little more than the traditional piety of a man seeking to ease his passage through purgatory. Other than electing to be buried at Worcester Cathedral, the only concern of the document is 'providing support to my sons towards obtaining and defending their inheritance'. That his nine-year-old son should succeed him was clearly an overriding concern to the dying king. Perhaps it represented the only hope to establish a meaningful legacy, but it is also likely that John knew failure by his appointed executors would almost certainly mean death for his two sons. He could expect no more mercy for them than he had shown his nephew Arthur of Brittany.

The choice of Worcester for his burial was in part forced upon John since Westminster Abbey was, along with the rest of London and much of the south-east, in the hands of Louis and the rebel barons. He may also have intended to be buried in the monastery he had founded at Beaulieu. However, John had links to Worcester, having spent Christmas there in 1206 and 1214, frequently enjoying the hunting in the area around Worcester. The shrine of Saint Wulfstan at Worcester may also have been a draw for John. In 1207 the king had visited the shrine of Wulfstan, who had been Bishop of Worcester from 1062 until his death in 1095 as the last pre-Conquest bishop in office. Wulfstan had been a social reformer, working against the Saxon slave trade in Bristol and focussing on the pastoral care of his diocese. He had been made a saint in 1203 by Pope Innocent, but the Angevin link extended back to John's parents. Henry II and Eleanor of Aquitaine visited Worcester Cathedral in 1158 when both of them placed their crowns on the shrine of St Wulfstan and swore never to wear them again. Worcester therefore also represented a link to John's parents and their rule, and John's son would emphasise the royal connection of the cathedral in the years that followed, as we shall see. Did guilt at his late betrayal of the father who had adored him contribute to John's decision? Perhaps, confronted by his own mortality and his sins, it represents the expression of a regret. His parents had laid their crowns at Worcester and now John would lay his head there forever.

With the king dead, it was by no means certain that any would see his wishes to fruition, either his funeral plans or the protection of his children. Louis controlled the south-east, barons in the north were in revolt, and Llywelyn the Great was using the disruption in England to expand his influence in Wales. The royalists were beleaguered on three fronts and the overwhelming majority of the barony was arrayed against them. The prospect of a child taking the throne was perhaps less than appealing, and there must have been a temptation to throw in the towel and recognise another as king. The situation bequeathed by John was not so simple, though. As Louis had swept through the south-east and the divide between the parties had become clear, each side had promised the same land to their supporters on the basis that if they could win it, it was theirs. Giving up the cause meant surrendering claims to great swathes of land and risking the positions of some of the most powerful barons in the land. Almost by accident, John had tied those loyal to him to the fortunes of his nine-year-old son.

Marshal had spent his long career amassing respect and epitomising the code of chivalry, but he could not have reached the baronage and acquired the vast lands and wealth he hoped to hand to his sons without being a political animal, too. Could he really risk all of this work on what must have looked like a lost cause? Retiring to Ireland again might well have been a strong temptation. Quite what caused William Marshal to throw dynastic caution to the wind is hard to fathom, unless it was simply the draw of the chivalric code that had dominated his life and led him to the success he had reached so far. Perhaps an inability to abandon not only an otherwise defenceless nine-year-old boy but also the dynasty he had served for virtually all of his adult life played its part in forcing him toward his decision.

The History recounts that on his deathbed, John had asked those around him 'to see that [Marshal] takes charge of my son and always keeps him under his protection, for my son will never govern these lands of mine with the help of anyone but Marshal', and it is clear that the attention of the entire royalist cause was instantly focussed on the elderly earl. Marshal had seen the political cunning of Henry II, the youthful ambition of Henry the Young King, the military and tactical prowess of Richard I, and the administrative drive of John, but he had also been witness to the worst of each of their characters. He had a strong set of examples to draw on and John may well have calculated – even from the very edge of death – that he could rely on Marshal's loyalty.

William despatched a small squad led by Sir Thomas de Sandford to collect the little king from Devizes Castle and rode to meet the boy on the road at Malmesbury. *The History* records that Henry was carried by a knight because he was so small, though it is possible that this means he was sitting on a saddle in front of a knight as he was too young to ride on his own. *The History* places in the boy's mouth the meek words, 'I give myself over to God and to you, so that in the Lord's name you may take charge of me.' Marshal replied, 'I will be yours in good faith [and] there is nothing I will not do to serve you while I have the strength', though it is unclear whether the sight of the boy hardened Marshal's resolve or caused him to doubt that such a little thing could be the figurehead of revival. Henry burst into tears and Marshal could not help but follow suit; the pair joined in grief and relief, their futures bound together. For Henry, though, the surrender of all authority and responsibility for his own cause may have set the tone for some of the problems in his future.

Together, Henry and Marshal rode to Gloucester, the most suitable place in royalist hands to stage a coronation. Plans were made swiftly and, on the eve of the coronation, a sudden, urgent question arose. The boy could not be crowned until he had been knighted, but who was there to confer this honour on the king? *The History* recalls one of the gathering offering the obvious answer:

Who should do it save he who, if we were a thousand here, would still be the highest and worthiest and bravest of all – he who has already knighted one young king – William the Marshal? God has given him such grace as none of us can attain. Let him gird the sword on this child; so shall he have worthily knighted two kings.

Marshal duly performed the knighting and all retired, prepared for the following day.

On 28 October, ten days after his father's death, King Henry III was crowned at Gloucester Cathedral in a ceremony overseen by Guala, the papal legate, who delegated the honour of performing the ceremony to Peter des Roches, the Bishop of Winchester. Henry stood before the high altar and, following the dictated words of the Bishop of Bath, he recited the traditional coronation oaths to protect the Church, deliver justice to his people and drive out evil laws and customs wherever they were found in his realm. The nine-year-old king next gave homage to the Pope on behalf of England and Ireland, vowing to maintain the thousand-mark tribute agreed by his father. Peter des Roches, aided by the bishops of Worcester and Exeter, anointed and crowned the new king. With the ceremony completed, and Henry apparently feeling the weight of the day, Peter d'Aubigné lifted the young king up and carried him back to his lodgings to change out of his heavy robes ready for the coronation feast.

The legate's presence gave the papal seal of approval to the new king's rule, and Marshal's support was squarely behind the boy, but there were many indications of the true extent of the trouble their cause faced. The very fact that the ceremony took place at Gloucester and not Westminster speaks volumes. Henry's coronation robes had to be begged and borrowed, cut down to fit him as he had none of his own and no time to have them made. The coronet that des Roches lowered onto Henry's head was a borrowed band, perhaps loaned by Henry's mother Isabella of Angoulême. Guala had excommunicated Prince Louis to prevent any member of the clergy crowning him, and the need for haste reflected the fear that Louis might be proclaimed king at any moment.

The coronation feast was a small affair, perhaps muted given the circumstances and the tiredness of the king, but proceedings were interrupted when a messenger burst in and delivered aloud to the room a desperate plea from the constable of Goodrich Castle for aid. The castle had been placed under siege by forces loyal to Louis and, most worryingly of all, Goodrich was only around a dozen miles from their current location in Gloucester. The pressing nature of Henry's predicament could hardly have been more pronounced. Here, on the day of his coronation, was a sharp reminder, if one were needed, that the enemy was all but at the gates. Even within the royalist camp all was not peace and unity. The most notable absence from the coronation was Ranulf of Chester, who had not arrived in time for the ceremony; many had called for a delay to await his arrival, but necessity had driven them to see it done. William might have been the obvious choice to lead their cause because he was on the spot, but Ranulf had at least as good a claim to the role as Marshal, and William seemed all too aware of the possibility that he might be seen as making a grab for power. According to *The History*, as the feast disbanded for the night William was asked to agree to act as the king's guardian, but he refused, telling the delegation, 'I cannot. I am old. The task is too heavy for me. Leave the matter until the Earl of Chester comes.' Was this deference genuine, for show, or did William really hope that Ranulf would relieve him of the task?

When Ranulf arrived the following morning there was a collective sigh of relief as he granted his approval for all that had been done so far. A few of his retinue seemed to wish to take offence that the coronation had taken place before their lord had arrived, but Ranulf himself brushed the criticism aside and paid homage to the new king. An early rift in the royalist camp had been avoided and they were able to turn their attention to the real work at hand. There had been no minority government in England since that of the Anglo-Saxon Aethelred the Unready, and there was no model for how the government should be handled – a question made all the more important by the disrupted nature of Henry's new kingdom. If they had casted about for some guidance, those who had been with the king's uncle, Richard I, in the Holy Land may have been able to fall back on the Assizes of Jerusalem, a set of laws for the government of the Holy Land that did have provision for the event of a minority: the relevant rule simply stated that the members of the council should elect one they felt best able to act as regent.

The History recounts the meeting that followed, preoccupied with the selection of 'a valiant man to guard King and kingdom'. Peter des Roches, Bishop of Winchester, called on a man named Alan Basset to speak, no doubt in a rehearsed bid to cut to the chase. 'By my faith!' Alan proclaimed, 'Fair sir, though I look up hill and down dale, I see no one fitted for this, save the Marshal or the Earl of Chester.' William repeated his plea of the previous evening, telling the gathering:

> I am too feeble and broken, I have passed fourscore years. Take it upon you, Sir Earl of Chester, for God's sake, for it is your due; and I will be your aid so long as I have strength in life, and will be under your command loyally to the uttermost of my power; never shall you command me aught, by word or by writing, that I will not do as well as I may by God's helping grace.

The room may well have deflated a little at this point. It was clear that Marshal was the man all desired to lead them, viewed as their only real hope, yet he offered the honour to Ranulf. The Earl of Chester was no doubt well aware of the mood and perhaps saw that Marshal protested as much to avoid the appearance of snatching at power as because of his age and the weight of the task at hand. The gathering must have buoyed again when Ranulf retorted, 'Out upon it! Marshal, this cannot be. You, who in every way are one of the best knights in the world – valiant, experienced, wise, and as much loved as you are feared – you must take it; and I will serve you and do your behests, without contradiction, in every way that I can.' It is perhaps too easy to see both men trying to pass the other a poisoned chalice, but that is far from the case. Both were tying themselves firmly to the royalist cause; the only question was who would give the orders. Chester perhaps held a small degree of social seniority but saw that Marshal's qualities and reputation were what men would follow and flock to, and he was not too proud to admit it. The qualities Ranulf listed – according to *The History*, which may have wanted those qualities listed whether Ranulf actually said it or not – were those that would have constituted a perfect king, and surely spoke to the desires and needs of a nation lacking a meaningful combination of those things for so many years.

The papal legate Guala then intervened, drawing Marshal, Ranulf and a few others into another room, perhaps fearing that a display of honourable deference could sink into disunity if it persisted in public. There is no account of little Henry being involved in these weighty discussions. The men may have felt that there was no time to indulge the boy king – although surely this kind of tense and critical negotiation should have formed a key part of Henry's education growing up in a minority. Perhaps a failure to hear the wrangling that great men undertook over weighty matters would leave a hole in Henry's experience, missing the aspect of statesmanship that allowed him to judge consequences and weigh alternative courses. Time, however, was not on the royalist side, and such niceties would have to wait. An impasse appeared to have been reached even in that more intimate and private meeting, until Guala, clearly displaying his preference in the matter, offered William full remission of all of his sins if he would take up the position. According to *The History*, William found himself unable to resist such a prize, telling the legate, 'If I am saved from my sins, this charge befits me well; I will take it, however burdensome it may be.' What amounted to a free pass into Heaven would surely have been too much for an aged soldier to pass up.

Without delay, Marshal set about enacting a plan that must have been taking shape in his mind over the days since John's death, even if he had not known whether he would be in a position to implement it. He was going to need all of the qualities Ranulf had seen in him and those he had divined in successive Angevin kings. With a pragmatism befitting Richard I, Marshal's first decision was to leave the little king behind in safety. Once more, hindsight will later see such decisions as being potentially harmful to Henry's kingly education, but in the pressure of that moment, Marshal saw clearly what must be done. 'My lords,' *The History* records him saying, 'you see the King is young and tender; I should not like to lead him about the country with me. So please you, I would seek out, by your counsel, a wise man who should keep him somewhere at ease.' William clearly intended to move quickly and did not think it the right environment for a nine-year-old boy. Had he thought back to his own precarious childhood, he may have reconsidered; Marshal had been a prisoner of King Stephen during The Anarchy for his father's good behaviour. When John Marshal turned to Empress Matilda's side, he had told Stephen that he may hang William, for he had other sons. Younger then than Henry was in the present predicament, William had been spared by Stephen's kindness and placed on the road to knightly achievement that now saw him at the head of government. He may have seen mercy in sparing Henry from hardship, but where would Marshal have been without enduring hardship of his own?

Nevertheless, all were in agreement with Marshal and left the decision of who should have responsibility for the king to the new guardian of both king and realm. A regent was traditionally a close member of the royal family entrusted during a king's absence, and it was clearly felt that this description was inappropriate. Instead, William was named official Guardian. Marshal quickly nominated Peter des Roches, the Bishop of Winchester, who had already served as Henry's tutor, offering the boy some continuity in the uncertain waters he now sailed. When news of the arrangements was made public, *The History* records that the people 'rejoiced greatly' at Marshal's appointment, but further recounts that once evening fell, darker thoughts plagued William again. With his back against a wall in the company of a few of his most trusted friend and knights, he pleaded for them to offer their advice, 'for, by my faith, I have embarked on a wide sea where, cast about as one may, neither bottom nor shore can be found, and it is a marvel if a man come safely into port'. Bemoaning their chances in the days to come, Marshal plainly told them the cause was 'like to miscarry', not least because 'the child has no possessions, worse luck, and I am an aged man'.

Emotion was high in the room as John of Earley, one of Marshal's closest friends and probably a source of the writer of *The History*, told him that, as long as he remained true to his course, his honour and reputation were secured. If all others turned to Louis and Marshal was forced to flee to Ireland, he would have done all that he could and remained loyal: 'And if a losing game could thus turn to your praise, how much greater will be your joy when you get the better of the adversary.' It was at this point that William uttered lines that have for centuries epitomised his character:

> By God's sword, your counsel is true and good, and goes so straight to my heart that if all the world should forsake the King, save myself, know you what I would do? I would carry him on my shoulders from one land to another, and never fail him, though I had to beg my bread.

The sentiment is dripping with chivalric honour, only replacing the figure of the damsel in distress with a helpless child, yet it also offers a view of the importance William placed on his reputation, almost to the point that Henry's success mattered less than the final securing of his own legacy. Whether Henry won or lost, Marshal was guaranteed a final flourish of victory in his old age. Perhaps that was the comfort an old man needed to draw him away from a warm hearth and back onto the campaign trail.

Letters were sent to sheriffs and castellans around the country ordering them to pay homage to their new king, and Guala instructed all loyal barons and bishops to attend a royal council meeting at Bristol on 11 November, a fortnight after the makeshift coronation at Gloucester. When the day arrived, what amounted to the full strength of the Church (excluding those such as Stephen Langton, Archbishop of Canterbury, who were out of the country, and the bishops of London, Salisbury and Lincoln, who were ill), turned out with all that could be raised of the baronial and knightly classes still loyal to the Angevin cause. Guala and Marshal must have worried that few, if any, would heed the call, and although their cause still looked light on support, it was an ember that they could nurture in the hope of a flame.

Guala, as the representative of Henry's overlord, the Pope, chaired the council meeting at which the actions already taken were confirmed. Marshal was formally appointed Guardian and began to sign documents written in Henry's name '*Rector nostri et regni nostri*' ('Our guardian and the guardian of our realm').

Wales was placed under interdict for its support of the barons, and Louis of France, along with all of his allies, were formally excommunicated.

This neat manoeuvre gave the royalist cause the thin sheen of a Holy Crusade and might have been inspired by Richard I's exploits in the Holy Land. If the cause appeared hopeless, what reason did men have beyond intangible notions of feudal loyalty and chivalry, which could neither secure their lands nor put bread on their tables, to offer their support? A holy mission offered them the same enticement that had secured Marshal's agreement: passage into the Kingdom of Heaven, with free rein to kill Frenchmen thrown into the deal. It seemed to work on those present, but they had already taken the greatest step toward Henry's cause simply by arriving in Bristol. The key was to win back those barons who had abandoned John for Louis.

What took place the following day, on 12 November 1216, was a stroke of political genius. It is probably the single reason Magna Carta is still recalled today rather than being a forgotten and failed attempt to secure peace. The Great Charter of the previous year was reissued in Henry's name with a few key changes. It was made known in Henry's name that he wished to see an end to the feud with the rebel barons, assuring them, 'We wish to remove it for ever, since it has nothing to do with us.' It was the first vital step in establishing distance between John's regime and the new one Marshal and Guala sought to establish for Henry. The truth was that most of the barons had taken issue with John, not the notion of kingship nor of the Angevin royal family itself. With John gone, the greatest blockage on the road to a peace that would allow Henry to keep his fragile throne was removed, and the royalist party were quick to make that very point. The most striking difference in the November 1216 reissue of Magna Carta was the removal of the 'security' clause that allowed a panel of barons to restrain the king and, if they felt it necessary, censure and punish him. This was probably the clause most offensive to John and one under which the regency government of a minor could not operate. In fact, it was simply not needed, since the king would not be exercising his will for perhaps more than a decade to come, and a degree of rule by council was probably inevitable during the minority.

Most of the clauses relating to the restriction of the imposition of arbitrary penalties, whether financial or requirements to give service, remained with only slight alterations. Protections for wardships remained, as did the pledge not to summon men from outside the forests to forest courts; that common pleas would be heard regularly at fixed locations rather than following the king around the country; and even the pledge concerning the removal of fish weirs everywhere but along the coast was retained. The clause that prevented constables seizing corn or cattle without immediate payment was adjusted to allow a deferment of payment of a maximum of three weeks if the owner lived in the township of the castle, and the prohibition on sheriffs and Crown officers using a freeman's horses or carts without his permission was amended to allow such a use subject to the payment of ten pence per day for a cart and two horses and fourteen pence a day if the cart had three horses.

In all, nineteen clauses were omitted completely in the new document, most of them relating to promised enquiries or the return of fines or land unjustly taken by John. The tactics in use are most clearly displayed in the absence of the clauses relating to the restriction of the raising of scutage (payment in lieu of military service) except for the king's ransom, the knighting of his first son, or the first marriage of his first daughter without the gathering and agreement of a counsel who would meet on a defined date to discuss the request. Along with the imposition of the council of barons to monitor the king's behaviour, this represented the most vexing restraint on royal power. Henry's minority all but negated the need for them – he was unlikely to need to be ransomed abroad as his uncle had been, and a son or daughter was a way off – and he would not be exercising his personal authority to necessitate it being checked. In fact, a baron was acting as Guardian and showing a willingness to be inclusive in his rule, so these protections were no longer necessary. The consequence of this careful balance of what remained and what was quietly redacted was the beginning of the restoration of royal authority. The 1216 Charter slipped the collar of baronial control whilst still seeking to give them victories they could hold on to.

The reissue was also a weightier promise of a longer-term commitment. It was sealed in the king's name by William Marshal, a man deeply trusted by even John's most vociferous enemies, whose word would have been enough even without his official seal. Guala also sealed the document, not only as the representative of Henry's liege lord but as a spokesman for the Pope, who had absolved John of his oath to abide by the original charter, effectively promising Rome would not undo this pact. On the one hand, this document is clear testament to Henry's weak position at the dawn of his rule and the need to give concessions to alienated men who might otherwise seek his downfall. On the other, it was a stroke of political genius. The barons had only turned to Louis because they could not deal with John or trust his word. What Marshal and Guala offered was enough of the original concessions to tempt all but the most hardcore of the rebels, and the fracturing of their unity was the first step toward a greater victory. If they had felt forced into rebellion by John's personality and his refusal to hear their demands, this document left them to question what they were still fighting against.

Although a few returned to the royalist side – the *reversi* as they were recorded in royal records – it was not an instant success. Those coming back to the king's camp were treated leniently, no doubt to encourage others, but they were slow to come. Men had tied their colours to Louis' mast and staked their future on his cause. Extricating themselves from oaths and giving up lands was not yet an attractive enough proposition. Neither was the royalist cause. Still, the aim was to destabilise the opposition, and the return of even a few demonstrated the success of the policy. The fault line simply needed to be allowed to crack further. The longer-term impact of this step was, however, utterly crucial. It is this reissue that ensured Magna Carta was not forgotten and which began its entrenchment into the fabric of what would become Western democracy, sitting eventually at the very heart of the United States' Constitution. What William Marshal, Guala and the others in the small band loyal to Henry III did was take the weapon of the enemy and turn it against them. Magna Carta had been a list of demands to be enforced on an unpopular and unruly king but was now an offer, a gesture of good faith proffered to men with whom the king wanted to be reconciled; fighting against the offer would only appear as bloody-minded and belligerent as John had been. The document sought to address issues of the Crown's relationship with the whole community of the nation, not to resolve the disputes of individuals, which was, after all, a matter for the courts. In an instant Magna Carta was transformed from a stick with which to beat a king to an olive branch, a promise from a king to his people. Therein lay the real secret of Magna Carta's long-term success: it was a compromise. It felt like a victory for the barons, but it was on the king's terms. That equivocal balance would define centuries of government extending far beyond England, and is the core of the constitutional monarchy that remains in the United Kingdom today.

Whilst the reissued Magna Carta worked its way under the skin of the rebellion, Marshal set about addressing the other problems his ward's government faced. The machinery of government, so carefully constructed by Henry II, and which had allowed Richard I a free hand abroad, had ground to a halt. The Exchequer was not bringing in money and royal justice was not being delivered or enforced. The Exchequer system of finance relied on sheriffs delivering tax income from their region to the government's central coffers. The sheriff would commit to raise an amount agreed between him and the king within the region, and twice a year the sheriff would account to the barons of the Exchequer for that income (the name of the system originates from the ten-foot-by-five-foot chequered cloth spread over a table to aid in the accounting process). If he managed to raise more than was agreed, that was his bonus to keep; the main portion was the income that fuelled government and war effort alike. At the earliest sign of trouble for the Crown, it became hard for sheriffs to collect the taxes due, harder still to deliver them to the Exchequer, and tempting for any but the most upright to pocket what they could gather – hence the reputation of sheriffs that lay behind Robin Hood's fictional but all too believable opponent. The Crown was also the fount of all justice in the land. The courts frequently followed the royal court around the country, meaning those who required access to it had to find the king. John's energetic, peripatetic style had seen the stationary courts at King's Bench in Westminster sit only erratically as he preferred to be the personal focus of justice.

The presence within the kingdom of a French prince who wanted Henry's throne posed another pressing issue. Until Louis could be removed from England, settling the young king into security would be all but impossible.

3

Saving England

On John's death, Louis had been laying siege to Dover, where the castle had stoutly held out under Hubert de Burgh as the rest of the south-east fell to the prince and the rebel barons. They held London, reaching as far west into Wiltshire as Marlborough and holding control over most of Yorkshire thanks to the northern barons. Royal resistance did stretch a long finger out from the west into the Midlands, with men loyal to John dug in at Windsor, Oxford, Buckingham, Hertford, Bedford, Cambridge, Northampton, Nottingham, Newark, Sleaford and Lincoln. In the east they retained control of the castles at Pleshy, Colchester, Norwich and Orford in enemy territory, while Newcastle-on-Tyne and Durham also held out for the king. This cut the invaders and rebels into two, but also left the royalist strongholds sandwiched between foes scrambling for their castles. Oxford, Buckingham, Hertford, Bedford, Cambridge and Northampton all lay under the control of Falkes de Bréauté, a man with no intention of turning from his former master's cause. There was something of a stalemate.

At Dover, Louis had been negotiating with Hubert for his surrender when John died. A channel of communication had been opened to allow Hubert to ask John for aid to avoid the fall of the castle, so news reached them promptly. Roger of Wendover records Louis telling Hubert 'I will enrich you with great honours and you shall be great amongst my councillors' if he would give up the castle. Hubert reportedly replied, 'If my lord is dead, he has sons and daughters who ought to succeed him,' before asking that he be allowed to consult the others within the castle. His comrades agreed that he should refuse Louis' offer 'lest by shamefully surrendering the place he should incur the mark of treason'. This was no throwaway rejection; the garrison could expect little relief before a slow decline into starvation and probable death, yet they bravely held out to remain an important thorn in Louis' side.

Warfare during the twelfth and thirteenth centuries was heavily focussed on control and besieging of castles, huge monuments to power and authority that could be used to dominate an area. Pitched battles were judged far too unpredictable and avoided at all costs, making up a tiny minority of any war effort. The growth of the tournament circuit on which William Marshal had made his name and fortune may make it seem like a practice arena for pitched battles, but in truth it served to reinforce the volatile nature of such encounters. William Marshal had risen from nowhere to be a rich and famous man. No great lord would seek to risk all he had on such a gamble, and even if a battle were won in the field, control of the castles was still the true test of power.

In the face of Hubert's valiant defiance Louis agreed to an extension of the truce, perhaps knowing he could not take Dover Castle quickly. It was this concession that had allowed Hubert to reach Gloucester and attend Henry's coronation and the subsequent discussions. It was an important act of resistance and chance attendance. Hubert was Justiciar, a role that might be roughly equated to the modern position of Prime Minister that had been in place since the reign of Henry I. The Justiciar frequently represented the king, acting as a regent when they were abroad, making them also a national equivalent to the local sheriff. Hubert had been King John's Chamberlain and, in 1215, had been appointed Justiciar, replacing Peter des Roches and leaving no love lost between the two men. Hubert was of lowly origins, his family holding small parcels of land around Norfolk and Suffolk; des Roches had arrived in England from a knightly family in Poitou and become hugely wealthy as Bishop of Winchester, though his secular and military activities always drew criticism from ecclesiastical commentators. They appeared, for the moment at least, to have lain aside their differences and found common cause in King Henry. Hubert returned to Dover, resisting Louis' attentions.

Hubert was not, however, entirely isolated at Dover. The Cinque Ports (Dover, Hastings, Hythe, Sandwich and Romney) had initially folded to Louis, but almost immediately returned to John, with a band of guerrilla warriors led by William of Cassingham hiding within the Weald of Kent and terrorising French troops. Roger of Wendover wrote of this man:

> A certain youth, William by name, a fighter and a loyalist who despised those who were not, gathered a vast number of archers in the forests and waste places, all of them men of the region, and all the time they attacked and disrupted the enemy, and as a result of their intense resistance many thousands of Frenchmen were slain.

The combination of these intransigent nuisances caused Louis to leave Dover with a group of his soldiers to loosely maintain the siege in the hope of quicker victories elsewhere. On 11 November, as the Great Council of the royalists sat down in Bristol to plan their revival, Louis arrived at Hertford Castle and began to bombard it with his siege engines. One of Falkes' men, Walter de Godardville, put up stout resistance, but on 6 December Marshal agreed to hand over Hertford and Berkhamsted castles if the men within were allowed to leave safely and a general truce be put in place. Berkhamsted's constable seemed more than happy to continue his resistance; a letter had to be sent in Henry's name on 20 December before he would give up the castle. With the expiry of this truce, another was secured by the handover of Orford and Norwich, with a further peace bought by Cambridge and either Colchester or Pleshy. Serious peace negotiations were initiated in late January when Louis gathered his council at Cambridge and Marshal brought little Henry himself to Oxford, but it seems Louis' supporters scented blood and had little intention of granting the royalists their peace. They laid siege to Hedingham before a truce was agreed that saw that castle and either Colchester or Pleshy, whichever had not been surrendered in the third agreement, given over to Louis.

Almost all of eastern England was now in Louis' hands without any serious effort on his part. The capitulations by the royalists must have given him and his rebel barons heart, though an English fleet still caused him trouble from the Channel, blocking his reinforcements and harassing ports that he held. The new gains left Louis needing more men to impose his authority effectively, and William of Coventry recorded that his allies were less than pleased when he announced to them in London that he intended to return to France to gather fresh troops. The English fleet made his route across the Channel less than easy but by the end of February Louis had sailed out of Dover and back to France, leaving his nephew Enguerrand de Coucy in command and with strict instructions to remain in London. The reality of William Marshal's manoeuvring is perhaps only easy to discern at a distance of intervening centuries and with the benefit of hindsight, neither being a luxury Louis possessed. The castles handed over by the royalists were isolated outposts surrounded by Louis' forces and well within his sphere of control. They were icons of power, but served no purpose other than to keep royalist soldiers cooped up and out of the real effort taking place. In handing them over to secure a truce, Marshal was able to gather all of his forces into one concentrated bulk whilst simultaneously stretching Louis' resources so thin that he had to leave the country to secure more men. It seems likely that Marshal's genius was to see the castles as pieces on a chess board. He had made tactical sacrifices in order to arrange his own pieces in precisely the way he wanted, and Louis had greedily snatched up the bait.

Within a week, the other benefit of the tactic paid dividends. On 5 March, after an evening spent in the Marshal's company, two of the highest-profile rebels were turned back to the royalist cause. William's own son, known as Young William Marshal, and his close friend, the king's half-uncle William Longspée, Earl of Salisbury, rode out from their meeting at Knepp to lay siege to Winchester in King Henry's name, while Marshal moved on Farnham, taking it about a week later before going to join his son and Salisbury. Marshal took over the siege at Winchester, where the town and Bishop's Castle had fallen but the town castle still held out. Taking over from the younger men, Marshal sent them to roll west through Southampton, Odiham and Marlborough, which fell only after a difficult siege. Philip d'Aubigné took Porchester back into royal hands; Chichester was regained before the end of April. Falkes de Bréauté added the Isle of Ely to this haul. These territories were carefully selected to extend the royal influence in a coherent block rather than the former patchy network whilst denying Louis access to ports on the south coast. The royalist regroupings and careful targeting of the rebel's resolve was working. Louis' decision to leave the country had proven a poor choice.

In late April, Prince Louis finally returned with fresh troops to renew his efforts, but found the landscape significantly changed. News must have been reaching him in France of the setbacks, which may have hastened his return. As he sailed into Dover on the morning of 23 April, St George's Day, he found the huts erected for the besieging force emptied of men. As he watched from the sea, a force led by one of John's illegitimate sons, Oliver, and the leader of the guerilla force, William of Cassingham, who had become known as Willikin of the Weald, ran into the town and set the huts ablaze. Louis was forced to divert to Sandwich, uncertain of what he might sail into amid the smoke and confusion of Dover. The following day, Louis rode to Dover priory to hear the full report of his losses. He immediately secured a further truce with Hubert and returned to Sandwich, which he had burned to the ground. On 25 April he set out for Winchester, meeting several of his allies en route and arriving on 27 April, only to find that it had fallen to the royalists.

When news reached Marshal of Louis' return he ordered the abandonment and destruction of all of the castles they had retaken, with the sole exception of Farnham, which held out to distract the French. It was clear that Marshal's tactics left no room for lengthy sieges that would consume manpower. What he had gained was expendable and he perhaps meant to do no more than provoke Louis. On 28 April, the French prince was visited by the Earl of Winchester, who urgently requested men to relieve the siege of his fortress at Mountsorrel. Winchester had received word from the garrison, pressed in for almost a month, that they would fall without immediate aid. Winchester petitioned Louis so passionately and relentlessly that he was sent back to London with the authority to raise men for the relief of Mountsorrel and the subdual of the rest of that region. On 1 May, this force marched out of London, but news of their approach ran ahead and by the time they reached Mountsorrel a few days later the royalist force had withdrawn to Nottingham. This would fit with Marshal's apparent tactic of avoiding lengthy engagements that he lacked the men and money to maintain. In the meantime, Louis set about rebuilding the castle at Winchester that Marshal had slighted. Once he was satisfied work was underway, he left the Count of Nevers to see it completed and returned to London, where he was immediately met by news that the garrison within Dover had breached the truce and killed some of his men. On 12 May, Louis was outside Dover Castle once more, this time watching his trebuchet being erected to begin the pummelling of the walls.

With Mountsorrel saved, the force that had headed north were able to respond to an urgent plea from Hugh of Arras to help him conclude the siege of Lincoln Castle, the last bastion of royalist resistance in the region. On the day that Louis arrived at Dover with his trebuchet, Marshal heard of the northern force's arrival at Lincoln whilst council was in session, with Henry present, at Northampton. His response, according to *The History*, was so swift and clear that it suggests his grand scheme had reached its end point:

> Hearken, loyal knights and all ye who are in fealty to the king! For God's sake hearken to me, for what I have to say deserves a hearing. This day we bear the burden of arms to defend our fame, and for ourselves and our dear ones, our wives and children, and to keep ourselves and our land in safety, and to win great honour, and for the peace of Holy Church, which these men have wronged and ill-used, and to gain remission and pardon of all our sins. Take heed then that there be no backsliders amongst us.

What Marshal proposed flew in the face of established military tactics, but he would not be deterred from a full attack on the French and rebel forces gathered at Lincoln; a pitched battle, with all won or lost in the space of a few hours.

It is likely that such a plan met with resistance because *The History* recounts that Marshal was required to make a further rousing plea.

> For God's sake, let us stake everything upon it! Remember that if we gain the victory, we shall increase our honour, and preserve for ourselves and our posterity the freedom which these men seek to take from us. We *will* keep it. God wills us to defend it! Therefore every man must bestir himself to the utmost of his power, for the thing cannot be done else. There must be no gaps in our armed ranks; our advance upon the foe must be no mere threat; but we must fall upon them swiftly. God of His mercy has granted us the hour for vengeance upon those who are come hither to do us ill: let no man draw back!

William seems to have failed to mention the fact that if they threw the dice and lost it would be the end of the royalist cause and Henry's hopes of a future, yet his assessment was probably correct. Louis had divided his force into two and they would never have a better chance to defeat them decisively than attacking one portion of his army whilst the other was far away and could be no help. The royalists could gather their full force and, if they could crush half of Louis' troops, that left only half to face. The harsh reality was that Henry's government could not sustain the prolonged sieges of castles: the passing to and fro of border fortresses might persist for years, but the royalists would run out of money and resources long before the rich Capetian prince did. In the turbulent atmosphere the papacy might withdraw its support at any moment, too. Right then, they had a chance of numerical equality, if not advantage, and the power of God's Church on their side. It was too good a chance to miss, and all of Marshal's manoeuvring over the preceding months might have been aiming for precisely this situation. Louis had been overstretched by Marshal's concessions; he had been forced to leave the country, giving men the window to return to their former allegiance, lost castles that the royalists had then slighted, and been forced to split his force, drawn north to relieve a siege that was abandoned before their arrival and placed temptingly close to Lincoln, which might have presented an apparently easy target.

With the agreement of the rest of the council, Marshal called a full muster of anyone loyal to Henry at Newark just three days later, on 15 May. Four hundred knights arrived at Newark, perhaps fewer than William might have wished for, but their number was swollen by two hundred and fifty crossbowmen and a large number of men-at-arms. Marshal and his son were joined by Ranulf, Earl of Chester, the warrior-bishop Peter des Roches, Falkes de Bréauté, two more earls and several other key figures in the royalist camp. On 19 May, the host was ready to leave. Mass was heard and Guala repeated the specific excommunication of Louis and reaffirmed the crusading nature of their venture before taking the king to Nottingham to await the outcome of the risky action. The military competence of those championing Henry's cause was clear even in their approach to Lincoln, perhaps informed, too, by Peter des Roches' understanding of the area from his time attached to the cathedral. The Fosse Way drove a straight line from Newark to Lincoln's south gate, but the north of the town was raised above the southern entrance and an attack there would have been hampered by the need to cross the River Witham at the narrow bridge and then fight uphill through the town. Instead, Marshal led the army in an arc that brought them to the north-western side of the town, where the castle stood up against the town walls.

Lincoln Castle had held out for so long through the sheer will of its castellan, Lady Nicola de la Haye. The death of Nicola's father without a son had left her hereditary castellan of Lincoln, and through two marriages she seems to have remained a strong presence. In 1191, Nicola's second husband, Gerard de Camville, left the town to support John in a dispute with King Richard's chancellor, giving strict instruction that Nicola was in charge during his absence. When the chancellor attacked the town, Nicola held the castle for more than a month before a truce was made. In 1216, before his death, John was apparently offered the keys to the castle by Nicola, then probably reaching toward her mid-sixties and pleading that she was too old for the task, but John refused and asked her to stay in her post. One of John's final acts was to appoint Nicola Sheriff of Lincolnshire, and, although this may point to a lack of reliable candidates for the king by this point, it is more likely an acknowledgment of the unswerving loyalty of the redoubtable Lady Nicola. Now a genuine damsel in distress, trapped within a castle by an evil invading army, Nicola's plight must have sung to Marshal's chivalric ideals.

By the time the royalist army arrived outside the walls, Lincoln Castle had withstood French and baronial attention for nearly three months. William sent his trusted nephew John Marshal forward to try and make contact with the castle garrison, but the lieutenant constable, Geoffrey de Serland, was already on his way out to report the state of the town to the approaching relief force. Peter des Roches then took it upon himself to make a daring reconnaissance of the town to look for a way in. He entered the castle through a postern gate in the town walls, presumably the same one used by Geoffrey but perhaps already known to Peter, and scouted out a gate in the north-west corner, above the castle, which he had probably seen was roughly blocked from the outside but clear inside. Returning to the army, a plan was settled upon. Falkes de Bréauté led a detachment of crossbowmen into the castle by the postern gate and took up a position on the castle walls. From there, between the castle and the cathedral opposite, he could look down on the besieging force and their stone-throwing machines. Next, Ranulf demanded the honour of the first charge and was allowed to lead a force to attack the barred north gate, in what must have been intended as a distraction, while Marshal and his men began the heavy work of clearing the blockade at the north-west gate.

As Ranulf attacked and the French force moved to the northern gate, Falkes' men unleashed a deadly hail of quarrels into the crowd, causing shock and panic. Emboldened, Falkes himself took a small group of men and charged from the castle's eastern gate, only to be quickly captured by the French and then freed again by his men. In the confusion, Marshal's force was afforded the time they needed to clear the gate and gain entry to the town unnoticed. Advised to wait for Ranulf to lift his attack and rejoin the army so that they were at full strength, the seventy-year-old Marshal could not be deterred from a charge, though he was reined in by a valet who pointed out that the old knight had forgotten to put on his helmet. Once properly armoured, he drove his steed fully three spear lengths into the enemy ranks and began to fight like a youth on the tournament circuit again (a tourney then being a wide-ranging mock battle rather than the formalised joust of the later medieval period).

Caught by surprise, there was panic in the ranks of the besiegers. *The History* enthusiastically boasted that a 'hungry lion never rushed on its prey so hotly as the Marshal on his foes'. The Bishop of Winchester followed him, calling out, 'God help the Marshal!', though the old knight seemed to need no assistance. Ranulf at almost the same moment finally breached the northern gate. The dice were cast and the royalist cause hinged entirely on the next few hours of close-quarters fighting.

As the royalists poured in they caught those inside the walls so by surprise that one man working a stone-throwing siege engine looked up from his work and assumed those crossing the open area were his own men. Turning back to his machine, he was about to fire when a royalist knight rode passed him and cut his head from his body. One of the English rebels, Robert of Ropsley, levelled his lance at the Earl of Salisbury, Henry's half-uncle, and shattered it on him, only for William Marshal, riding at Salisbury's side, to deliver the man such a blow that he was knocked from his horse and crawled away to lick his wounds. The leader of the French forces, the twenty-two-year-old Count of Perche, described in *The History* as 'handsome, tall and noble-looking', rallied men to him to try and hold the attackers while the rest of his force fell back. When he was finally surrounded and his surrender called for, the count, according to Roger of Wendover, swore to them that he would never give in to men of a race 'who had been traitors to their king', perhaps identifying a cultural split within Louis' force that could never properly have healed. Indeed, many of the *reversi* cited the high-handed behaviour of the French as their reason for abandoning Louis.

Reginald Croc, one of Falkes' knights, then thrust his spear at the count and caught his helmeted face. Marshal jumped down and took the reins of the count's horse, concerned that he had been hurt, only for the count to smash William on the head three times with his sword, denting the helmet he might not have been wearing but for that vigilant valet. With that, the count fell from his saddle. Presuming he had fainted, his helmet was removed, only to find that the spear had pierced his eye and gone into his brain. If a pitched battle was a novelty, the death of a member of the nobility was a source of deep shock to all. High-status combatants were taken as prisoners or ransomed; only those not worth ransoming were fair game to kill. The French forces raced down the hill to follow their comrades, only to find them regrouped at the bottom and ready to push back up the hill. The attempt was short lived, though, and the French eventually routed. Their escape was hindered by the bridge over the Witham and by an odd mechanism on the gate that caused it to close behind each man so that the next had to dismount and reopen it. At one point, a cow managed to get itself wedged in the other side of the gate and blocked their passage until it was killed and dragged out of the way. Several French and a large proportion of the rebel barons were taken prisoner, and the fleeing army was pursued, though *The History* notes that family ties probably caused the chase to be less than committed as men decided against riding down fleeing relatives.

Only three Frenchmen of note and two hundred knights made it back to London, the unfortunate men-at-arms abandoned to the vengeance of the folk of the countryside they passed through. Within Lincoln, only five men were reported as killed in the fighting, a testament to the less bloodthirsty nature of battles entered by those more accustomed to the notion of a tourney. Indeed, what is now known as the Second Battle of Lincoln was quickly referred to as the Tournament of Lincoln, later translated as the Fair of Lincoln. Marshal's gamble had paid off and, apparently without waiting to eat or refresh himself, he rode directly to Nottingham to tell the king of their victory. Despite this, in his absence the royalists sacked Lincoln and 'despoiled the whole city, even to the uttermost farthing', using Guala's order to treat the canons there as excommunicates for their opposition to Henry as an excuse to loot churches. Women gathered up their children and took to small boats, trying to row to safety, but in their inexperience many capsized and were drowned, their valuables washing up on the banks and being added to the booty. It was a disgraceful episode and it must be suspected that it would not have occurred had William Marshal stayed. To add insult to injury, Nicola de la Haye was removed as sheriff and castellan and her positions handed to the Earl of Salisbury, who further rode to Mountsorrel and took custody of it when news arrived that the French garrison there had also fled south. Nicola journeyed to the king in person to plead her case. He immediately gave her everything back, though a compromise was later agreed that gave Salisbury the position of sheriff and returned to Nicola the castle and town, though Salisbury also ensured his son was married to Nicola's granddaughter, her sole heiress. Mountsorrel was also given over to Ranulf, who had it torn down.

The royalist victory was as complete as it was shocking. At Nottingham there was uncertainty as to the next move. Some wanted to march on London, others to meet Louis and relieve Dover. Marshal decided instead to allow everyone to take stock and a breath. He sent everyone home to secure their hostages and set another muster for a few days later. When news reached Louis on 25 May he was equally shocked. After consulting with his councillors he reluctantly had his trebuchet dismantled and returned to London on 1 June to regroup. Around one hundred and fifty notable men flocked to Henry's cause over the weeks that followed Lincoln. The royalists, then at Chertsey, made contact with London to try and tempt the city back to loyalty, with a promise of a confirmation of its liberties to be given under royal seal – though the fate of Lincoln served to strike doubt and fear into the capital, too.

Louis ordered the city gates locked and a renewal of its oath of loyalty to him. The momentum of the conflict was now clearly with the royalist cause, and in early June the Archbishop of Tyre and the abbots of Citeaux, Claivaux and Pontigny arrived in England, ostensibly to preach the new crusade. Instead, they set about the task of resolving the conflict in England, perhaps at the behest of Louis' father Philip Augustus who, according to *The History,* declared Louis' cause lost on hearing Marshal had taken up young Henry's cause: 'We shall take nothing from England now; that brave man's good sense will defend the land – Louis has lost it. Mark my words! When the Marshal takes the matter in hand, we are undone.'

Several parleys took place between representatives of both sides, and a draft treaty was apparently discussed by Louis's councillors. Negotiations fell apart when Louis, quite commendably, refused to agree to the exclusion of four clerics whom Guala would not readmit from their excommunication. Unwilling to abandon even these four, Louis refused to sign up to the deal.

Caught within London, Louis began to resort to raiding outside the city for supplies, his men heading into East Anglia to steal the treasures of the Abbey of St Edmund. Louis' wife, Blanche of Castile, began to try and raise reinforcements within France and gather them at Calais, though English ships harassed and hampered the effort. By the end of June, the Earl of Warren had returned to the royalist fold, and Henry and William Marshal called a council at Oxford for 15 July, by which time the Earl of Arundel was also back with Henry. A further meeting was summoned for 6 August from which the royal host felt strong enough to divide. Guala and Henry moved toward London while Marshal and Hubert de Burgh made for the south coast to prepare for the threatened invasion by the gathering fleet. At Dover, Marshal called out the men and ships of the Cinque Ports for a muster at Sandwich. The seventy-year-old was desperate to join the fleet, but his comrades would not allow it for fear of what would happen to their cause if he was captured or killed. Apparently Lincoln had frightened them as much as it had excited and reinvigorated William. Instead, the Justiciar Hubert was given the command.

As his cause began to disintegrate, Louis made one last bid to reverse his fortunes with the aid of a famous pirate, Eustace the Monk. Eustace had been employed by John at the outbreak of war but had invaded and occupied the Channel Islands in 1205, to John's irritation. When Eustace began attacking English shipping in the Channel he was outlawed by John and turned to the French side. On 24 August 1217, Eustace headed toward Dover with a fleet and an army from Calais. As they rose on the clear morning of 24 August, Marshal and the royalists could see the fleet, consisting of around eighty ships, including ten large warships packed with some of France's finest knights and plenty of soldiers, looming in from Calais. The most notable men were to be found on the flagship with Eustace, who appeared to have control of the French armada. The English had, at best estimate, half the number of available ships and were disheartened by the sight of so many well-arrayed enemies. Many abandoned their ships for small boats as though they intended to flee. With characteristic vigour, Marshal offered to join the sailors again, but his men told him once more that he should not. Instead, he offered a rousing speech to remind them of their land-bound comrades' victory and that God was on their side, until they found heart and went back to their posts.

With the wind and tide against them, the English fleet moved out of the harbour to pursue the French as they made for the Thames Estuary. As they neared the French fleet, Hubert's lead ship suddenly veered off course and sped up. Those following copied the manoeuvre, which gave all the appearance of avoiding and slipping past the French, who hurled abuse at the fleeing English. Whether those on shore panicked or were aware of what was going on is unclear, but the English sailors had used the cover of an apparent escape to get themselves into a better position to attack. With the wind behind them, they pulled alongside the French and launched powdered lime into the air so that thick clouds blew across the French decks and blinded their crews into panic. Eustace's ship was boarded and captured along with all of its prestigious crew and cargo, including fine horses and another trebuchet. The English ships up and down the line fired crossbows into the confused French crews and ploughed into the side of their ships with their iron clad prows. In utter disarray and with their flagship captured, the French desperately turned back for home, making for Calais with the English in hot pursuit. Only fifteen of the eighty-strong fleet made it home, the others captured or sunk. Eustace was found hiding below deck and dragged up to be summarily executed, though not before a sailor had recited his list of crimes to explain their refusal to accept his offer of ten thousand marks and service to King Henry in return for his life.

Eustace's head was placed on a spear to let all know that the infamous pirate was really dead. Apparently heeding the warning of Lincoln, Marshal sent Philip d'Aubigné to relay the news of the victory to Henry and Guala while he remained behind and took control of distributing the huge amount of booty captured. The prisoners were sent to Dover Castle under Hubert's care and the treasure distributed fairly so that all men were pleased with their lot. With what was left, Marshal ordered the foundation of a hospital for the poor, named for the saint on whose day the victory had been granted, Saint Bartholomew. Louis had lost most of his English allies at Lincoln and now his reinforcements from France had been unable to reach him. He had suffered two unexpected and crushing victories on land and sea and his cause must have appeared a tattered dream. To add to his immediate problems, Guala was outside London with the other half of the royalist forces, coming as near as Kingston, though Henry seems to have been left at Windsor with his mother. There were fresh attempts at peace led by various parties, but still no agreement could be reached.

According to *The History*, safe passage was given in Henry's name for one of Louis' men to travel to Marshal's camp at Rochester. The following day that man acted as surety for the release of one of the captured French knights, who rode back to London where Louis had moved into the Tower for safety. Now Louis asked for a parley with William himself. Some demanded a siege of London but many who had fought the French saw things the same way as Marshal: the only way to end the conflict was to get Louis out of England for good, whatever the cost, 'for they would help him to the utmost of their power, with hearts and bodies and possessions'. Marshal marched to join Guala's half of their force and ordered the fleet to blockade the Thames. Louis was faced with the stark reality of making terms quickly or being starved into imposed terms, which might be considerably harsher. When Louis met Marshal and Hubert he asked them for their terms, assuring them that he would agree provided only that they should not seek to dishonour him or his companions.

It took several tense days for the negotiations to begin. When the royalists sent their terms, Louis called a council of those within London and presented the offer to them. Roger of Wendover notes that this represented the only offer from the royalists:

They, with whom the whole matter rested, and who desired above all things to get rid of Louis, sent back to him a certain form of peace drawn up in writing; to which if he consented, they would undertake to secure for him and his adherents a safe departure from England; if not, they would use their utmost efforts to compass his ruin.

The terms were final but temptingly fair. Lands and rights on both sides were to be restored to the position before Louis' invasion. All prisoners held by either side were to be released, though any ransoms already collected were to be kept. Any English subjects who had been in rebellion were to give homage to Henry and renounce any allegiance to Louis, who was to release them all from any pledge. Louis was required to write to the brothers of Eustace the Monk, still occupying the Channel Islands, and order them to surrender the land – if they failed to do so they were to be considered outside the peace this treaty would ensure. Louis was also to urge Llywelyn to give up his insurrection in Wales. To sweeten the deal further, all debts owed to Louis were still to be paid, and there was an offer of a payment to encourage his departure from England. Louis might have expected harsher terms and hurried to accept the deal.

On 12 September, the royalists arrived at one side of the Thames near Kingston and the French on the other. Louis and his council rowed to an island in the centre and were joined by the queen, legate, Marshal, the royalist council and by King Henry himself. Louis and his men swore to respect the Church and the Pope and to uphold the treaty, Louis adding an apparently voluntary promise to convince his father to return Henry's lands in France. Henry, along with Guala and Marshal, then swore to return to the rebel barons what had been theirs before the war, and Marshal offered personal security for a payment of ten thousand marks to Louis when he left England. The absolution of Louis and his men was postponed until it could be arranged properly, not least because, according to *The History*, Guala, with typical belligerence, refused to absolve Louis unless he arrived in the traditional dress of a penitent, 'barefooted and shirtless, clothed in a woolen gown', though he did concede after much pleading by Louis' men that the prince should be allowed to wear a robe over his gown to protect his honour. It was done the next day, and in those that followed the peace was repeatedly proclaimed and confirmed around the capital.

Finally, on Michaelmas Eve, 28 September 1217, Marshal watched as Louis sailed away from England. He would later be criticised for failing to exact harsher terms from Louis, but this is to miss the true crisis that Marshal was seeking to extricate Henry from. Starved of money and resources, it is astounding that Marshal was able to keep the royalist effort afloat for a year. That he was willing to risk the uncertainties of open battle at Lincoln and Sandwich is testament to the urgent need he saw to bring matters to a head rather than engage in a prolonged and unaffordable campaign of siege warfare. If the handovers of castles were deliberate and meant to stretch Louis, it surely worked, and if it was only meant to buy time then it achieved that end, too. Louis and the rebels were lured into dividing their force in two and then half was crushed. A victory on land and one at sea, neither assured by any means, won the war and saw Louis sail out of Henry's kingdom. That had been the mission and it was achieved. Louis had shown himself willing to refuse if the peace infringed his dignity or excluded any of his followers. Marshal just needed to be sure he was gone, even if it meant packing him off with bags of gold to see it done. Irrespective of later criticism, William Marshal had performed an act of heroic valour that would seal his reputation. He had saved a boy king, the Angevin throne and fought off a French invasion that had been destined for success, all at the age of seventy. He had won a war. There was only one remaining question: could the peace be won?

4

The Regency

Although the barons were treated evenly and returned to their lands, the clergy who had supported Louis were not so fortunate. These rebels came under the papal jurisdiction of Guala and did not have to be pandered to in order to secure peace. On 27 October, the legate fell upon St Paul's, whose canons had been excommunicated but cared little and had continued to preach in defiance of his ruling. He ordered all of the altars and chalices destroyed, the vestments burnt and everything replaced anew. The canons were deprived of all their offices and income and also replaced, and many of the clergy who had sided with Louis and the rebel barons were ordered to leave England by 22 March.

Two days later, on Sunday 29 October 1217, a year and a day after his coronation, King Henry III entered his capital city for the first time. William of Coventry records that the ten-year-old was 'received with glory, and fealty and homage were done to'. In the days that followed 'many discussions were held by the King's guardians and the leading men of the kingdom concerning the ordering of the realm, the establishment of peace, and the abolition of evil customs'. What followed, perhaps in an attempt to settle and reaffirm the peace, was the issue of another new version of the Great Charter. As with the first reissue under William Marshal, there were amendments and omissions: a widow's dower was now defined; the articles concerned with justice were altered to modify the make-up of panels; the time limit for payment following requisition of corn or cattle was extended from twenty-one days to forty, though carts that were the property of clerics, knights or ladies could no longer be seized at all; shire courts were permitted to sit less regularly. Although it sought to reaffirm a fragile peace, there are also traces of Marshal's steady intention to recover royal authority for Henry. One article allowed that 'Scutage shall be taken henceforth as it used to be taken in the time of our grandfather King Henry,' re-establishing the Crown's right to extract taxation but carefully ignoring the reigns of both Henry's father and uncle, harking back instead to his grandfather (scutage was a payment in lieu of military service by a knight, ostensibly to allow the hiring of mercenaries to replace the men he should have provided).

Although this issue of Magna Carta is not dated, it was most likely published on 6 November 1217 alongside a document that was arguably far more important to the people of England. The original 1215 document had tried to deal with some issues relating to the royal forests. The 1216 Charter had promised a separate document to deal with these as distinct from the political disputes with the barons. In 1217 the first Charter of the Forest was published. Royal forests covered great swathes of England at the time and were not restricted to actual forested land, but covered arable land and waterways, too. Since the conquest, kings with a passion for hunting had extended the limits of the royal forests, essentially their private property, and deprived those living in the countryside of the right to hunt, forage and gather firewood in places that had traditionally sustained their communities. Again carefully stepping back in time over the recent troubles and referring to what might by then have been considered a golden age of Angevin kingship, Henry's government used his grandfather as a template. If the Great Charter sought to balance the relationship between the king and his barons, the Forest Charter was aimed squarely at the people living across the land.

Clause 3 of the Charter stated that 'all woods made forest by King Richard our uncle, or by King John our father, up to the time of our first coronation shall be immediately disafforested unless it be our demesne wood', and Clause 9 reinstated the ancient right to graze pigs within royal forests and to keep them there overnight without penalty. Clause 10 would have been of great concern to many as it removed the death penalty for poaching deer, imposed by Richard I, with the assurance that

> no one shall henceforth lose life or limb because of our venison, but if anyone has been arrested and convicted of taking venison he shall be fined heavily if he has the means; and if he has not the means, he shall lie in our prison for a year and a day, and if after a year and a day he can find pledges he may leave prison; but if not, he shall abjure the realm of England.

This Charter represented the reversal of 150 years of erosion of the rights of free men – and it is an important distinction that it was aimed only at free men, which was around half the population of England by this point. Access to pasture, food and fuel closed off for years was suddenly reopened, and the removal of the death penalty for poaching deer marked a rebalancing of the relationship between the king and his people – a promise to punish their transgressions less harshly. The Charter of the Forest was the longest-standing statute in English law, remaining in force until 1971, over 750 years after it was enacted.

It is tempting to wonder whether this was also a part of a bigger scheme Marshal was slowly bringing to realisation. The barons had got what they wanted in Magna Carta, though he was slowly chipping away at the mechanisms that would restrict Henry's authority. With the Forest Charter he allowed the king to communicate directly with his people, rather than through the medium of feudal lords. Henry was offering his people a direct social contract with him just as the barons had been granted in their earlier charter. This would surely guarantee a swell of popular backing for the young king and place clear distance between him and his father, but it would also give the barons something to think about. If they wanted rights, others would get them too. It is unlikely that the barons entirely approved of the idea of giving back power, in however small a way, to those they had to control in order to remain in authority. The very act of giving away rights in the Forest Charter proved that those rights were Henry's to give away, no one else's. By separating the two into distinct documents, it also meant that one could be reviewed without reference to the other, and this issue of Magna Carta appears to explicitly provide for future revision. Whether the barons saw this as being to their benefit is unclear, but Marshal surely meant to leave himself a mechanism through which to transfer more power back to the king.

The revival of the Exchequer was the preoccupation of the Great Council meeting convened in London after Henry's arrival. It had ceased to function years earlier when John's control slipped and the ensuing chaos prevented it from exacting its taxes. When Marshal had tried to set it in motion the sheriffs had struggled to meet the submission deadline of November 1217 and were given until Easter 1218 to enter their accounts. The first Pipe Roll, the Exchequer account records, of Henry's reign covers the period from Michaelmas, 29 September 1217 to 29 September 1218. Significantly, it made no mention of a requirement to account for the months during which the Exchequer was closed, no doubt an admission that such a tangled mess would be too complicated to unravel, with any attempt risking the revival of problems and rivalries that must still have bubbled beneath the surface. The Great Council sanctioned a scutage tax, knowing that it was urgently needed to pay for the secured peace, and also set about re-establishing the judicial system, not least to collect oaths of fealty from across the nation.

Although Louis was gone, problems caused by the war lingered at England's borders. King Alexander of Scotland had crossed the border and taken Carlisle in the period of unrule and had refused to retreat when Marshal ordered him to in September. In early November Alexander was given an escort to bring him to meet Henry at Northampton, and the two kings met in mid-December. On 19 December, Alexander gave back Carlisle and gave homage to Henry for his English earldom of Huntingdon, the confirmation of his right to which seems to have been the lure that brought Alexander to peace. Ragnald, King of the Orkneys and of the Isle of Man, was ordered to come and pay homage to Henry in January 1218 but failed to arrive, perhaps because of the remoteness of his location, and he did not give his oath until September 1219. Equally tardy was Geoffrey de Marsh, Justiciar of Ireland, who enjoyed a great deal of autonomy in his role. Despite constant instructions to return to England not only to swear his fealty to Henry but also to report on the state of Ireland and deliver the income due from there to the Exchequer, Geoffrey delayed and pleaded that he could not leave until finally the Archbishop of Dublin was sent by Henry back from England to keep watch on Geoffrey.

Nowhere was the work of settling the peace with England's neighbours more difficult than in Wales. Llywelyn the Great had taken advantage of the fighting to expand his own influence. Many of the Marcher Lords and the Normans with property in Wales had an odd relationship with the Welsh lords and princes, frequently using them and backing one or the other in local disputes or just as often staying out of Welsh matters altogether. Guala had placed Wales under interdict because the barons based there had sided against the king and, despite efforts to bring one of the most powerful, Reginald de Braose, back into the fold, it was not until the victory at Lincoln that he could be induced to submit to Henry in return for the confirmation of his lands and titles. On 18 November 1217, the bishops of Hereford and Coventry travelled to Wales to receive the oaths of fealty from the Welsh princes and lift their excommunication. Hugh de Mortimer was amongst the barons who were then to escort the Welsh princes to meet Henry at Northampton whilst he was there to see Alexander, but the Welsh did not come. Negotiations to secure peace in Wales and a desire to make their presence felt may explain why Henry and Marshal spent Christmas 1217 at Gloucester, near to the border. A safe conduct was sent to Llywelyn in February 1218 to allow him to meet the king at Worcester. He had given his homage by mid-March, when the castles of Cardigan and Carmarthen were given into the care of Henry's 'beloved brother-in-law Llywelyn, Prince of North Wales' (Llywelyn had married an illegitimate daughter of John named Joan in 1205). On 25 May, at Woodstock, Henry received the homage of other Welsh princes, constituting those who could be cajoled to give it without a renewal of hostilities.

William of Coventry was at pains to note the almost impossible nature of subduing so many different factions with their own grievances and agendas, writing that 'it was difficult speedily to satisfy the desires of all men, and to ally in a moment the rancour of so many dissidents', yet Marshal and Henry had set about the task with vigour and found eventual success. The other challenge was to get the country off a war footing and used to peace again. There seem to have been early attempts to bring tournaments to England, because as early as October 1217, just after Louis' departure, William Marshal found himself in the hypocritical position of publicly banning tournaments, declaring in Henry's name that 'we will and ordain that this tournament be not held, for no other reason than this, that we fear a disturbance of our realm'. It seems that there was fear that tournaments might not only perpetuate the militaristic culture that had taken hold in the country but also provide a way of reigniting and settling old scores.

Another outlet seems to have been the persecution of Jews, targeted particularly by those who had been in the Holy Land. In March 1218 Gloucester, Lincoln, Oxford and Bristol were ordered to appoint twenty-four citizens to protect their Jewish communities. In a measure we may view as disturbing but which was designed to make the task of protection easier, Jews were required to wear two strips of white linen on the front of their clothes. The job of securing peace was made significantly easier when, over the months following the Treaty of Kingston, several of the leading barons, including Ranulf, left England to join Honorius III's crusade. Two of the rebel leaders, Robert FitzWalter and Saer de Quincy, took the cross, as did John's illegitimate son Oliver. The evacuation of some of the chief protagonists in the common cause of Christianity was a boon to Marshal and Henry in their efforts to settle civil matters at home.

On 2 December 1218 a new papal legate, Pandulf, arrived in London. Guala, pleading exhaustion, had submitted his resignation to Pope Honorius III, who had accepted it and appointed as his replacement the new legate, a man well known in England and who knew England well in turn, having worked with King John after his submission to the papacy and earning the trust of Henry's father. Around the time of the publication of these charters, Guala left England for other duties, and Pandulf arrived on 2 December to take up his duties. Guala was probably legitimately exhausted. His efforts had helped ensure the success of Henry's cause as much as Marshal's, not least because the papacy might have tried to assert a feudal right to the role Marshal was given; Guala likely realised that foreign interference would only have made matters worse. He operated strictly from the sidelines of the political game, supporting and advising William Marshal without seeking to dominate. He offered the weight of papal power when needed through the use of excommunication and crusading vigour and maintained his right to deal with rebel clerics, to whom he was not lenient. In two years he had done plenty and no doubt rightly felt his job was complete. The peace was for another man.

When it was known that this change was coming, no doubt combined with a knowledge that William Marshal could not sustain his own efforts indefinitely, Henry's first royal seal was commissioned from a goldsmith referred to as Walter of the Hithe, perhaps locating his workshop in London's dock area. The Close Rolls record that it was made of silver with a weight of five marks. The first document to which the seal was applied in early November 1218 was aimed at preventing its abuse but would have far-reaching and long-lasting implications. The Patent Rolls record that it was used to seal letters ordering that no grant of land or title could be made permanently during the king's minority. The measure was no doubt designed to prevent the wholesale loss of Henry's lands before he had reasserted control of them and to prevent corruption that could not be later undone. The restriction also served to keep those hoping to make their gains permanent loyal to Henry during the minority, but there was a downside too, since it necessarily denied those rewarded by the king the security many craved and which had already been in short supply for years.

Whatever the drawbacks, the preparation was shown to be prudent when, on 2 February 1219, William Marshal fell ill. According to *The History*, he travelled back to London from Marlborough 'in pain', lodging at the Tower with his wife and continuing with the business of government until mid-March, when he must have realised his end was closing in. He travelled along the Thames to his manor at Caversham, preferring to prepare for his death at a place he considered home, but he did not shirk his duty, realising that he must hand over power rather than risk a scrabble after his death. Henry and the rest of the council moved along the Thames to Reading, as close to Caversham as they could get, a clear signal of the reliance still placed on William. At Marshal's request, they all visited him at his manor and, according to *The History*, he spoke plainly to Henry:

> Fair sweet sir, in presence of these barons I wish to tell you that when your father died and you were crowned, it was arranged that you should be given into my charge, and so you were, that I should defend your land, which is not easy to hold. I have served you, I can truly say, loyally and to the uttermost of my power; and I would serve you yet, if it pleased God to enable me; but everyone can see it is not His Will that I should abide longer in this world. Wherefore it is fitting that our baronage choose someone who shall guard you and the realm in such way, if he can, as to please both God and men.

Peter des Roches, Bishop of Winchester and tutor to the king at Marshal's appointment, stood and staked his claim to the regency on the basis that Marshal had given him control of the king eighteen months earlier. William chided the bishop from his sickbed for overreaching himself in his untimely demand. Perhaps Marshal had considered the bishop's merits and might have selected him for the role, but, if so, this early play destroyed any chance he might have had, and may have caused William to realise just how much was resting upon the appointment of his successor. Two of the most powerful men in the realm, Peter and Hubert, had no love for each other, and the appointment of either might push the other into rebellion again. As his pain increased, William asked Pandulf to take the king back to Reading, promising that if they would return the next day he would name his successor. The following morning, William called his wife, his son Young William, his faithful nephew John and others of his advisors and told them of his plan, complaining that 'in no land are the folk of so many different minds as in England, and if I committed him to one, the others, you may be sure, would be envious'. With their agreement, he waited for the king and council, who appear to have gathered around his sickbed. Taking Henry by the hand, William told the legate of his decision: 'Sir, I have thought long and carefully about what we spoke of yesterday. I will commit my lord here into the Hand of God, and into the hand of the Pope, and into yours, you being here in the

Pope's stead.' His decision made and his duty discharged, William turned his attention to the boy at his side:

> Sir, I pray the Lord God that, if I have ever done anything that pleased Him, He may grant you to be a brave and good man; and if you should go astray in the footsteps of any evil ancestor and become like to such, then I pray God, the Son of Mary, that he give you not long life, but grant you to die at once.

It was a bold way to address his king, but Marshal surely by now had such a relationship with young Henry, who owed him so great a debt, that on his deathbed he might be excused such a manner. The message was blunt: don't make the mistakes your father's made or it will be the death of you. 'Amen', was the king's simple reply, accepting the advice. It is easy to believe that this message rang in Henry's ears many times in the years to come, and it is possible that Marshal's sharp reminder saved him more than once. With his life fading away, the king left William to his family. Realising that the decision had not been openly communicated, Marshal sent his son after the group to ensure that all of the barons knew his mind. Again, Peter des Roches, laying a hand on the king's head, claimed the position for himself, only to be told by Young William that it was not his to take. Pandulf stood and received the king, reproaching the bishop for his ambition.

On Tuesday 14 May 1219, in his early seventies, William Marshal, Earl of Pembroke, regent of Henry III and saviour of Angevin England, slipped from the world surrounded by his family and close friends. It was no small achievement, given the events of his long life, to end it at home, in his bed, at peace with the ones he loved. Shortly before he passed away, William's friend Aimery St Maur, head of the Templar Order in England, visited at Caversham and, apparently in fulfilment of some old promise to Marshal, performed the ceremony that made William a Knight Templar. Whether the promise was real, imagined or fabricated is uncertain, but it entitled him to a burial within the Temple Church in London where his tomb and effigy can be seen today. On 20 May, two years to the day since his monumental victory at Lincoln, William's funeral took place at the Temple Church. To try and assess which of William Marshal's virtues and which of his achievements were his greatest seems futile. His was an extraordinary life, the impact of which is best summed up by the comments passed upon him by very different men, recorded in *The History*. When William had been accused of treason to Richard I, the Lionheart had roared, 'God's feet! I have always held him for the most loyal knight in all my realm. I do not believe he has ever been false.' King John, on his deathbed, had committed his son and his realm to Marshal, saying, 'He has always served me loyally; in his loyalty, above that of any other man, I put my trust.' His reputation, even amongst those opposed to him, who might still never have wished to call him an enemy, was summed up by the French king Philip Augustus, who, when all about sought superlatives to describe William Marshal upon his death, told those gathered, 'You have well said – but what I say is that he was the most loyal man I ever knew in any place where I have been.' Perhaps the final word should go to Stephen Langton, the Archbishop of Canterbury, absent from England during the latter part of the troubles but an architect of Magna Carta in 1215. At William Marshal's funeral, the archbishop stood over his open grave and pronounced him 'the greatest knight of all the world that has lived in our time'.

5

The Legate

There can be no doubt that the death of William Marshal left a huge hole in Henry's government that had to be filled. The Marshal had proved a unifying force, willing to operate a consultative government and capable of delivering real victory and peace. A part of the reason for Marshal's success, apart from his personal reputation, had been the inclusive nature of his government. Keen to avoid the whiff of self-aggrandising tyranny and needing to unite a splintered nation, William had been forced to deliver precisely what the barons had demanded at Runnymede. They were involved in government but the model was as incompatible with medieval monarchical rule as it had been in John's reign. For now, the barons had what they wanted. The question was whether they would ever be willing to return to the autocratic, exclusive style that was inevitable when Henry came of age. Precisely when that might be was a matter of some uncertainty, but there was to be years of a minority to navigate first.

In the same month that William Marshal passed away, the truce John had secured with Philip Augustus expired. In July Honorius secured a further year of peace and Philip's condemnation of his son's invasion of England, followed in January 1220 by a four-year truce, which appears to have been negotiated in secret – Pandulf only advising Hubert as Justiciar of the plans as late as 10 January. Honorius was still concerned to pursue his crusade, and tension and mistrust between two of Europe's most important kingdoms was not conducive to getting numbers of nobles and knights to leave for the Holy Land. In England, Pandulf had the unenviable job of stepping into the Marshal's shoes. He may have been intended for the post of legate for some time, as he had been recommended to the bishopric of Norwich by John though never consecrated, perhaps because that position would have made him subservient to the Archbishop of Canterbury and compromised his papal authority. The powers previously invested in Marshal and Guala were now united in Pandulf.

The papacy no longer kept to the background during this period as Guala had done. Honorius was a passionate administrator, and in June 1219 he had been forced to leave Rome by a quarrel with some of the powerful families of the city, not returning until the following year with the aid of Frederick II, who, in return, insisted on being crowned Holy Roman Emperor. Despite what was happening in Rome, Honorius maintained a strong interest in the affairs of the papacy's most prestigious fiefdom, evidenced by the flood of letters relating to England and King Henry that poured across Europe. In January 1219 the Pope sanctioned a plan to translate the remains of St Thomas Becket from his original tomb to a grand shrine, offering an indulgence of forty days to all who assisted in the matter. In May, as Marshal's regency was ending, Honorius wrote to his legate in France, Cardinal Bertrand, to warn him of rumours that Prince Louis was planning to snatch Poitou and Gascony from Henry, authorising Bertrand to make it known that the Pope ordered the preservation of the lands of the King of England and that none could be taken from him.

In England, Pandulf was making his presence felt. In May 1219 he wrote to Hubert and Peter to tell them that 'being solicitous about the king's affairs, we direct that Walter Malclerc be joined to the sheriffs for the collection', no doubt to provide Pandulf with eyes and ears for the attempt to collect money, writing in an imperative tone 'we strictly warn and order' the Justiciar and Bishop of Winchester to make sure that it was done. This tone persisted and, on 4 July, Pandulf wrote to both men again 'strictly commanding' them to see justice done for one of his servants so that 'it may appear that you desire to procure the peace of the king and kingdom'. This may have dented the pride of both Hubert and Peter, but the first signs of what would become a crucial triumvirate in England were emerging when Pandulf added to this letter, 'We send you a copy of the letter from the king of Scotland, which we have received. When you have read it, write to us your opinion.' Later in July, the legate demonstrated his personal involvement by explaining, 'We can hardly tolerate any longer the constant complaints of Christians as to the usury practised by the Jews,' but ordering 'the said justices not to judge the above cases until we come into those parts.'

What remained of Henry's Continental possessions in Gascony and Poitou were far from secure in spite of the Pope's intervention, because the threat did not come, at least directly, from Philip Augustus – though it is not beyond the realms of possibility that the French king was happy to see the trouble erupting.

The main culprits were the de Lusignan family, who had been at odds with John for years and had not ended their feud with his death. Hugh de Lusignan the Elder had been betrothed to Henry's mother, Isabella of Angoulême, when John had taken a shine to her and whisked her away to marry him. Hugh had never forgiven the English king and, although he was now absent on crusade, his son Hugh the Younger had taken up the mantle of vengeance. Geoffrey de Neville was despatched to resolve the problems and found Hugh the Younger attacking Henry's lands and castles. Although he attempted to negotiate with de Lusignan, Geoffrey ended up writing to the triumvirate in England in terms that make no effort to disguise his frustration. Geoffrey bluntly explained that, having sought peace with Hugh the Younger, 'he answered that he would not cease from infesting your land for us or for anybody else', encouraged by the fact that 'he and others can see how poor we are both in men and money'. Geoffrey finally threatened to leave his post in exasperation, warning,

We greatly fear that unless speedy and effectual counsel be taken for the defence of your land, the said Hugh and the magnates will usurp it, and it will pass to the rule of a stranger. And we do you to wit that unless you take strong measures for its defence, we intend to set out for Holy Land on Midsummer day, for we will on no account stay here to your and our own damage and disgrace; because the said Hugh has let us know that he will not cease from molesting you until you give up the English lands of the count of Eu. For the love of God, write back quickly what you wish us to do.

Ordered to remain where he was, Geoffrey persisted in his belief that the local Gascon barons, who should have been loyal subjects to Henry, were the true danger to his lands rather than Philip Augustus. Hugh and the others, Geoffrey complained, 'make no more account of me than if I were a foot-boy', and this time threatened to return to England if he was not given firm direction and sufficient resource, concluding this letter by warning, 'Do not say that the King's land is lost through us; you are casting it away yourselves for lack of counsel.' Clearly, very real problems and threats still remained.

The year 1220 began with the extension of the truce with France for a further four years, as Pandulf had belatedly advised Hubert, but bad news from Henry's own territories kept on arriving. In March, letters arrived claiming that William Larcheveque, Lord of Parthenay, was reportedly running amok, and the burghers of La Rochelle, Niort and St Jean d'Angely in Gascony complained that William 'seizes [...] and holds them to ransom; he carries off their beasts of burden', adding that he had

> put out the eyes of the bearer of this letter, and those of two men, without any offence or fault of theirs, and though they were not even on his land when he captured them. And all this evil he does to us, so he declares, because of a hundred marks of silver which the late King promised him, and on account of a certain traitor whom you, Sir Hubert de Burgh, hanged when you were our seneschal.

The plaintiff burghers insisted that they did not want Geoffrey de Neville to return since 'our former governors have been somewhat slack in dealing with your enemies', going as far as to explain,

> When Sir Geoffrey was here, he could not protect us; he was not sufficient for these things, nor for other things either. If he were here now, he would be of no use. Send us some one more useful,

more competent to manage the country, and to provide for the welfare of its people and uphold the rights and interests of the Crown.

Hard on the heels of this report arrived news that made the problem with William Larcheveque seem insignificant. Henry's mother wrote to him, having returned home to Angoulême, that she was set to marry none other than Hugh de Lusignan the Younger. Hugh's father had died serving in the Fifth Crusade at Damietta in November 1219, and not only was Isabella planning to marry the son of her former intended who was causing Henry great trouble but she was ousting her own daughter, Henry's sister Joan, who was already in Angoulême and betrothed to Hugh the Younger. When Isabella wrote to her son to break this disturbing news she tried to give the impression of doing her son a favour, telling him,

We do you to wit that the counts of La Marche and Eu being both dead, Sir Hugh de Lusignan was left, as it were, alone and without an heir, and his friends would not allow him to marry our daughter on account of her tender age, but counselled him to make such a marriage that he might speedily have an heir; and it was proposed that he should take a wife in France; which if he should do, all your land in Poitou and Gascony, and ours too, would be lost. We therefore, seeing the great danger that might arise if such a marriage should take place, and getting no support from your counsellors, have taken the said Hugh count La Marche to be our lord and husband.

The reaction of the twelve-year-old king is not known, but Honorius wrote to Isabella insisting that she should cease from embarrassing her son. In spite of Isabella's assurance that she was working in Henry's interests, Hugh almost immediately stepped up his campaign against the king's lands, leading to a flood of complaints to the court about his behaviour.

At home there was still palpable tension. On 3 April 1220 Pandulf wrote to Hubert that he intended to be at Windsor for Easter and asked the Justiciar to meet with him there to discuss pressing matters of state. Hubert had written to Pandulf previously to make him aware that William Marshal the Younger, now Earl of Pembroke in his father's place, was fortifying his castle at Marlborough. Pandulf's response was a sharp reminder that such action was still a cause for fear and suspicion. The legate told the Justiciar, 'In regard to what you have told us, namely, that the castle of Marlborough is being fortified, we order you, without loss of time, to send royal letters to the marshal, couched in the most stringent terms you can devise, expressly prohibiting these fortifications.'

On 28 April 1220 Pandulf laid the foundation stone of Salisbury Cathedral, which today remains one of the great Gothic masterpieces of the medieval period. It is hard to discern how involved Henry was at this point in decisions about where and what to build. At thirteen years old it is perhaps likely that this early exposure to new projects and emerging idioms, and the prestige afforded to those who funded and laid foundations stones for them, influenced Henry's later obsessive love of building rather than Henry driving proceedings at this point; but it is undeniable that this century would rework the landscape of England and leave us so many jewels that we are still able, if not compelled by the same impulse, to wonder at. It had not been an easy start to the year, but the young king's government was back on an even footing, with the laying of the foundation stone perhaps meant to symbolise more than just a new cathedral at Salisbury. It was the launching point for another busy year for the teenage king.

The first sign of an issue that would dominate Henry's reign for decades to come appeared in April. Pandulf wrote to Ralph Neville, the vice-chancellor, forbidding him to leave the Exchequer for any reason, ordering him to deposit whatever money was available with the Temple Church, the home of the Knights Templar, and advising him that he was not to disperse any funds 'without our order and special licence'. Pandulf's concern from the outset with the Exchequer and the collection of funds, as demonstrated by his appointment of Walter Malclerc in May 1219 and reinforced by the stringent restraints placed on Ralph Neville, was probably only in part a reaction to the

Crown's lack of funds. It is true that the government needed money and that the systems designed to ensure the income the king was entitled to flowed to his Exchequer had broken down and needed to be patched up, but over the years and decades that followed it became clear that there was another agenda at play, too. Rome was determined to retake the Holy Land, and both Innocent III and Honorius III displayed a strong commitment to seeing it done by means of crusade. These huge military enterprises required vast sums of money and it seems likely that in 1213, when accepting England as a fiefdom of the papacy, Innocent III had envisaged plenty of funds being available from the rich Angevin lands in France and England to help fund these endeavours. Although John had promised an annual tribute of 1,000 marks, Innocent may well have viewed his protection of the deeply unpopular king as an investment that would pay dividends, capable of greatly bolstering the papal war chest. It had not happened yet, and Pandulf's interest suggests that Honorius was looking for the pay-out. He would be disappointed – but neither he nor his successors would ever give up on this theme.

On 4 May a meeting took place between Llywelyn and Henry, Pandulf, Stephen Langton, Peter des Roches and Hubert de Burgh at Shrewsbury to try and resolve the ongoing troubles caused to the English Crown by Llywelyn's successful expansionism. The meeting was cordial and productive, with Llywelyn promising to return the property of Hugh de Mortimer that he had seized. Henry instructed all of the other Welsh princes to be loyal to Llywelyn and his oldest son, Dafydd, effectively giving Llywelyn control of most of Wales as Henry's liegeman. In return for this recognition of his de facto position, Llywelyn agreed to leave Dafydd with the English court as security for his good behaviour. A precarious peace seemed to have been attained in the Marches and Wales, at least for now.

Also during May, Henry wrote to his new stepfather Hugh de Lusignan offering his approval for the marriage. It is hard to see what the young king's disapproval, which he surely felt, might have contributed other than to further enflame Hugh's hatred and encourage his bad behaviour, but this must have been an early lesson in diplomacy for the young king. He could do nothing practical to undo the union – voicing anything other than approval would only make matters worse – though he did take the opportunity to charge Hugh with returning his nine-year-old sister Joan to La Rochelle. The twelve-year-old may well have taken a lesson in biting his tongue as he congratulated his mother and Hugh, although it would remain to be seen whether the lesson would stick or leave a bad taste. Honorius was also busy on Henry's behalf in May, since he had previously instructed that the young king should undergo a second coronation ceremony at Westminster Abbey to correct the lack of dignity and poor attendance at his first. The Pope wrote to Pandulf instructing him that appropriate tutors should be put in place for Henry:

> We are wishful that our beloved son in Christ, the illustrious king of the English, should be prosperous through every temporal assistance, and ever grounded in virtue before God. We hope that this will be the case if he has for instructors men who are prudent, upright, and observers of God's law. By the authority of these letters, then, we commit to your discretion the charge diligently to cause the said king to be under the guardianship of prudent and honest men, who are with-out suspicion in their country, who may instruct him in good morals, and teach him to fear God and love his subjects. In this way, through your care and their teaching, he may visibly grow up moral and virtuous.

On 14 May Honorius wrote to the barons of England instructing them to give all of the king's castles back into Henry's keeping and charging them to give Pandulf every assistance that they could to keep Henry and the country safe. On the same day a letter was addressed to Pandulf on the same matter ordering him 'not to allow anyone in England, no matter how true and near to the king he may be, to hold more than two of the royal castles, because we do not think that it is a good thing for the king's interests'. The hint at the mistrust and tension still rife in the country is clear and Honorius was exercising caution in preventing any baron from gaining control of too many castles. On the Continent, the Pope wrote to two bishops in Poitou instructing them to inquire into a rumour that certain nobles there were stirring up trouble for Henry: if they found any truth in the story, the bishops were to immediately excommunicate the offenders,

> For since our beloved son in Christ, Henry, the illustrious king of England, is a *cruce signatus*, a ward and an orphan, specially left to the guardianship of the Holy See, we, not without reason, look upon injuries and annoyances to him as done to ourselves. We consequently desire to act vigorously against such disturbers of the peace, as indeed we are bound to do.

The term *cruce signatus* means 'one signed with the cross' and marks Henry as a crusader, even at his tender age, offering him the same particular protections that his father had taken the cross to gain.

Marking the beginning of a lifelong passion, Henry laid the foundation stone of a new Lady chapel that was to be built at Westminster Abbey on 16 May 1220, the day before his second coronation. Honorius had instructed that Henry

> should be a second time raised to the office of king, with due solemnity, according to the custom of the realm, because his first coronation, on account of the disturbed condition of his realm, had been performed less solemnly that was right and fitting, and in another place than that which was the usage of the kingdom required ...

He continued that this was to be a far better-planned and attended ceremony than the first at Gloucester. This coronation represented the first for which a full list of the royal regalia is still available, including a 'golden crown entirely adorned with divers stones', referring to the crown of St Edward the Confessor which was used that day. A set of golden spurs, a silver-gilt rod and a golden sceptre are also listed in Honorius's letter, along with a tunic and dalmatic (an ecclesiastical tunic) of red samite (a heavy silk) with a jewel and stones in the orphrey (the ornamental stripe on a dalmatic). Amongst the rest of the items was a golden ring with a ruby set in it, two golden brooches, one with a sapphire and one with a pearl, and five swords to be used in the ceremony. Simon Langton, the Archbishop of Canterbury, presided over the ceremony on this occasion; the Archbishop of York appears to have been the only notable absentee. William of Coventry recorded with delight that 'this crowning of the King was done with such great peacefulness and splendour, that the oldest men amongst the nobles of England who were present asserted that they never remembered any of his predecessors being crowned amid such concord and tranquillity'. The coronation was also to be the last to take place in Saint Edward the Confessor's Anglo-Saxon abbey at Westminster, as Henry's great love of building was to reach its zenith with the rebuilding of the great abbey erected by his favourite royal saint.

Rome's real interest in England became starkly clear just nine days after the coronation ceremony, when Honorius wrote to Pandulf to complain about the financial state of the country, clearly blaming the English Church for the king's poverty. 'Of old,' he wrote,

> The English kings were wont to be rich, not only in comparison with other kings of the earth, but beyond them all. This was greatly to their glory and honour, and that of their faithful subjects. It is not, therefore, without cause that we wonder how it is that our well-beloved son in Christ, Henry, the illustrious king of England, even though as a minor he spends less than his predecessors, is said to be in such want that he hardly ever, if ever, has sufficient to provide adequately for his royal dignity; a state of affairs which is a reproach to his people and to such a kingdom. This condition of things, to speak plainly, is imputed chiefly to the archbishop, bishops, and prelates of England.

Honorius blamed the prelates for taking possession of so many of the king's castles and manors that he was left all but destitute, and ordered Pandulf to remedy the situation without delay, 'For we cannot permit the king to be injured. We look on his cause as our own, for he is a *cruce signatiis*, an orphan, and a ward under the special protection of the Apostolic See.' It was becoming clear, though perhaps not yet to Henry or his country, that the papacy saw in England a deep chest from which they could finance the crusades to retake the Holy Land. It seems that, after seven years as a vassal state, Rome was losing patience with England's inability to provide those funds.

A busy year for the young king continued as he travelled north in June to meet with King Alexander II of Scotland. The two monarchs met on 11 June in York and, in a cordial conference, it was agreed that Alexander should marry Henry's sister Joan, though she was still in France and Hugh was dragging his heels in returning her, hoping to extract terms relating to Isabella's dower lands before handing her over. A date for the union was fixed, although when Joan was still not returned by that date, Alexander graciously offered to wait for her rather than risk the peace he and Henry had agreed when the two met again at York on 13 October the same year. The *Barnwell Chronicle* records that 'the King with his tutors perambulated his realm, to know whether those whom his father had made custodians of fortresses in England were minded to give up those fortresses quietly to himself as their lord'. The court slowly moved south from York to Nottingham, then to Leicester and on to Northampton. On 25 June they reached Rockingham Castle, in the possession of William de Forz, Count of Aumale, to find the gates locked and entry denied to them. Aumale was not inside Rockingham but appears not to have been too far away. Messages were sent to him ordering that he surrender the castle, and Falkes de Bréauté laid siege to it. Aumale requested a safe conduct to the king, and on 28 June he officially handed Rockingham and Sauvey Castles over to Henry. The episode was a demonstration that ambitious men within the country might still prove hard to divest of properties that rightfully belonged to the king, but in return Henry and his guardians had shown themselves unwilling to accept anything short of obedience. Their tactic had paid off, quickly and without a fight.

Another momentous occasion, which surely influenced the pious young king, took place on 7 July 1220 when the mortal remains of St Thomas Becket were translated from their original resting place to a new, magnificent shrine. The event had evidently been planned for some time but may have been made to wait for this year, which was the fiftieth anniversary of the murder of the former Archbishop of Canterbury during the reign of this king's grandfather. Walter the Sacrist of St Albans had been commissioned to build the stunning monument and the ceremony was attended by not only the king but the present Archbishop of Canterbury, Stephen Langton, though it was conducted by William de Joinville, Archbishop of Reims. The Prior of Christ Church had secured permission from the Pope to offer an indulgence to any who visited the shrine in celebration, and Henry, no doubt well aware of his history, may have reflected on the harm done to his grandfather by an act supposedly perpetrated in his name, even if not at his instruction. The *Crowland Chronicle* recorded of the ceremony:

> So great was the lavishness, and so munificent the bounty of the said archbishop, and so worthy to be proclaimed to the whole world, as being displayed towards all who devoutly attended the translation of the martyr, that no one then living in the flesh could remember any such solemnity being celebrated in such manner in England at any previous time.

For a deeply religious boy there were lessons to be learned as well as a saint to be celebrated.

In August 1220, the troublesome Geoffrey de Marsh, Justiciar of Ireland, was found guilty of mismanagement, though nothing more substantial could be proven against him. The triumvirate took the view that it might be better, at least for the time being, to allow Geoffrey to get away with his bad practices rather than destabilise a region which, poorly managed as it might be, was nevertheless at peace and not causing the Crown undue trouble. In the same month Stephen Langton set out for Rome to visit the Pope. It is not clear whether the true purpose of his visit was known on his departure, but his return the following year would make it clear that he had an agenda to push in the Eternal City. As Henry settled in to enjoy Christmas at Oxford, he must have reflected on a momentous and incredibly positive year in his young life and younger kingship. Although trouble in Gascony had not been fully resolved, and his own mother probably made matters worse, he had found a route to peace with Llywelyn that calmed the trouble in the Marches and Wales, found a friend in Alexander II of Scotland, who was to become his brother-in-law, undergone a second, successful and well-celebrated coronation, watched the translation of one of England's most important saints to a new shrine, and even nipped a potential military threat from the Count of Aumale in the bud. Given the troubles of previous years, it was something of an unprecedented success and demonstrated a progress in dealing with several of the major issues facing the Crown. If Henry was pleased, the triumvirate must have been overjoyed at the improvements. For all four, the pleasure was not to be savoured, not even until the end of the Christmas celebrations.

Aumale, apparently not yet over his clash with the king and his guardians earlier in the year, stormed out of the Christmas court and stomped into Lincolnshire where he set about fanning the flames of rebellion. An army was raised and sent to bring Aumale back to heel. Henry, Pandulf and Ranulf were at Bytham Castle when, on 2 February, it was surrendered by Aumale's forces and his brief flash of revolt was extinguished. Aumale himself had fled into sanctuary, though he emerged quickly to obtain Henry's forgiveness. Roger of Wendover complained that his pardon without any real punishment set 'the worst of examples, and encouraged future rebellions', though the position Henry and his triumvirate were in was a difficult one. To punish Aumale too harshly was to risk inflaming the barons again and shattering the fragile peace. Aumale had admitted his fault and it was perhaps considered prudent to allow the matter to end as quickly as it had begun. The king's party had demonstrated that uprisings could now be effectively snuffed out without needing to make more determined enemies. Following the disturbing news of Marshal's building work at Marlborough and Pandulf's insistence on its prohibition, the earl was asked to handover Marlborough and Luggershall castles, which he seems to have done on being given the hand in marriage of Henry's sister Eleanor to take the sting out of the loss.

In May, representatives were sent to the coronation of Henry's old foe Louis as joint king with his father, Philip Augustus – a practice common on the Continent but which never really took hold in England. Fifty years earlier, Henry's grandfather Henry II had twice had his eldest son, Henry the Young King, crowned as joint monarch but had found himself unable to slacken his iron grip on every aspect and corner of his empire, leading to confrontation and frustration. The Young King had predeceased his father and Henry II had not repeated the process for any of his other no less troublesome sons. On the Continent, it was viewed as a mark of the more gradual handover of power and designed to ensure the trouble-free succession of the king's chosen heir. Philip Augustus was approaching his fifty-sixth birthday and might well have considered his job complete, with the near expulsion of the Angevins from land he had long wanted to bring under the crown of France. Although he had been forced to condemn his son's invasion of England publicly, this was an equally public display of unity from the Capetian house. Henry's government sought to heal old wounds and offer a European presence that would serve to promote the stable image of the English Crown, even if that was to deliberately obscure the true situation.

Stephen Langton arrived in Rome during May to deliver a complaint to the Pope. The archbishop had spent twenty years teaching theology in Paris, the centre of European theological learning, and he had become an incredibly persuasive orator during that time, learned in the subject but also able to charm and influence with astounding success. Langton complained bitterly to Honorius about Pandulf's constant and excessive interference in England. The gist of the argument was that the weighty influence of foreigners had gone a long way toward alienating the barons under John, who hired Continental mercenaries and imported support as it dried up at home. Now, in Pandulf, England effectively had a foreign ruler acting as regent for the minor king, and Langton voiced concern that this might serve to upset the apple cart that had been so painstakingly righted. This was almost certainly, at least in part, disingenuous. As long as Pandulf was in England he represented not only supreme temporal authority as regent but a spiritual power above the archbishop's own. After years in exile and opposition to John it is likely that Langton could see no opportunity to flex his own muscles as head of the Church in

England while a papal legate could always outrank him. Langton asked a lot, though. The legate was Honorius' eyes and ears in his fiefdom and Langton was asking him to sacrifice them both. A refusal would risk antagonising a powerful and influential man.

At home, Henry celebrated Midsummer at York in order to attend the wedding of his sister Joan – finally back in England after the wrangling with his mother and step-father – to King Alexander of Scotland. Alexander was twenty-three and Joan was just approaching her eleventh birthday when they married, but it was the political significance of their union that mattered to all. Joan would pass away in 1238 without providing Alexander with any children, but their union appears to have been a relatively happy one and certainly went a long way toward binding England and Scotland more tightly together. A sign of the burgeoning confidence of the government was to be seen around the same time, in July, when the troublesome Justiciar of Ireland Geoffrey de Marsh was finally removed from office. Although he did not formally relinquish the post until 25 October, moving against him was a sure sign that the prevailing concerns about doing so just under a year earlier had been relieved.

During August, the Archbishop of Canterbury returned to England after his visit to Rome. The outcome of his efforts had reached England before him, though. The confirmation of Eustace de Fauconberg as Bishop of London on 25 February 1221 was to prove Pandulf's final official action. The Pope must have written ahead of the returning Langton to deliver his decision to Pandulf, because on 19 July Pandulf announced his resignation as legate before the bishops of Winchester, Salisbury and London, his term to end on the following Michaelmas, 29 September. Langton had secured three concessions from the Pope that the chroniclers felt important enough to comment on. Firstly, the Archbishop of York was only to be permitted to carry the cross in his own province, settling a matter of seniority in favour of the See of Canterbury. The second noteworthy news was that Honorius had agreed that he would not give any English benefice to a foreigner in succession to another foreigner. The greatest victory, though, was the removal of Pandulf. Stephen had secured a promise from the Pope that he would not appoint another legate to England during Langton's lifetime. This assured the archbishop supremacy in ecclesiastical matters in England, but he must have been conscious that it would increase his temporal power, too. Pandulf had wielded unparalleled power which also curtailed the political influence traditionally enjoyed by the Archbishop of Canterbury.

With peace in place with Scotland, Wales and France the future must have begun to look bright. The security felt at home is evidenced by the decisions of Peter des Roches and Falkes de Bréauté to undergo the ceremony of taking the cross on 19 September 1221. The ceremony had grown from rites relating to pilgrimage, since crusaders were first and foremost pilgrims. As well as the cloth cross which was to be worn on the shoulder, those taking the crusading vow were endowed with the staff and purse symbolic of a pilgrim. A handful of records of the ceremonials remain intact and most follow a similar line. The cross is blessed, bestowed on the crusader with a verse and then a series of prayers to conclude the ceremony. Crusaders were given up to three years to set their temporal affairs in order before being required to begin their pilgrimage, but for two such important men to feel able to commit to leaving the kingdom shows that matters were more settled than they had been for some time.

The end of Pandulf's role as legate does not appear to have diminished his interest in or care for the papacy's newest and most favoured territory. On 12 October, Pandulf was given a safe conduct to allow him to travel to negotiate with Isabella and Hugh de Lusignan. Henry's government was insistent that Hugh give homage to Henry for his lands but he refused to do so until the dower lands he and Isabella believed they were due had been handed over. In turn, the government refused to deliver the lands until Hugh gave homage to the king. A dangerous stalemate had set in and Pandulf was tasked with resolving it. To ramp up the pressure, all of Isabella's English lands were taken into Crown hands until her husband submitted. By April of the following year, Pandulf seems to have achieved this not inconsiderable feat, and Isabella's English lands were restored to her.

Christmas 1221 was spent at Winchester. There were riots in London, though they don't appear to have been too serious. Of more concern was a dispute that had erupted between Ranulf,

Earl of Chester, on the one side and Henry's half-uncle William Longespée, Earl of Salisbury, and the Justiciar Hubert de Burgh on the other. Quite what caused the argument is unclear but it served to demonstrate once more the fragility of the peace that had been clung onto for another year. In a demonstration of his newly won authority, Stephen Langton intervened, and his threat to 'wield the spiritual sword against disturbers of the realm and assailants of the King' worked to bring the parties to terms.

It had been another good year, but it closed as the last one had, with a stark reminder of how close civil war still remained.

6

The Rise of the Justiciar

The following year, 1222, marked a further stabilising step on the long, bumpy road to recovery. The events worthy of note during this year are a clear demonstration of the progress that had been and was being made. In April, the Archbishop of Canterbury, Stephen Langton, still perhaps buoyed by his victory in Rome, called a synod at Osney Abbey near to Oxford. The result of this meeting of the Church was a wide-ranging constitution, composed of fifty articles, designed to give form to what Langton saw as the role of the clerics under his control within the country and the society they served. The constitution was designed to give clearly defined duties to ecclesiastical roles. For example, a priest was required 'often to teach' the flock under his care, ensuring that they knew the articles of the Creed and Christian practices, without knowledge of which, the articles warned, 'faith is dead'. Archdeacons were required to make sure that the clergy of their district were well versed in the practice of their faith, as set down in Innocent III's Fourth Lateran Council in 1215. If necessary, this was to be ensured by practical testing, by having the cleric perform rites before the archdeacon. Details of the Catholic faith were to be taught to congregations '*domestico idiomate*', in the vernacular, and congregations were to be encouraged to say the Creed, the Lord's Prayer and the Hail Mary frequently. Children were to gather regularly for religious instruction. Clerics were to ensure that where possible a couple of children of higher ability were equipped to teach their peers to pray, whilst parents and heads of households were to be reminded of their duty to see to the religious education of children in their care.

The traditional, but frequently flouted, requirement of celibacy was affirmed, as was the need for both personal poverty and charity within the community. All priests and beneficed clergy were reminded that they were 'bound, according to the measure of their revenues and resources, to dispense charity and not to manifest avarice where the poor are concerned'. Priests were not to live in ostentatious estate and were warned that, if they did, 'those who abuse the patrimony of the Crucified, either by living a life of luxury or by not practising the virtue of charity, shall be punished according to the canons, when we shall have information of such people'. It was a weighty and worthy effort to put the Church's house in order after years of interdict followed by the long shadow of direct papal interference – and it is a glowing testament to Langton's towering intellect and commitment to his role. Just as importantly, it speaks, as Peter des Roche and Falkes de Bréauté's taking of the cross did, of a more settled kingdom in which issues pushed into the long grass could be retrieved and receive the attention they had been missing.

On 13 April Honorius penned a slightly odd letter to Ralph Neville, Bishop-elect of Chichester and Henry's Chancellor, advising him that the king, now aged fourteen, was to be considered to have reached the age of majority. It is not, however, clear quite what that meant in practical terms. Fourteen was not an unusual age for a step toward adulthood, though nothing was entirely clear and in the case of nobles inheriting land, majority might not be reached until eighteen or twenty-one. The stipulated age of twenty-eight was not unheard of. Peter des Roches' decision to take the cross the previous Christmas could be a sign that his tutelage of the young king was deemed to be at an end, and there were rumours that the Justiciar Hubert de Burgh was behind the marginalisation of the warrior-bishop of Winchester. Honorius may well have had an agenda in declaring Henry of age which enabled his desire for money, since if the king reached his majority he could take possession of all of his castles and their associated income. In real terms, there is little sign of Henry's hand on the tiller of government yet. That was gripped firmly by Hubert.

Less than a week after that letter Honorius despatched several others. He wrote to Philip Augustus, encouraging him to go on crusade, and simultaneously wrote to ask Henry to exempt crusaders from tolls as they travelled across England in order to ease their passage. He also wrote to Henry to suggest that the king might wish to consider joining the Holy Roman Emperor Frederick II on crusade. This seems premature at fourteen, though taking the cross allowed three years for the fulfilment of the vow and the Pope perhaps sought to bind Henry in preparation for his later teens. The Pope might well simply have been driving the crusading message home and trying to kindle a crusading ardour in the boy who would serve Rome well in years to come, not least financially. In a side note to a busy spring in religious affairs, Pandulf was finally consecrated as Bishop of Norwich on 29 May. He seems to have retained an interest and genuine affection for English affairs until his death in 1226, when he asked that his body be transported to Norwich Cathedral for burial. He doesn't appear to have held any grudge against Langton or Honorius for his abrupt removal from high office.

The only real disruption during 1222 came from the citizens of London and, troublesome though it was, it must have been a relief that it had nothing to do with the king or his barons. In its aftermath, though, there was a cruelly barbed reminder of past trouble. In the fields next to the Tower of London a friendly series of wrestling matches took place on 25 July – friendly, that is, until a team put out by the citizens were victorious against the Abbot of Westminster's steward's team. The steward was not best pleased and sought revenge in the guise of a rematch arranged for 1 August, offering the tempting prize of a ram for the victors. During the match, the steward's team produced weapons and set about the citizen's team, cudgelling them into retreat. The following day, the citizens ransacked Westminster, tearing the steward's house down. Hubert was away from the capital at the time, but Philip d'Aubigne had just returned and the abbot pleaded with him to help. The disquiet was eventually extinguished, but when Hubert was once again in London about ten days later he demanded the names of the ringleaders from amongst the citizens. Remarkably, one Constantine Olaveson stepped forward and unrepentantly claimed full responsibility. He and his nephew were hanged for their actions in the unrest, but it must have chilled Hubert to hear Constantine proudly boast that during the riots they had chanted in the streets, 'Montjoie! Montjoie! God and our lord Louis be our aid!' It was a reminder of quite how emboldened even the citizens of London, never mind the barons, had become since the First Barons' War.

Throughout the summer safe conducts were granted to Hugh de Lusignan to allow him to come to England to pay homage to Henry. Peter des Roches was sent across the Channel to escort Hugh, suggesting that there was a real belief that he might come this time. He didn't. Honorius, his patience with Hugh exhausted, ordered the publication of the excommunication he had passed two years earlier but never published. The council hurriedly pleaded with the Pope for more time, fearing that Hugh and Isabella might be pushed back into open rebellion. They were given a reprieve in an exchange that shows a mature confidence along with a willingness and ability to operate with a lighter touch than previously. They were in a position to begin to pick their battles. In the autumn there were even plans afoot to provide increased aid in the bid to gain firmer control over Poitou. In all, barring a sharp reminder of previous troubles, it had been a quiet year of gentle progress.

By February 1223 the tactic of mollifying Hugh and Isabella had paid off, and Philip d'Aubigne, with the Abbot of Boxley, had secured a truce to last until 1 August – though on 25 June Honorius threatened once again to finally publish the bull of excommunication against Hugh. Just when it must have felt like real progress was being made, Llywelyn ap Iorwerth reared up in Wales once more. Young William Marshal had been in Ireland attending to business there, and Llywelyn had used the opportunity presented by his absence to seize and destroy Kinnerley and Whittington Castles in the Marches.

During March, Henry and Hubert were in Shrewsbury to find a resolution. Ranulf, Earl of Chester, offered to act as surety for Llywelyn's good behaviour if the prince would be given time to make amends and make good the damage he had done. Although this served to postpone any hostilities, Marshal, having heard report of Llywelyn's actions, arrived in the south of Wales with a large fleet. The council swiftly dropped previous demands that Marshal hand over Caerleon Castle in order to ensure his continued loyalty. He was proving a capable enforcer for the Crown in unruly Wales, as the *Brut Chronicle* records. It tells how he took Cardigan Castle on 24 April, Easter Monday, and that 'on the Wednesday following he drew to Carmarthen, and obtained that castle also'. Llywelyn sent his second son Gruffydd 'with a very numerous army to oppose the Earl', and the two forces met at Kidwelly where they fought 'for the greater part of the day' before Gruffydd 'for lack of provision returned back to his country'. Between 6 July and 10 July Henry met with Llywelyn and Marshal at Ludlow to try and resolve the matter but, as the *Brut Chronicle* confirms, the parties could not be reconciled'. Marshal and William Longespée, Earl of Salisbury and Henry's half-uncle, marched into Wales at the head of an army. To reinforce their efforts, the sons of Gwenwynwyn, the last real ruler of Mid Wales, who had died in 1216, were brought out of Bridgnorth Castle to show them as compliant Welsh princes loyal to Henry.

On 14 July King Philip II Augustus of France died at the age of fifty-seven. During nearly forty-three years on the throne he had driven the expansion of France to absorb most of the Angevin Empire – it looked much more like the France we would recognise today at the end of his rule than it had at the beginning. Henry, approaching his sixteenth birthday, issued a demand to Philip's heir, Louis, for the immediate return of Normandy in fulfilment of Louis' vow on leaving England six years earlier. The demand was delivered by the persuasive Stephen Langton, accompanied by the bishops of London and Salisbury along with a letter of protest to the Archbishop of Reims insisting that Louis should not be crowned until he had returned the duchy. Pandulf, still supporting English affairs, lobbied in Rome, according to the *Annals of Dunstable*, for Honorius to forbid Louis' coronation, though this doesn't appear to have been achieved. Henry despatched letters patent to Normandy calling for the barons there to return to their allegiance to him 'since the opportunity is now at hand', and offering the return of English lands lost by those who remained in Normandy as a prize if they would support him. The Patent Rolls record on 9 August that the barons of the Cinque Ports were summoned to Portsmouth 'with the whole service which they owe to the King, and with their ships, with the first favourable wind, to go with the King in his service'. Wood was ordered from the southern forests and ships entering English ports were requisitioned, emptied and readied to cross the Channel.

The preparations for an invasion of France made the securing of the sure support of Hugh de Lusignan vital. Two areas in dispute, the town of Cognac and the castle at Belmont, were handed over to Hugh until Henry came of age – it was still not possible to make permanent grants, again making the papal statement that Henry was to be considered of the age of majority seem odd – subject to a requirement noted in the Patent Rolls that Hugh give an oath 'for his good and faithful service, and that he would faithfully do his utmost to advance the King's interest and procure his honour till the term before mentioned'. To reinforce this, the *Annals of Dunstable* record that the papal mandate for Hugh's excommunication was put at the discretion of two of Henry's envoys to ramp up the pressure. On 6 August 1223, before the Archbishop of Canterbury and the others arrived in Paris, Louis VIII was crowned. Henry's efforts were to no avail.

At the beginning of September, John of Brienne, titular King of Jerusalem, arrived in England to drum up men and money for a fresh assault on the Holy Land. A tax had been granted during the previous year to send toward the crusade but had not yet been collected, and it was for this that John made the journey to England, as well as for the opportunity to attract knights and barons. Henry met John at Canterbury and escorted him to London where he gave a lavish gift of four large sapphires 'than which we never saw finer' according to Matthew Paris, who also records that John, on his journey back to the south coast, left the sapphires as an offering at the new shrine of St Thomas of Canterbury. In spite of his plans, Henry had little other option than to make time to receive John even if he could not deliver the money John hoped for. He may have been a king on paper only, one looking for support to regain his lost kingdom, but he was an emblem of the Holy Land and the Pope's beloved Crusade and, even if Henry had wanted to, he could not ignore the visit. There was also an important family connection, since the father of Geoffrey, Count of Anjou, and therefore the grandfather of

King Henry II, was Fulk, King of Jerusalem, and John was the widow of Fulk's great-granddaughter Maria of Montferrat. John's heir was Maria's daughter Isabella II, making Henry and Isabella third cousins, and giving the plight of Jerusalem a personal edge that made it even harder to ignore.

On 12 September Henry was forced to divert his military efforts from the south coast and set a muster for Gloucester when an urgent plea arrived from Reginald de Braose. He had been besieged at Builth Castle by Llywelyn, who perhaps saw in Henry's preparations to travel abroad another opportunity to press his own cause. The approach of Henry's army was enough to cause Llywelyn to abandon the siege and withdraw from Builth. By 23 September Henry was back in Hereford, before he and Hubert led their army north along the Marches through Leominster and Shrewsbury before turning west into Llywelyn's heartland. Montgomery Castle was swiftly snatched from Llywelyn, and Stephen Langton excommunicated the Welsh prince. The pressure paid off quickly, and on 8 October, encouraged by Ranulf, Llywelyn arrived at Montgomery to submit to Henry and receive absolution from the archbishop.

With his plans to take an army into France derailed, Henry sent Pandulf, John of Ely, Philip d'Aubigne and Richard de Rivers to France to obtain a final answer from Louis on the issue of the lands Henry claimed as his by right. They were also tasked with trying to extend the truce that was due to end in April 1224, suggesting that Henry and his council were beginning to accept that it might be a leap too far to make a serious military attempt on lands outside the kingdom whilst the interior remained only delicately at peace. Louis replied to the envoys that he considered the lands formerly making up the Angevin Empire now legally the property of the French Crown and saw no reason to give them to Henry. Louis also instructed emissaries to return to England with the threat that, at the first available opportunity, he fully intended to invade England again and press his own claim there on the basis that the Pope had taken the crown, which had been offered to Louis by the English barons, from John. It is not clear whether this was a genuine threat by Louis, though it seems unlikely whilst Henry remained the Pope's favourite son. It seems more likely that Louis was posturing and warning Henry that if he was thinking of attacking Louis he would end up regretting it. If Henry persisted in claiming land Louis now considered firmly and legally his, then Louis would claim Henry's in return.

In April 1223, Honorius had written to Peter des Roches, Hubert de Burgh and William Brewer to clarify the previous year's declaration that Henry was to be considered of age. The king, Honorius explained, 'ought no longer to be debarred from disposing usefully and prudently of his realm and its affairs' and his guardians were to give him 'free and unfettered disposal of his kingdom, resign to him without any difficulty the lands and castles of his which they held in wardenship, and procure a like resignation of all Crown lands and castles similarly held by other persons'. Ranulf received a similar letter, and the vice-chancellor was instructed to use the royal seal at the instruction of Henry and no one else from that moment on. The king was still prevented from making gifts in perpetuity so this could only be considered a partial coming of age, which might seem odd still unless seen in the light of the papal desire for funds from England. By allowing Henry to retake possession of castles that had been held by others during his minority his income would be significantly increased and his ability to contribute to Honorius' plans equally improved. It seems that the Pope was growing tired of waiting for the river of gold he believed existed in England to begin flowing to Rome, but his measure caused only more trouble for the young king.

Henry instructed that Hereford and Gloucester Castles be handed over to Hubert. There was outrage. Ranulf, Gilbert de Clare, Earl of Gloucester, William, Count of Aumale, Falkes de Bréauté, Robert de Vipont, John de Lacy, Peter de Mauley, Philip Marc, Engelard de Cigone, William de Cantelupe and many others were deeply unhappy at the move. Hubert was becoming more and more unpopular as he became more influential at the centre of Henry's hybrid government. As the tension escalated Hubert took Henry to Gloucester Castle, apparently having convinced him that the angry barons were planning to attack him. The lords vented their frustration by attacking the Tower of London, so that by 28 November Henry and Hubert were back in the capital to meet with the aggravated men and settle the issue. The talks descended into chaos as Peter and Hubert vociferously blamed each other; Peter stormed out, followed by Ranulf and his party. It was far from ideal, though there was no lasting fallout since the sting was taken out of the argument when a reply came from Honorius, dated 20 November but which probably arrived in England a couple of weeks after the meeting. Henry had written before the meeting with des Roches and the others to ask Honorius whether it was possible for those ordered by the Pope to hand over their castles immediately to retain them if Henry trusted them and wished it. Honorius seems to have realised the effect his order was likely to have had and took a step backward in order to preserve peace. He wrote:

We have been humbly asked on your behalf (the following difficulty): Certain letters have been received from us, by which we ordered our venerable brother, the bishop of Winchester, and our beloved sons, Ralph, earl of Chester, Hubert de Burgh, Justiciar, and Falkes de Bréauté, to surrender their charges and their care of the royal castles into your hands; but because occasion of discord may arise from this command, since, like faithful subjects, they are ready, on a proper occasion, to give an account of their stewardship, and since there are no hands to which these charges may be more safely committed, will we allow this order in their regard to remain void. Now, seeing that the said letters were issued for your benefit, and asked for and granted for that end, you should not be compelled to act upon them. But, lest it should seem that they were issued without consideration, we conclude not to withdraw them further than to declare that they need not be acted upon against your will.

Henry had been granted the option of respite from more conflict and was entitled, though not compelled, to leave castles in the hands of men he trusted if he so wished. It is an important marker of Henry's move toward governmental maturity, at least in the eyes of the Pope, that he was permitted to use or ignore Honorius' letters of authority. He was now being given permission to act as he pleased rather than his guardians being compelled to do as Rome said. Between Henry's temporal and Langton's spiritual freedom, 1223 might have appeared to mark a year that slackened the restrictive bindings of papal authority, but it remained to be seen what might happen if Church or Crown were to attempt anything to which the Pope was strongly opposed.

In November there appears to have been a baronial plot to remove Hubert de Burgh, his unpopularity swelling along with his influence. Henry returned from Wales to London on hearing of the plot, and it soon evaporated, though some barons approached Henry directly to request Hubert's removal. The king refused – Hubert's unassailable position was made crystal clear. On 18 December the king, now just past his sixteenth birthday, penned a pleasant and friendly letter to the Pope ruminating on the benefits their relationship had brought him as a boy. 'By means of the many benefits conferred by your great affection,' he explained, 'we have come out of the cloud into the sunshine, and by your help have been established in the rule of our kingdom. This we rightly regard as your work.' The letter was accompanied by one signed by Hubert and others in the king's circle that flattered the Holy Father in equally grateful terms for his contribution to Henry's progress to date:

For indeed, your Holiness has been pleased to exercise your authority in promoting his every good, and in furthering his every interest in a way beyond all praise. But seeing that you have never refused nor feared to undertake the greatest burdens and labours, and have never spared yourself to make sure his rule over us, we do not hesitate to beg your Holiness, with loving insistence, to continue your efforts, and to prevent what has been brought thus far safely, from being trodden under foot by the enemy of mankind.

Christmas 1223 was spent at Northampton with the Archbishop of Canterbury and a group of bishops. Many of the barons were gathering at Leicester like a dark storm cloud, still unsure what was going to happen to their possessions. In Northampton Stephen Langton and his bishops published a papal bull they had secured excommunicating all disturbers of the king's peace and those who attacked the rights of the Church. After this solemn ceremony the archbishop sent messengers to the gathering barons to warn them that unless the castles the king had identified were returned by the following day they would be excommunicated by name. This threat, along with Henry's promise that the castles were to be reclaimed in a fair and unbiased manner, caused the barons to submit. True to his word, Henry did not target those who had threatened to rebel. Hubert was required to hand over his castles along with those of the other barons. It appeared to be a fair measure in line with papal instruction, though Ralph of Coggleshall insisted, 'When the castles were surrendered the King gave back to Hubert his wardenships, the others castellans being deprived of theirs.' The records are a little hazy on this matter and cannot quite support Ralph's charge, though that may have been by design; Falkes de Bréauté would later level the same complaint.

Whatever the truth, it was clear that a new force, missing from English politics for almost a decade, was entering the tournament field: the will of the king. Henry was easing into his majority and nowhere is that more clearly exhibited than in the official documents of government. Never again was the form 'Witness Hubert de Burgh, my Justiciar' seen giving force to royal documents. It was replaced with 'Witness myself'.

In January 1224 Henry made an attempt to flex his newly found muscles in both the temporal and spiritual arenas, and the month was to display one of the key aspects of Henry's emerging personality. After the initial problems of Henry's demi-majority at the close of the previous year, and to mark the transition to a new phase in the government of the realm, Archbishop Langton, according to Roger of Wendover, led calls for a fresh reissue of the Great Charter, telling Henry that he 'could not evade doing this, since at the departure of Louis he and all the nobility of the realm with him had sworn that they would all observe, and cause to be observed by all others, the liberties written down aforetime'. William Brewer answered for the king, perhaps to save Henry having to bind himself early in the proceedings. If that was the case, it shows that Henry was testing the waters without fully intending to commit to a course of action. Brewer told the archbishop, 'The liberties which ye ask for ought rightly not to be observed, because they were extorted by violence.' Henry perhaps leaned forward on his seat to hear the response to this challenge. Langton scolded Brewer, warning him, 'William, if you loved the king, you would not thus stand in the way of the peace of his realm.' Those within earshot must have held their breath as Henry contemplated his reply, and let it out in relief when he told them, 'These liberties we have all sworn, and what we have sworn we are all bound to observe.' This represented Henry's first recorded, voluntary confirmation of commitment to the Charters previously made in his name, but it also demonstrates a key facet of his personality. He had pushed, but ceased pushing before plummeting over a precipice.

Also during January, Peter des Roches felt compelled to write to the Pope complaining of his treatment at the king's hands. It is likely that his alienation had more to do with his long-running feud with Hubert than a real falling out with Henry, but it also provided the king with an opportunity to test the boundaries of ecclesiastical control. The Pope's reply demonstrates his willingness to support the Church in England against the authority of the king. Honorius reminded the king that both he and his father owed the Bishop of Winchester a debt created 'at a time of great need', and told the king he 'has heard, and since hearing has not ceased to wonder' that Henry would forget such a debt. Henry was warned not to demean the Church of Winchester, since doing so would offend the Apostolic See, which held Peter's diocese under special protection. The Pope was also dismayed to hear that Henry had tried to forbid the bishop from 'coming to us and to the Roman Church his mother, for this is really no more an injury to him than it is to us and the Apostolic See'. Honorius expressed the hope that what he had heard would prove to be a false rumour and that Henry had not been so 'forgetful of the reverence due to the Apostolic See and to the true fidelity of the said bishop'.

If Henry was testing the slack on his leash as part of his assumption of more power, then he had found that the bindings were still quite tight, though at least he now knew where he stood. The early spring brought news of unrest in Ireland. Walter de Lacy was blamed either for failing to prevent the trouble or for being involved but he quickly made his peace with the king, offering one castle in Ireland at Trim and one in England at Ludlow for two years in reparation, and also promising to 'fight to the uttermost of his power, with the King's help, against the men who had done these things'. On 23 April, Young William Marshal was married at the age of thirty-four to Henry's nine-year-old sister, Eleanor, before he also departed for Ireland to give his assistance to the Justiciar there. By far the biggest problem in April, though, came from across the sea in the other direction. The truce with Louis in France had expired during April in spite of letters written by Honorius in February and April encouraging the King of France to renew them and maintain the peace. Louis punched into Poitou and most of Gascony fell swiftly behind the weight of the blow. Frustratingly, Louis was assisted in his incursion by Henry's stepfather, Hugh de Lusignan.

Once more, time to focus on one matter was denied to Henry. On 15 May he issued letters patent announcing that the truce with France was at an end. If it was a prelude to a planned attack to retake his lands, it was derailed by fresh trouble at home. On 16 June formal charges of thirty counts of *novel disseisin*, misappropriating property, were brought against Falkes de Bréauté – and he did not take the move against him lightly. Falkes was something of an enigma in England during a turbulent period. By turns, he had been precisely the kind of brutal foreign interloper the barons had railed against during the final years of John's reign and the very reason John had been so hard to unseat; he had been a large part of the reason Henry had clung to power during the first months and years of his reign in one of the hardest regions to hold onto, the Midlands, sandwiched between Louis in the south and irate barons in the north, but also represented a lingering and still resented foreign influence holding several castles from the king. Falkes had been valuable to John and his son because of his brutal, often cruel but effective methods and he seemed not to fit well in a realm now trying to be at peace with itself. Falkes perhaps represented the largest elephant in the kingdom, and the time had come to confront the matter head on.

It is hardly surprising that Falkes refused to take the accusations against him lying down. He must have known that it was about more than disagreements over property. In a fit of rage that he doubtless believed righteous, Falkes kidnapped Henry de Braybrook, the justice at Dunstable responsible for bringing the charges, and two other men, throwing them into Bedford Castle and settling himself in, daring the government to try and get him out. Henry had begun a muster at Northampton for an excursion across the Channel but was forced to divert this force to Bedford and lay siege to the castle, arriving on 20 June. Henry's father had fortified Bedford to withstand precisely the kind of siege his son now needed resolved quickly. It took almost two months before Falkes slipped out of Bedford and fled into Wales so that the siege could be ended on 14 August. One of his father's men in one of his father's castles had cost Henry the chance to try and regain lost Angevin lands. At the beginning of the siege, when Falkes and his men refused to deliver up the castle, Henry had sworn on his father's soul that he would hang every one of them if they resisted him, and this threat was perhaps a signal that he had better things to do with his army and had no time for this business. The garrison refused to give up even after Falkes had left, until Henry's miners made their way under the keep and set a fire.

The huge stone keep smouldered and filled with smoke all night with no sign of any movement inside. Only in the morning, with the worst of the blaze over, did the bedraggled garrison emerge sooty and feeling the effects of a night in the smoke-filled building. They received absolution and were hanged, just as Henry had promised. The king had perhaps learned the lesson Roger of Wendover had taught after the Count of Aumale's revolt in 1221, the forgiveness of which Roger complained was 'the worst of examples, and encouraged future rebellions'. It was not a mistake Henry would make again and, although we might view his treatment of defeated enemies as harsh and unnecessary, he was following the established rule of siege warfare – to do anything else, as Roger demonstrated, was perceived as a weakness.

When a town or castle was besieged there was a very strict code, part of the chivalric rules of warfare, which guided both parties in the engagement. Upon laying siege, the attackers were expected to allow the defenders the opportunity to parley and try to agree terms for their surrender. If no agreement was reached, the siege began in earnest, though the attackers were expected to allow a channel of communication between the besieged and their master, if they had one. The defenders would frequently eject non-combatants – women, children and the elderly – from the town or castle in order to allow provisions to go further and prolong the siege. An attacking force was entitled to trap these civilians in no man's land between the two forces and allow them to starve, those within forced to watch the helpless people they had sent out starve if they would not give up. The defenders were permitted to ask their lord for aid or permission to surrender, and frequently a deadline was imposed by the defenders for their relief, after the expiry of which they would accept that no aid was coming and were entitled to surrender. If they gave up at that stage the attackers were required to treat them fairly and allow them to live, though their goods and property within might well be forfeit. If they resisted beyond this point and forced a siege to its conclusion, they could expect no mercy and effectively sentenced themselves to death. Henry's threat at the outset of the siege was little more than a reminder of the rules of engagement and his fulfilment at the end no less than both sides would have expected. Henry V's Agincourt campaign of 1415 was executed strictly according to these rules and, although he draws criticism now for behaviour we find unacceptable, contemporaries, even amongst the French, praised his adherence to the laws of war.

There was a hard reminder of Henry's anomalous position a few weeks later when a letter from Honorius, written on 17 August, three days after the siege had been brought to an end, arrived in England. The Pope was not appreciative of the king's adhesion to the rules of engagement and reminded Henry that he had told him on numerous occasions before to deal with his subjects in 'a spirit of mildness' and 'to strive to keep peace and concord'. He was not pleased to hear that 'despising these warnings, you have rashly taken up arms against that noble man, Falkes de Bréauté, who in time of need has risked his life and property for your father and for yourself', and complained to Henry that

> those who have counselled you in this are as unwise as they are faithless. It is not the time to turn your arms against your own subjects. Even if they have gravely injured you, at the

present moment you should rather strive to win them by your royal favours to unite heartily in defence of your kingdom and yourself.

In a crushing blow to Henry's tentative moves toward an independent rule, Honorius thundered on:

> We warn your Highness, therefore, and earnestly exhort you, as well as strictly order you by these Apostolic letters, at once on sight of them, to desist from the siege of de Bréauté's castle without delay, and not to punish the foresaid nobleman, nor allow him to be punished in any way ... Prefer not any other counsels to our salutary admonitions and commands; but do what we suggest and order as you trust to our favour and help.

Falkes appears to have had great sympathy in Rome, as Peter des Roches had, and also seems to have blamed Hubert completely for his persecution.

Henry was placed in an impossible position. The Pope was his feudal overlord and Henry was bound by every conceivable tie to obey him, not least because he could hardly demand loyalty from men within his kingdom if he himself was seen to flout those terms, but Falkes was increasingly hated in England. By the time the siege of Bedford ended, Louis had scooped up all of Poitou and, with the help of Hugh de Lusignan, had bent it to his rule. Falkes' behaviour was widely blamed for the loss of Poitou and most of Gascony that summer since the distraction he caused prevented Henry from defending his lands. Xenophobia was swelling to a dangerous flood tide and Henry was being ordered to refrain from punishing Falkes. Whether he believed himself wronged or not, Falkes was subject to legal proceedings and, rather than using the law to defend himself, he resorted directly to war. In response to this, Henry was told he was only able to use 'a spirit of mildness', which simply poured fuel onto the fire. At such a distance, the subtleties of England's cultural politics perhaps evaded Honorius, though he was still ordering that a breach of the law should not be punished. A foreign ruler protecting a foreign mercenary from the law in England did not sit well, but Henry had little choice.

Honorius was even more authoritarian and severe in a letter addressed to Archbishop Langton at the same time:

> We have not yet been able to force our mind to credit what has been suggested to us about you by many, though they have striven to enforce the truth of what they say by many evidences. We thought indeed of that eminent knowledge of Divine Scripture which you possess; of that uprightness, which you should have put on with the bishop's office and dignity; and of that abundance of love which has been shown to you by the Apostolic See in so many ways; and turning these things over in our mind, we could not bring ourselves to think anything evil or unworthy of you.

The Pope seemed irritated that Langton sent constant word that 'all things in England were peaceful and tranquil, so as to prevent by every means in their power the mission of any legate', whilst others at the Curia were 'telling us of disturbances in the kingdom and eagerly beseeching us to dispatch a legate thither'. Honorius went on to all but call Langton a liar, railing,

> Trusting to you, though not indeed without suspicion (for why do you fear the eyes of the Apostolic See), we desisted from our design to send thither a legate, and determined to send simple messengers. When they were ready to start, so that in two days' time they would have left the city, your letters arrived containing assurances that peace was fully established in England.

Honorius raged yet further regarding news of Langton's treatment of Falkes, complaining that he had heard

> that you with other bishops had published an excommunication against him and his. What can you say to this? Will you reply, that after your letters had been dispatched to us discord broke out against your expectation? If so, why did you not inform us about it at once? Perhaps you will say, that justice required arms to be taken up against the foresaid noble? But most certainly prudence would have required the contrary, and at the present time prudence should rather be considered. Where then is your great

wisdom, if it has been done by your advice? We consequently warn your Fraternity, and strictly order you, by our Apostolic letters that ... you cause the king at once to abandon the siege of the said noble, and that you, without delay or difficulty, relax the sentence you have laid upon him and his followers.

In what amounted to a threat, the Pope concluded that only by 'faithfully carrying out our order, you may justify our trust in you and give us greater hope of your love'.

Henry took a firm stance to this challenge to his growing authority. He wrote back to Honorius in a tone that was firm but polite to tell the Pope that he had acted on the advice of men who knew the circumstances in England, detailing some of Falkes' transgressions to support the action that he maintained was not only warranted but required to secure the peace of the kingdom. Henry expressed his own concern that the cases of both Peter des Roches and Falkes de Bréauté had been misrepresented to him and that the Pope was defending men who did not deserve his concern and protection. It is perhaps possible to hear Hubert's voice guiding the king's pen, but Henry is also likely to have been chafing at the papal bit restraining his kingship. Christmas 1224 was spent at Westminster: the year to follow would be a defining one, if not necessarily for Henry then certainly for every year that followed in Britain and further afield.

7

The Truth of Magna Carta

In response to Henry's letter, which might represent an incipient sign of the young king bucking papal control, Honorius replied in a tone that was far more conciliatory and paternal, offering Henry advice on the ruling of his kingdom rather than chastising and ordering him. It is possible that Honorius accepted Henry's point, that he did not have the full story, or perhaps the Pope realised that Henry was no longer a boy and that to push him too far might risk an outright revolt by Henry against the papal presence in England:

> Remembering this, since you are the common lord of all in your kingdom, it is well that you should strive to act fairly to all, showing yourself kind and favourable to everyone. If differences arise, as amongst so great a number will happen, take neither the one side nor the other, but correct, rule and govern all with like affection, care and watchfulness. In this way your subjects, seeing in you the uprightness proper to your royal dignity, will not hesitate to leave their cause to your decision, and will put their trust in you as every loyal vassal does in his loving lord, and every dutiful son in his affectionate parent. We therefore beg your Highness to write these principles carefully on the tablets of your heart. Lay them up in the treasure-house of your mind and make use of them when need shall be. In particular, we would counsel your Highness and suggest in all good faith to you, that at this time you should not exact a full account from your

vassals, nor alienate them by requiring the full payment of your revenues. This settlement and other matters which might cause discontent you should prudently defer to an opportune occasion. We would beg you to recognise, however, that your agents, whom we send back to you with every commendation for their fidelity, have presented your requests on these and other matters, and have strenuously and with insistence laboured to promote them. Some of them we have granted; others, by the advice of our brethren, we have thought proper to defer for a season. We think this is expedient at present; but when the time is fitting, we will listen to these requests and any others you may think proper to urge, for we love you with the fullest affection, as the special son of the Roman Church. We have hitherto striven to secure your peace and that of your kingdom within and without, even when we have not been asked, and by every watchful care; we will continue to guard this for you, and to afford you the favour, grace, counsel and help of the Apostolic See in all things, whensoever it is fitting.

The wisdom of Honorius' advice is plain to see and it offered the seventeen-year-old a model for just kingship that the Pope believed would serve him well. Accompanying this letter, though, was one to the Archbishop of Canterbury and addressed to the bishops of the English Church that demonstrates clearly that one aspect of Honorius' interest in England had not waned at all:

The Church is ever ready to relieve the necessities of secular princes, by liberally affording them help when it is called for. This is no prejudice to the liberty of the Church, but must be regarded rather as a work of charity. And, since our beloved son in Christ, Henry, the illustrious king of England, is said to be greatly in want of your help, we earnestly request and exhort all of you, and by these Apostolic letters command you to give him a contribution fitting to the condition of your churches.

In order to allay a common fear amongst the clergy in this period, Honorius added the caveat, 'We are, however, unwilling that this special favour of ours, and the fact of your charitable assistance should be hereafter pleaded as a precedent, or claimed as a right.' The Church was always wary of setting a precedent for taxation that would impinge upon the freedom it claimed from the state, and Honorius pre-empted this objection in order to prevent delay in the collection of a supplement for the king. Honorius was keen to test the wealth of the Church in England and see if it was ready to support his desire to further a crusade.

In January 1225, Henry found himself in urgent need of money, a state that was to be a constant and ever-present theme of his kingship, which moulded the events of the start of 1225 and was to shape centuries to come. The siege at Bedford had exhausted Henry's limited funds and victory there bought no reward and only scorn from his liege, though it was popular amongst the English barons and bishops. At a council meeting in January Hubert de Burgh requested a tax of a fifteenth (referring to a levy of one fifteenth of the value of each person's moveable goods) and asked that the Church should be included in the tax. As Honorius' letter demonstrates, and as Hubert perhaps knew, the bishops were all but required to grant the request. The ever-resourceful Stephen Langton, though, held one card up the sleeve of his archbishop's robes. Langdon politely requested that the liberties of the Church be confirmed, in a move that led to a wider discussion on the reissue of Magna Carta and the Forest Charter.

Another moment of great importance took place during the deliberations over this matter. On 2 February, Henry knighted his younger brother Richard, and eleven days later, on 13 February, issued letters patent to create Richard as Earl of Cornwall 'with all that pertained to the King in that county, to support himself in the King's service, during the King's pleasure'. It is likely that it was at this time, too, that Richard was made Count of Poitou. At sixteen, Henry's younger brother was emerging onto the political scene at a time when Henry was in need of support, and he doubtless saw Richard's promotion and empowerment as a method of bolstering his own position. Richard was to have a huge part to play during the rest of his brother's reign as well as on the world stage. February 1225 saw the emergence of a truly global figure who, even when disagreeing with his brother, was a pillar by which Henry's kingship was made much steadier.

In between these two illustrious events, on 11 February the Charters were reissued. The 1225 versions of both Magna Carta and the Charter of the Forests, which were from this point onward inextricably linked and known as the Charters, represents the final iteration of both, preserving the wording that remained on the statute books in England for centuries. The general wording of both Charters remained the same as the 1217 versions, but there was a crucial difference in the preamble. The 1215 Charter had been forced upon John. The 1217 version, though granted as an olive branch rather than extracted, was given on behalf of a minor, sealed by a papal legate and the king's regent. The preamble of 1217 had stated that the Charters were given by the king 'by the advice of our councillors', but in 1225 this was changed to state that they were granted by Henry 'of his own free good-will, to the prelates, magnates, and all the people of England, to be kept in the realm of England for ever'. This was, crucially, the first ever granting of the Charters by the truly free will of the king and they were given a new level of force, authority and meaning in that subtle alteration.

Even this distinction did not mark the greatest impact of the 1225 reissues to the very heart of the establishment of England. Matthew Paris notes that,

> Moved by his desire to obtain the money, Henry consented, and forthwith the royal Charters were dispatched under the king's seal into every county, and judges were appointed to view the forests and determine their limits. Simultaneously the royal agents were directed to gather in the aid of a fifteenth, by which these privileges had been purchased for the nation.

In forwarding Honorius' letters to his bishops, Stephen Langton wrote that 'in these days, grave needs are pressing heavily upon the king, and considering how upright and good he is, and how upon his peace, the peace of the Church rests', he therefore wanted the bishops to not only accept the fifteenth but, in response to Honorius' request, find as much as they could to offer support to the king, suggesting a twelfth or at the very least a fourteenth.

Within the records of discussions of the Salisbury chapter a decision was reached: they believed the Church needed to act with unity in order to prevent the establishment of a precedent, but expressed their desire to help the king as far as they were able.

The fundamental fact was the reissue of 1225 created a new relationship between the king and his subjects, or at least the most significant portion of them, a relationship that furthermore would be the foundation of rule for centuries to come and the ignoring of which would almost always lead to civil war, deposition or even death for the king. The grant of a tax to meet the Crown's financial needs was given on the condition that either liberties were granted or confirmed, or that issues concerning the magnates were suitably addressed. The grant of funding from the nation was, for the first time, made conditional upon the good rule of the monarch. In medieval terms, it was a complete novelty. No French monarch would ever have recognised the need for such a bargain with his subjects, and no Norman or Angevin king before Henry III would have reached such an agreement. Indeed, Henry's father had lost his life fighting precisely this kind of measure. Richard I feeling obliged to give to his magnates in order to secure a tax from them is unthinkable. William I had commissioned the Domesday Book in order to work out what *his* country was worth to *him*: he owed it to nobody and required no man's permission to take what was rightfully his. The deal struck by the 1225 issue was genuinely groundbreaking. It gave the magnates the kind of control that the security clause, so repugnant in the 1215 Charter, had tried to establish without granting them licence to go to war with the king. If the monarch consulted them, listened to them and demonstrated good governance, he would have their financial and military support; if not, they reserved the right to withhold that aid. It was the birth of checks and balances on the autocratic rule of the king.

To Henry III, in that January and February of 1225, it was probably viewed as little more than an expedient, a motion to go through in order to secure the money he desperately needed to try and claw back his rapidly shrinking territory abroad. Matthew Paris notes that, 'Even at the time, however, in the minds of many, there were not wanting suspicions of the king's honesty of purpose, which subsequent events showed were not unwarranted.' By March, Richard, Earl of Cornwall, was despatched at the head of an army to Gascony. It was the opening of the campaign season, and Henry had time and peace at home to focus on the recapture of lands his father had lost and which were slipping beyond his grasp. It is hard to judge the level of dismay that must have been caused by a letter, dated 22 March, received by Henry from the papal legate in France requesting an immediate truce. Louis had taken the Cross in order to lead what would become known as the Albigensian Crusade against the Cathars in the Languedoc region of southern France. Catharism had been declared a heresy and Louis had been tasked with its eradication. One of the most committed and effective persecutors of the Cathars had been Simon de Montfort the Elder, who had died in the wars in 1218 and whose work had been continued by his oldest son Amaury. His younger son, Simon de Montfort the Younger, was to inherit his father's fierce reputation for military competence and was to seek his fortune in Henry's England to shattering effect. With the Crusader's protection, which had served King John well, Henry was forbidden from attacking Louis' lands, including those currently in dispute.

A letter from Honorius to Henry in April made the situation very clear. One of Louis' conditions for agreeing to undertake the crusade Honorius desperately wanted was that the Pope order Henry not to attack any of his lands. This Honorius duly did – Henry was ordered not to attack any of Louis's territory on pain of excommunication. Henry called a council meeting to discuss what could be done but there was little option other than to obey the Pope. England and Henry were not only beholden to Rome but owed their security to a special relationship with the Pope that could not be put at risk for the opportunity of an easy land grab. According to Roger of Wendover, Henry consoled himself with the prediction of an astronomer, William Pierpunt, that the Albigensian campaign would cost Louis either his life or his crown. It was small comfort against the frustration of the only decision available: to delay action.

Throughout mid-1225, rumours that a papal nuncio was on the way to England caused concern. The legate in France, Romanus, would only tell English representatives that the nuncio's name was Otto and that he was keeping his purpose very much to himself. Langton had secured assurances that no legate would be appointed during his lifetime; a nuncio was effectively a papal envoy for a specific purpose rather than holding the general and supreme powers of a legate, but even a specific purpose was sufficient to raise anxiety. Whilst in France, word reached Otto of the apprehension his imminent arrival was causing and he wrote a letter of reassurance to Henry:

> I am astonished and not a little dismayed to understand that the lord king is at all angry or disturbed at my coming to him. It is not my intention to do aught, or to engage in any business which might issue in loss or injury to him, nor is it the design of the Roman Curia, that has sent me, that I should do so. My mission is rather for the advantage and honour both of the king and of his kingdom. I therefore hope that when I shall meet him and shall have fully explained what I have been ordered to do, I shall not only satisfy him about myself, but in regard to the business I have with him and with others, I shall earn his gratitude.

The nuncio made slow progress on his journey, though, only arriving later in the year.

Meanwhile, Henry had decided that he was not willing to wait any longer to press his claims in Gascony and Poitou, even if it meant incurring the Pope's displeasure. In August Richard was sent once again into Gascony with a war chest and the resources required for a serious campaign. In September, Henry was able to attend the opening of the new Salisbury Cathedral. Work was not finished and the consecration would not take place until 1258, but Henry was donating timber from his Wiltshire estates and from Ireland to support the work there. Alice Brewer gave marble from her Purbeck quarry for a dozen years, too, before building was completed. As earlier mentioned, a keen interest in building works was to define Henry's rule and his impact on the landscape of England almost as much as his efforts with the Charters would, but his mind may have been elsewhere at this time as his brother Richard enjoyed unprecedented success. On 13 November 1225, La Reole, the last town still in opposition in Gascony, fell to Richard's army. The entire region had been recaptured – the first positive step England had taken on the continent in years.

Christmas at Winchester must have been a buoyant affair. Henry could look back on a year in which he had reached agreement with his magnates to secure funding that previously had been denied to him, recovered from a setback in his desire to send a campaign into Gascony to see the whole region taken back into his possession, and visited one of the great Gothic masterpieces of medieval England. Perhaps the only fly in the ointment was Otto's arrival carrying the Pope's demand for English money to be sent to Rome. When council was summoned to Westminster on 13 January 1226, it was an oddly stage-managed and cagey affair. Henry sent word that he was unable to attend through illness, and Stephen Langton similarly sent his apologies since he was required to remain with the king and attend on him whilst he was ill. It is likely that both were excuses to ensure that the two people who might be expected to make a decision on Otto's request were not there to give it. As Otto had kept his business a secret, Henry and Langton probably sought to avoid being placed in an awkward position and being pressed for a decision. Their absence meant that Otto's requests could be heard and delivered to them with time to be digested and to formulate a response.

Otto may have realised what was going on but delivered his message anyway. The plan originating with the Pope was clear, but frightening to the Church in its implications. It was possibly the full realisation of the papacy's plans in England, though it was a plan that was being explained to all Christian countries. Otto proposed that in every cathedral in England two prebends (a portion of the cathedral's income that would be granted to a canon or member of the chapter) should be set aside for the Pope, one that would usually have been in the gift of the bishop and one in the hands of the chapter. All monasteries in England would be required to send a portion of their income that would represent one monk if their income was divided up and also a portion of the abbot's income.

The recorded answer given to Otto was surely in the form expected and designed:

> Sir, what you have proposed to us specially touches the prerogative of the English king and generally the interests and rights of all patrons of churches in this realm. It touches, too, the archbishops and their suffragans as well as numberless other English prelates. Since then the king by reason of his illness is absent, and the archbishop and some of the bishops and other beneficed clergy are not here, we neither can nor ought to give you any answer in their absence. Did we presume to do so we should be prejudicing the rights of all the absent prelates.

Langton used the time brought by this stalling to complain to Honorius about Otto's presence. In the meantime, letters arrived from Honorius forbidding Henry from taking any further action in Poitou while Louis was engaged in the Albigensian Crusade and ordering him not to make any truce or alliance with Raymond of Toulouse, traditionally Henry's ally. Raymond was Louis' cousin but the leader of the Cathars and so an enemy of the Pope. The only consolation was that the Pope also wrote to Romanus, the legate in France, that he should ensure Louis did not move against any more of Henry's lands in France, either. In April, Henry opened negotiations with another of Louis' enemies, hoping to tempt the Duke of Lorraine into an alliance that would spring into action once the prohibition on action against Louis was lifted. Otto was heading north during Lent collecting procurations (payments extracted from clergy for the support of papal officers in the course of their work) when letters from Rome overtook him at Northampton ordering him to return to the Curia and removing all of his special powers. Roger of Wendover records that, 'Looking askance at them, he threw the documents into the fire, and forthwith changing all his plans he left England in distress, and with empty saddle bags.' The Pope, however, had imposed one requirement on the Archbishop of Canterbury in return for Otto's removal: he wanted an answer to his plan.

On 4 May 1226 a council met at St Paul's to thrash out a response. There is no doubt that they wanted to refuse the plan, but they had to work out whether they could do so in a manner that wouldn't incur the wrath of Honorius. Henry and his brother Richard were held in a special station by the Pope; neither could be excommunicated without a direct notice from the Pope himself, and they would not wish to risk that nor to upset their feudal overlord. Light was seen in the news that the plan had been rejected outright in France already. The legate in France was reported to have admitted that he did not agree with the scheme and had promised that he would not ask for its implementation again until the other major kingdoms of Europe had agreed to it, 'which I do not think will be the case'. This chink was seized upon, and Henry wrote to Honorius:

> What the lord Pope asks us to do is a matter which affects the whole Christian world. We are placed, as it were, on the very confines of the world, and consequently desire to see how other kingdoms will act in regard to these proposed exactions. When we shall have the example of what others do before our eyes, the lord pope will not find us more backward in obedience.

The king managed to refuse without refusing. Honorius must have known how the plan would be received across Europe but was desperate for cash for his planned crusade. He perhaps hoped that his vassal state would set the precedent that others would then be all but forced to follow, but the plan failed to be ratified even in the surest centre of papal authority.

This year also saw Henry's passion for building moving closer to home and being applied increasingly to royal as well as religious edifices. The Palace of Westminster attracted Henry's attention and, in 1226, he commissioned work on the Painted Chamber at Westminster, designed to be a stunning and colourful private apartment with immense murals bringing the walls to life and a canopied bed at one end. The significance of the spot was immense for Henry too. The room was said to stand on the spot where Edward the Confessor, a king and saint that Henry was utterly obsessed by, had died. The bedposts were painted green and sported golden stars, whilst a painting of Edward the Confessor was placed directly above the bed.

October saw the death of Francis of Assisi, whose Franciscan order of friars had arrived in England and established friaries in Canterbury, London and Oxford. Their public preaching, combined with a commitment to help the poor and sick, was making them very popular in the communities they entered and served. Of far more importance to Henry was another death during the following month. On 8 November 1226, the prediction offered by William Pierpunt eighteen months earlier came true. Louis VIII of France was returning to Paris from a campaign that formed part of the Albigensian Crusade when he fell ill with dysentery and died at the age of thirty-nine. Louis had been Henry's arch-enemy, a man occupying half his kingdom when he had come to the throne who had also continued his father's work of snatching Angevin lands. The only thing that had restrained Louis was the support for Henry offered by the Pope, which had seen continual extensions to truces until Louis had finally snatched Gascony and Poitou, only to shield himself quickly from reprisal with a crusader's vow, just as Henry's father had done. Of great concern to the French was the fact that Louis' heir, crowned King Louis IX on 30 November, was only twelve and in need of a minority government. His coronation was as poorly attended as Henry's first ceremony had been as the nobility began to divide. The new king's mother, Blanche of Castile, led the regency government, but it was easy for Henry to see his family's former Angevin territories becoming unsettled. His brother Richard was working hard to pick the ripening fruit in the Angevin orchard.

That December there was another sign of a more settled politics at home in England when Henry wrote to Honorius with regard to Simon Langton's prohibition from returning to England. The brother of the Archbishop of Canterbury had sided very firmly with Louis and the rebels in 1216–17 and had not been forgiven by the Pope, so that he was forbidden entry into England. Honorius had blocked Simon's election to the Archbishopric of York, which would have placed the Langton brothers in the two highest roles of England's Church. Henry wrote that Stephen Langton 'was strenuously exerting himself to shield him from anything hurtful and to help him to everything good', but the king believed that if the archbishop 'could occasionally enjoy the society of his brother

Simon, of whom, as is not to be wondered at, he thinks not a little, he would pass his life in less sadness, which we would much desire, and would devote himself to our affairs with even greater ardour'. Henry therefore requested a lifting of the prohibition so that Simon could return to support his brother. This move is clear evidence of a strong working relationship between the king and the highest ecclesiastical officer in England and, indeed, of a close personal rapport, but it could also point to a level of influence the charismatic archbishop held over the impressionable king. It was already widely thought that the Justiciar Hubert had too much influence, and Stephen Langton perhaps sought either to balance that out or to further his own agenda by exploiting a weakness in Henry's character.

Christmas 1226 was spent at Reading, but immediately after the celebrations Henry rode to London and demanded a gift of 5,000 marks from the City on the basis that the citizens had willingly given Louis the same sum. London must have been slightly bemused by the random levy, no doubt sought to support Richard's efforts in Gascony and Poitou, but paid nevertheless, perhaps in recognition of their past infidelity. The demand perhaps shows that there was still a nail in the boot of the relationship between the monarch and his capital city. The fact that Henry felt he needed cash urgently to capitalise on recent gains on the Continent and the current instability in France was even more clearly demonstrated at the beginning of 1227.

On 8 January 1227 the council met at Oxford. Its discussions and business were consumed by an announcement from King Henry. At the age of nineteen, perhaps as much as two years before it might have been more fully expected, Henry declared himself of full age, ending his minority. He formerly ended his tutelage under Peter des Roches, which may practically have been over for some time but which technically remained in place, and removed the bishop without apparently consulting him. Frustratingly for some, particularly Peter des Roches, Hubert was confirmed in his role as Justiciar – which had not been created because of the minority but had enjoyed increased power during its term – and rewarded for the good service Henry discerned with the earldom of Kent. Disturbingly for many, Henry openly repudiated the Charters during the meeting, too, on the basis that he had given them, or rather they had been given on his behalf, only as a minor, and the law had clearly stated that nothing given or granted during his minority could be permanent until the king reached his majority. It may well also have been a reaction to the failure of the barons to pay the fifteenth they had agreed to in return for the Charters of 1225 and which the Church does appear to have paid.

Henry also told all of the barons and bishops that he would not be bound by any, even ancient, charter or privilege, but that any charter or privilege claimed would have to be presented to receive the new king's seal of approval. A letter dated 21 January was circulated throughout the kingdom explaining the new position:

> Be it known to you that by the common counsel of the Archbishop of Canterbury, the bishops, abbots, earls, barons, and other our magnates and faithful men, we recently at Oxford provided that henceforth we will cause charters and confirmations to be made under our seal. And we therefore bid you without delay publicly proclaim and make known to all persons in your bailiwick who have, or claim to have, lands or tenements or liberties by grant or concession and confirmation of our ancestors the Kings of England, or by our precept, that they come to us without fail before the beginning of this approaching Lent of the eleventh year of our reign, to shew us by what warrant they have, or claim to have, those lands or tenements or liberties, as they desire to keep or to recover them. You are also to make known to all persons in your bailiwick, and cause to be publicly proclaimed, that whosoever shall desire to obtain at any time our charter or confirmation of lands, tenements, markets, liberties, or anything whatsoever, let them come to us before the same term, to ask for our charter or confirmation thereof.

This was a significant turn of events. After years of civil war followed by over a decade of minority government, England would now have a king operating fully in his own name. It must have been a tense moment for the country. The cancellation of all charters and privileges, the repudiation of the Charters and the need to secure afresh any grant might appear terrifying and destabilising, yet it was most likely not in reality. From the beginning of the minority it had been clear that nothing would be held in perpetuity until Henry came of age, so this moment was always going to arrive. For the barons and other ambitious men in the country it opened the door to permanent reward and advancement that had not been available for over a decade. Royal patronage was about to become a real force in the kingdom again.

There were very clear reasons, too, for Henry taking this action. After civil war and a long minority, during which there had been continual rumour of mismanagement, it was a perfect opportunity to take stock, settle all property disputes and update royal records of privileges and properties held throughout the realm. Repudiating the Charters allowed Henry to negotiate again and he may not have seen any obligation to be bound by the bargain struck if the barons were not going to pay the tax they had promised in return for the grant; it had to be a bargain that worked both ways and must be observed by both sides to be effective and binding. In most cases a large part of the reason few were fazed by the announcement was that the re-granting of all charters and privileges was a mere formality without much contention. However, payment was required for each re-grant, which served as a huge revenue-generation drive for Henry, who was in desperate need of funds to keep the campaign abroad going and was clearly annoyed by the barons' failure to pay the promised fifteenth. Causing everyone who held, or wished to hold, anything from the Crown in the centre of administration to apply for the permanent grant of their rights was also an opportunity to cause each of those people to swear again fealty to the king as a ruler of full age, so that none might later deny an oath made to a minor should hold in relation to a man in his majority.

Henry was marking himself as his own man, showing that he expected his barons to honour their side of any deal if they were to expect him to be bound by his word, causing anyone who held property or right within the kingdom to swear fealty to him and raising revenue for the continuance of a successful campaign in France. It was a fine start to a majority, with the king able to demonstrate that he was no pushover without unnecessarily or excessively antagonising his barons. There was a question mark lingering over the assertion that he was fully independent whilst Hubert and to some extent Stephen Langton were still in place holding some degree of influence, perhaps over-emphasised by their enemies, but nevertheless a lingering shadow of the minority. What none probably realised and what, even if anyone could have predicted, was probably unavoidable was the threat posed by a sharp change in the style and direction of government brought about by the close of a minority that had nothing to do with the king's personality or abilities.

King John had been brought down by an insistence that he should relinquish some of the control inherent and traditionally vested in the position of king in order to provide a mechanism by which barons might protect themselves and, probably to a lesser extent, the country from the ravages of a tyrant. No king could realistically hand over that power, any more than he could admit that he was the kind of bad king who needed restraining, and whilst John doubtless mishandled the matter and created an atmosphere of brinkmanship, almost every king in Europe at that time and probably beyond throughout the medieval period would have fought against such a diminishment of their power. By John's early death during the war the sting of personality was drawn, but it was not over. Marshal and Guala had worked hard to conciliate and save a kingdom for Henry to grow into. The very nature of a minority government, particularly one trying to get to grips with a splintered nation and even more so one led by a man like Marshal, whose nature and experience narrowed his outlook to notions of chivalry and brotherhood, was inclusive and consultative. No one person really wanted to be seen to be taking the king's power to himself, hoping to emerge from the minority able to hold onto whatever they had gathered. By virtue of the accident of Henry's age, the barons had effectively got what they had wanted at Runnymede: they were involved in government and could not be dominated by the personality of a king. Whilst Marshal's achievements are the stuff of legend, and he was unlikely to have succeeded by any other method, his inclusive instincts had created a monster. The question at the end of the long minority was whether the barons could ever willingly hand back what they had won and enjoyed for ten years and, assuming that they would not, how a seventeen-year-old desperate to regain territory his father had lost would handle the expectation that had developed of inclusive, consultative rule when that style was completely at odds with every conception of medieval kingship. England's barons had ceased to view themselves solely as the fingers of the Crown's long arm but sought instead to control both that arm's reach and its scope. Was there to be a crisis arising from Marshal's success?

8

The Last Great Justiciar

Pope Honorius III died on 18 March 1227 aged seventy-seven. During his nine years on the throne of St Peter he had largely continued the administrative reforms, political expansionism and crusading drive of his predecessor Innocent III. He had also been key to Henry III's survival as king of England, shielding the government of the country from storms at home and abroad, though at times restraining them, too. If Innocent hadn't, Honorius certainly seemed to have identified the rich Angevin lands as a potential war chest for his crusading passion. Even having lost much of the Continental empire, Honorius' letters show that he believed England to be a traditionally wealthy land that now belonged to the papacy. Honorius was succeeded by the almost eighty-year-old Ugolino da Segni, nephew of Innocent III, who took the papal tiara as Gregory IX. In May Gregory wrote to King Henry telling the English king that he looked on him 'as a special son of the Roman Church', encouraging him 'ever to strive to honour and revere the Holy Roman Church, your mother, thus walking in the footsteps of your ancestors' and 'as becomes a Christian prince, humbly and devotedly to help us, who by God's providence are called to rule it'.

Accompanying this formal announcement of his election, Gregory sent a more personal letter written in more paternal terms that mirrored those of his predecessors in which he expressed a desire that Henry would continue to endeavour to cultivate the Roman faith in his country and to demonstrate Christian devotion in his actions. As friendly as the tone was, it was also a gentle notice that

Gregory had no intention of relaxing the papacy's hold on England. Gregory also replied to Henry's request regarding Simon Langton's return, which had remained unanswered before Honorius' death, willingly granting that Simon might return to England. On the same day, Gregory addressed a letter to Simon himself telling him of the decision, explaining,

> Though the Roman Church may pour out the wine that you may experience its discipline, still together with the rod of a father it has the affection of a mother, and we who, though unworthy, hold on earth His place, who in wrath restrains not His mercy nor forgets to take pity, now pour out for you the oil of mercy, after you have experienced the bitterness of the punishment, and after the rod offer to you the salve.

Before the end of May, Gregory continued his free support to Henry by penning a strongly worded rebuke to the King of France, Louis IX, or at least to his regency government. Gregory reminded the king that successive popes had not shied away from working to prevent French kings from assaulting Henry's territory, 'since the kingdom of England specially belongs to' the Apostolic See. Gregory recounted the manner in which the present king's grandfather had invaded English possessions in the face of papal prohibitions whilst King John should have enjoyed a crusader's protection, and how Louis' own father had since snatched most of the rest of Henry's possessions in France despite similar papal protections. Now, news had reached Rome of a plot to take all that remained of Henry's territories in France, and Gregory warned the French against such a course in the strongest possible terms and ordered Louis to immediately return all of Henry's possessions that he currently held. It was a strong start and must have been music to Henry's ears since Gregory seemed determined to see done what his predecessors had not.

Events beyond his control were once more to conspire against Henry, though, and Gregory's nineteen years as Pope, a term which might not have been anticipated given the age at which he assumed the position, were to be utterly dominated by a vicious and irresolvable dispute between the Pope and the Holy Roman

Emperor Frederick II. Indeed, not only did this hamper Henry's cause but he was drawn into the heart of the conflict between his feudal lord and a family tie. Frederick's grandmother was Matilda of England, the eldest daughter of Henry II. Her son, Otto IV, had been John's nephew, and Frederick could count himself first cousin once removed to the English king. He would not refrain from calling on that family connection for support Henry was bound not to give. Henry would be forced to walk a tough line, writing to Gregory to express sorrow at the troubles the Pope suffered, confirming that he had written to Frederick under the eye of Master Stephen, a papal representative, and that the Emperor should not rashly 'depart from the duty owing to you and the Church, but humbly to obey and follow your directions', hoping in return that the Pope would welcome Frederick with open arms if he were to seek a reconciliation. On the same day, Henry despatched a letter to Frederick in which he expressed sympathy for the Emperor's dented pride but voicing his concern that the 'enemy of mankind', meaning Satan, had been able to sow discord. He added that he hoped his own words and prayers would move the Pope, since Henry was 'bound to him by great and special obligations than to other earthly princes', and equally trusting that his cousin would not 'despise the hand of the Church, which is stretched out against him'.

All of this did nothing to aid Henry's cause in France, where Richard was running out of resources and money. In March 1227, Blanche of Castile managed to negotiate the Treaty of Vendomme, which brought much-needed unity and security for her son. As part of the agreement, Hugh de Lusignan, son of Henry's step-father and mother, was betrothed to one of Blanche's daughters, Louis IX's sister Isabelle, showing clearly where Henry's own mother had placed her loyalty. Richard, knowing that he was about to hit a united wall of opposition in France, managed to hop onto the coat tails of the negotiations to secure a one-year truce for England which, at least technically, retained Poitou in English hands. By July, Richard was back in England and, worryingly, he was reported as storming out of Henry's court after an argument with his brother over possession of a manor which traditionally formed part of the patrimony of the earldom of Cornwall but which

Henry had, for some reason, withheld from his brother. Richard must have seen in it scant gratitude for all of his efforts on Henry's behalf, but Henry may not have been pleased by his brother's truce, which now bound Henry to inaction for a year and might, in the new atmosphere of his full majority, have been seeking to ensure that Richard, like all others in his kingdom, knew who was in charge. It was a dangerous game to play with such a reliable ally who possessed the same volatile Plantagenet blood that Henry did.

Just under a month after Richard had fled, the brothers met at a council meeting in Northampton on 2 August. Richard had met with William Marshal and Ranulf of Chester and the three expressed concerns to the king on several matters. Concessions appear to have been made to Richard, and the brothers were reconciled. By Christmas, this year celebrated in York, peace was secured and any rebellion averted. In managing this, Henry had shown that he was no pushover or soft touch, but he had also demonstrated that, unlike his father, he was willing to make concessions and review decisions his most senior nobles took exception to. It was a vital facet of his emerging kingly personality and appeared to offer the promise that he would not belligerently push the country into revolt if there was a deal to be struck.

Since his announcement at Oxford, Henry had been seeking papal approval for his assumption of full authority in England. Honorius' death saw the matter sidelined and it wasn't until the early part of 1228, a year after the declaration, that Rome seemed to focus on the matter. Gregory wrote to order the cancellation of a number of tournaments in England, events the Church routinely objected to as a cause of frequent deaths. Gregory had, however, heard reports that tournaments were being used, as they had during John's reign, as a cover to foment unrest in the kingdom and create alliances of barons against the king. Gregory therefore forbade tournaments in England and gave permission to a selection of bishops to excommunicate any who took part in such gatherings. The final confirmation of Henry's decision came in April when Gregory wrote to explain that,

Though our beloved son in Christ, Henry, the illustrious king of England, is in years a youth, he is already, as we rejoice to hear, possessed of a man's mind, and has made such progress [in the qualities] of age and prudence, that what is wanting to him in years seems to have been made up to him in the virtue of discretion, and so there is no longer any reason to prevent his ordering, usefully and prudently, the kingdom and its affairs.

It was official: Henry was a man in command of his realm. It is unfortunate that no contemporary description of Henry's appearance as an adult has yet been found. As a child he was described a good-looking and intelligent, and as a man, judging by his tomb effigy, he appears to have stood around 5 feet 6 inches tall, as his father had done. He probably had a drooping left eyelid that covered up to half his eye, perhaps impairing his military performance (though his son, the future Edward I, would inherit the same droop and suffer no impediment on the battlefield) and giving him the appearance of narrowing his eyes, in turns suspiciously, menacingly and slyly. He is thought to have been stocky, also like his father, and perhaps inclined to be a little plump, though this is all drawn from speculation and sadly nothing beyond the likeness held in his tomb effigy can be confirmed.

Another potential flashpoint was avoided in July 1228. Tensions had begun to manifest between the king and the Archbishop of Canterbury over the rights of the archbishopric, but, on 15 July, Stephen Langton passed away. His career had been a difficult one since accepting the post of Archbishop of Canterbury but he had found peace and worked well with John's son. He came to the post with a glittering record and might be the most intelligent, articulate and charming man to hold the highest post in England's Church. He left behind him a set of rules for the structure and duties of the clergy that were relied upon long after he was gone and managed to secure for himself ecclesiastical supremacy in a kingdom that belonged to the Pope. Stephen Langton's death also threatened to reopen old wounds as, for the first time in Henry's reign, the See of Canterbury was vacant and a new appointment had to be made.

On the same day as Stephen Langton shuffled off the weight of his mortal coil, Henry wrote to Frederick II again to try and bring the Pope and Emperor together, not least because their feud sucked focus away from his own priorities in France. Henry told his cousin that his only desire was 'to bring about the peace of the Church and to wrest a triumph from the enemies of the cross of Christ', imploring the Emperor not to forget 'the honour due to God and Holy Church', though his personal appeals did little to break the deadlock. Henry also wrote to Gregory to ask for permission to move his father's remains from Worcester Cathedral to Beaulieu Abbey. John had apparently intended to be interred at Beaulieu, an abbey that he had founded, but circumstances at the time of his death had made that impossible. Henry wrote that 'kneeling at the foot of your holiness', 'by the bearer of this present letter we beg you lovingly to permit' the move. For some reason, it was not granted, or at least King John was not moved to Beaulieu Abbey.

By September, the vacancy at Canterbury was beginning to allow the kind of problems that had dogged the Angevin kings. Richard Poore, Bishop of Salisbury, was translated to the bishopric of Durham in May so that an election for the vacancy created at Salisbury was required. By royal licence, the chapter at Salisbury met in September and elected Robert de Bingeham, writing to the king to request his approval of their choice. Henry, apparently faltering in his bid to grip total authority and perhaps already missing the guiding hand of Stephen Langton, wrote to Gregory for confirmation that 'as the See of Canterbury was then vacant, such confirmation of the elect belonged of right immediately' to the Pope. Of course, such a delay, as letters moved to Rome and the matter worked its way up the list of papal business, and a reply wended its way across Europe, prolonged the time during which Henry was entitled to take the income from the vacant See. If that formed a part of his thinking, he was walking a road dangerously close to his father's, though the effectiveness of this as a method of securing large amounts of unexpected cash is undeniable and must have been tempting.

During the Christmas celebrations at Oxford letters arrived from the barons of Normandy and Poitou inviting an invasion from the King of England. Both regions were chafing under the regency government of France, and although Richard's truce had nominally left Poitou in English hands, it was all but cut off and might as well have been under the French Crown – as their invitation of an invasion suggests. Preparations began and the news must have been exciting, but it was a prelude to another frustrating and expensive year for Henry. 1229 was characterised by problems over Canterbury and the planned incursion onto the Continent. Henry opposed the candidate elected by the monks of Canterbury and proposed his own, Richard le Grant, Chancellor of Lincoln Cathedral. Henry sent representatives to Rome to secure the Pope's support for his candidate, and when Gregory heard Henry's offer of a tax of a tenth on all of England's property to fund his war with the Emperor, the Pope was unable to refuse the boost to his cause. It was a reckless offer from Henry which would never be popular in England and which he would struggle to fulfil, particularly in a year in which he was also trying to pay for a large military campaign. However he planned to meet his commitment, Henry got his man in the post. Missing the campaigning seasons of spring and summer, Henry finally welcomed Peter, Duke of Brittany, at Portsmouth to join him as he set out for Normandy. After several days of maddening frustration, too few ships turned up to transport the army; splitting it into different trips was decided to be too risky. The invasion was abandoned and Henry, in a fit of pique, blamed Hubert for failing to get him enough transport. Henry celebrated Christmas at York with the Scottish King Alexander II with fleet preparations already underway for 1230.

On 30 April 1230, Henry and his fleet finally sailed out of Portsmouth. The campaign was initially successful and most of Brittany and Poitou were quickly secured. It must have felt to Henry as though all of his waiting was finally going to pay off and that glory might at last be restored to the Angevin dynasty. It took just two days from Henry's departure for the domestic peace to quiver. On 2 May 1230, Llywelyn, who had been quiet for some time now, publicly hanged William de Braose, whom he had taken prisoner in 1228, ransomed for the huge sum of £2,000 and then made an alliance with, which saw Llywelyn's son Dafydd married to William's oldest daughter Isabella. The *Chronicle of Ystrad Fflur* records that Llywelyn took the action against William 'after he had been caught in Llywelyn's chamber with the king of England's daughter, Llywelyn's wife'. William was a member of a wealthy and powerful Marcher line and his treatment risked the reopening of old hostilities, though such an eruption was fortunately avoided.

Henry was at Nantes, having just secured Mirebeau Castle, when he wrote a letter expressing his intention to return home, not least because both he and his brother Richard had been severely ill. By October, the army was back in England – though the Christmas celebrations at Lambeth may have been a little subdued. Henry had personally pinned a lot of hopes to this invasion of France. He had been invited, which ought to have greased the hinges of doors that had been shut for decades and secured early successes, but created an advantage only until the French began to organise themselves in resistance. Henry had punched hard into Brittany and Poitou in his enthusiasm to take back what he believed was his and perhaps to try and redeem his father's reputation, something his request to the Pope about John's removal to Beaulieu demonstrates remained high in his thoughts. Early success had perhaps drawn the inexperienced king in too deep too quickly, and the campaign seems to have lacked any overarching plan either in terms of a direction of attack or a set of provisions for securing what was taken. As Henry's army marched forlornly out of France, young Louis' forces quietly and quickly mopped up behind them, taking everything back. Perhaps illness explained the faltering scheme, but the king returned to England with news of a failure that was financially expensive and politically unwelcome.

In January 1231 an uncomfortable council met to thrash out the military, financial and political impacts of the failures of 1230, though little progress was made and no resolution reached. In April, William Marshal, Earl of Pembroke, and oldest son of the legendary Marshal, died at the age of about forty shortly after celebrating the marriage of his sister to Henry's brother Richard, cementing the relationship between their families. Henry was reported to have lamented, 'Woe, woe is me! Is not the blood of the blessed martyr Thomas fully avenged yet?', counting the loss of Marshal as a stroke of bad luck that felt like a punishment from God. Henry was right to see trouble on the horizon, and 1231 would see the re-emergence of unrest at home. England had been relatively peaceful for several years, the last real trouble having ended in Wales in 1223, giving Henry the freedom to focus abroad. Had he been successful, it is possible that he would not have seen the kind of backlash at home that might seem predictable as a disappointed and depleted warrior class returned home in frustration. Llywelyn exploited the vacuum left by the loss of the immensely capable William Marshal to reignite his own resistance to Henry, raiding up and down the Marches before attacking a royal force near Montgomery.

Letters appeared on the desks of bishops and cathedral chapters all over the kingdom from an unknown group who called themselves 'men ready to die rather than tolerate the Romans beneficed in England' and who wrote that they were utterly determined to end the slavery and abuse of England by the papacy. They wanted nothing less than the expulsion of all Romans holding benefices in England, a method by which the popes had been able to enrich their Roman faction within the English Church, tightening the grip and increasing the influence of the Pope. When a court in St Albans broke up at the end of its business a Roman canon of St Paul's by the name of Cincio was kidnapped by this secretive society, robbed and held for several weeks. John de Ferentino, Archdeacon of Norwich, only narrowly escaped the trap and fled into hiding in London.

The Earl of Chester and William Marshal's brother and heir Richard Marshal had been in Anjou and Normandy, but their failure to make progress led to a truce with France, sealed on 4 July. To add to the troubles of this unsettled year, Archbishop le Grand died on 3 August whilst travelling back to England from Rome. In January he had, in common with other bishops, opposed Henry's request for a scutage tax to fund the war abroad and had fallen into dispute with Hubert. The archbishop had travelled to Rome to seek approval for measures he wished to implement to deal with the problems regarding pluralism still lingering in England and was on his way back when he died. The See of Canterbury was vacant again, and that might well mean more trouble in an already difficult year.

Christmas was spent at Winchester with Peter des Roches, who had returned from crusading in the Holy Land and been warmly welcomed back by Henry. Peter instantly rose to higher favour than Hubert, who was increasingly being blamed by Henry for everything that was going wrong. Peter's exotic tales from the Holy Land and complete detachment from the recent problems Henry had suffered doubtless contributed to the enthusiasm with which the king took to his former tutor once more. The Bishop of Winchester was also a hard man, and Henry might have believed him more capable of solving the present unrest than Hubert.

1232 began as 1231 had ended. The attacks on the property of foreigners were becoming more numerous and more serious. One Roman clerk at Wingham in Kent complained to the sheriff that his barns had been attacked, and when the sheriff and his men went to investigate they found armed men occupying the barns. All of the clerk's corn within had been either sold cheaply or given away to the poor and those within produced letters from the king ordering that their work should not be interfered with. The papers were forgeries but the matter reached the ear of the Bishop of London, who summoned ten of his colleagues that together excommunicated all of those involved at Wingham and in similar attacks elsewhere, plus the men who had seized Cincio at St Albans and those who had written the letters threatening Romans. A Yorkshire knight named Robert Twenge, operating under the name of William Wither, was identified as the ringleader of the organised unrest. The Pope would surely not be happy to hear of the attacks on his countrymen.

The culmination of this lawlessness and increasing trouble was the dismissal on 29 July 1232 of Hubert de Burgh from the position of Justiciar that he had held for seventeen years, from the last years of John, throughout Henry's minority and into his majority. The position had given Hubert unrivalled authority during the minority but that only brought heavy accusations of abuse of his position. The articles of accusation against Hubert are recorded in the papers of State Trials and make grim reading for the Justiciar. The nine articles were a comprehensive indictment of Hubert's performance as chief minister. In the first, Hubert was required to provide 'an account of all the revenue of the kingdom, for the fourteen years next following the death of King John his father, from which time he took upon him the keeping and management of the same, without any authority'. This set the scene for the rest of the articles. Providing fourteen years' worth of accounts would be no mean feat, but to accuse Hubert of taking control of the kingdom's finances without authority was simply untrue. His role as Justiciar, particularly during a minority, required him to take full responsibility as if the king were not present in the realm, and, even if he should not have done so, no Pope or legate had removed those powers in a decade and a half. From the first article Hubert must have known his downfall was a done deal.

The second article required an account to be provided for 89,000 marks of silver, which should have been collected for a fifteenth tax and not spent without the permission of six bishops and six earls or on the defence of the kingdom but which was, allegedly, missing. Henry was now seeking to blame his constant pecuniary embarrassments on his chief minister. Next, Hubert was blamed entirely for the loss of Poitou, with a far-fetched claim that the Justiciar had, instead of sending money and supplies, 'sent barrels filled with stones and sand, so that when the Barons and great men of our lord the King, and the burgesses, perceived that default, they abandoned the homage and service of our lord the King, and turned themselves to the enemies of our lord the King, by means whereof our lord the King lost Poitou'. The fourth article added to the accusation of costing the king Poitou with a claim that the expensive and lengthy siege of Bedford had been not only wrong but entirely Hubert's doing. In the fifth article, it was explained that Hubert had written to Rome to obtain Henry's period of demi-majority without permission and with the sole intention of enriching himself and his friends by increasing his own power. Article six referred to the agreement John had made with the late King William of Scotland regarding the marriage of one of William's daughters to Henry. The article explained that whilst the king was still a minor and unable to decide upon a marriage for himself Hubert had seen himself married to Henry's intended, and that the breach of John's promise had cost the Crown not only honour but land and money to compensate the current Scottish King Alexander for the failure to meet the terms agreed. The seventh article named Hubert as the driving force behind the current attack on Romans as a petulant action in response to a papal order that he divorce his wife, whilst the eighth accused Hubert of breaching a promise to the king that he would not escape his custody whilst awaiting trial (which he then proceeded to do), and the ninth not only alleged that Hubert had 'spake base and scandalous words of the lord the King' in the presence of witnesses but also ominously stated that 'the lord the King still has many things to be proposed and alleged against him, which, for the perusal, he reserves in his mind to propose when it shall please him and occasion shall serve'.

Hubert was doomed, whether he was guilty or not. A king did not bring such charges against a subject to see them dismissed. Peter des Roches may well have harboured a jagged grudge against Hubert and used the high favour of his return to undo a man he believed had undone him and driven him from the king's favour. This is evidenced in some small way by the fact that Poitevins associated with Peter quickly rose to fill gaps left by Hubert. Stephen de Segrave replaced Hubert as Justiciar and Peter de Rievaulx, a man officially recorded as the bishop's nephew but rumoured in some quarters to be his son, was appointed Treasurer. For the rest of the year Englishmen were squeezed out of influence and replaced by Poitevins. By August, Peter de Rievaulx held nineteen of the thirty-five offices of sheriff in England. The removal of Hubert also served a purpose for Henry, even if the Bishop of Winchester worked hard to encourage it. Hubert's dismissal marked the final clear break from Henry's minority but it also allowed him to park all of the troubles, failures and disappointments of recent years at Hubert's cell door, rinsing himself clean of their stains and creating a new start for the king which, he may have believed, would be brighter. It perhaps shows a lack of the maturity and independence that he sought to demonstrate that he was heavily influenced by his former tutor and instantly replaced Hubert's influence with Peter's.

Although Hubert was not the last man to hold the post of Justiciar of England – four more would sporadically occupy the office during Henry's reign – he can be rightly considered the last of the great, powerful Justiciars. From the first appointment, that of Roger of Salisbury in 1102 by Henry I, the post had held a prestige second only to that reserved for the king. The Justiciar was chief minister, the king's deputy and his regent when he went abroad. During the absentee rule of Richard I, the country was ruled by his Justiciars for years. In Hubert, with the first minority kingship since the Norman Conquest, the post had taken on even more lustre and authority. The post was the nearest England would come to a Prime Minister in the modern sense for several centuries more and the authority they wielded, though partly absorbed by an increasingly self-aware and self-confident Parliament over following centuries, would not be focussed in one man again until Cardinal Wolsey and Thomas Cromwell administered the government for King Henry VIII. It has become an archaic, almost unknown, foreign-sounding title, but during the twelfth and early thirteenth centuries the holder wielded unrivalled power.

In October 1232, Ranulf de Blondeville, Earl of Chester, died at the age of around sixty-two. He had variously been a powerful supporter of Henry, particularly against Louis' invasion, and a strong critic when he felt the young king needed to be drawn back into line. His death left Richard Marshal, Earl of Pembroke, as the most senior noble in the land and with the unenviable task of trying to fend off the tide of Poitevins sweeping through the corridors of power. Ranulf has been considered the last bastion of the old Anglo-Norman feudal barony; this was proving to be a year of significant endings. Henry spent Christmas at Worcester with Peter de Roches and his attendance marks another of those endings. Over the previous few years, Henry had been involved in the rebuilding of the east end of Worcester Cathedral and had taken the opportunity to erect a permanent monument for his father. The effigy that rests before the altar today is the oldest royal effigy in England and is believed to be a true likeness of King John, though the base upon which the effigy now rests is a later, Tudor addition, installed when the cathedral quire was reworked to house the remains of Prince Arthur, Henry VIII's older brother. On either side of John's head are representations of saints Wulfstan and Oswald – when the tomb was installed it stood between the two shrines to these saints. Faint traces of the bright paintwork that originally decorated the effigy and a gilded cage originally wrapped over the top of the effigy give a hint of the colourful environment medieval churches were.

Quite what Henry thought as he inspected the work and looked on the face of his father, albeit in stone, for the first time in nearly twenty years is impossible to tell. Did he resent the treatment his father had received at the hands of his barons? Had he been waiting for the end of his minority to impose himself in true Angevin style? Did his father's fate act as a warning which Henry could constantly use to remind himself of the dangers of tyranny? Perhaps the deathbed words of William Marshal rang in his ears as he looked upon what he had done for his father, reminding him not to follow in John's footsteps if he hoped for a long life. The fact that such questions were on the mind of the twenty-five-year-old king is suggested by the sculptures that look down on his father's tomb. Standing on the south side of the quire, with Prince Arthur's chantry at your right hand and the choir stalls in front, looking up reveals a set of carved figures that tell a story and may offer a glimpse into the mind of King Henry III, who paid for much of the work. It is not known with certainty who the figures are, but it is believed that one pair, on the far left, represent King John and his wife Isabella of Angoulême. At the far right is another pair thought to be Henry himself and his future wife Eleanor, demonstrating that they were added some years after the tomb effigy. In the four sculptures between the father and son is a pondering on kingship.

Between John and Henry are images of Edward the Confessor, Henry's personal hero, King David, another kingly figure with legs crossed and a toad on his shield, marking him as a bad king, and a king playing a harp. The image of Edward the Confessor depicts the story of the saint-king, the pilgrim and the ring, in which Edward, lacking coin to give a beggar as alms, removed a ring from his finger and handed it over. Years later, two Englishmen were stranded during a pilgrimage to the Holy Land when they met an old man. On learning that they were from England, the old man told them that he was John the Baptist, gave them a ring and asked them to return it to Edward, who had given it to him, and to tell the English king that in six months' time he would join John in Heaven. It is unsure when this series was completed, though it was clearly later than 1232 given the appearance of Henry's wife, but it is a fascinating insight into Henry's thoughts. Does he mean the viewer to understand that kings are made up of good and bad elements and can be brave warriors, tyrants, saints and patrons of the arts all at once, in varying degrees and in response to circumstance? Perhaps Henry sought to distance himself from his father's reputation, placing distance and a saint between them. It is hard to discern with any certainty what the message was, but it does clearly demonstrate that notions of what constituted a good king or a bad king, and how aspects of kingship made up the whole or might dominate a reputation, were firmly in Henry's mind during this period of his life, and we can perhaps read a good deal into the fact that it preoccupied him to some degree.

During May 1233, Henry's brother Richard struck an odd deal with the king. The earl swapped three of his manors for a small plot of unusable land on the windswept, sea-battered Cornish coast. The deed referred to the spit of rock as 'the island of Tyntagel'. Richard lavished money on this unlikely spot, building walls and an outer bailey on the mainland and using the small land bridge to the island to connect to an inner bailey and new residential buildings almost detached from the coast. Tintagel was already, by the thirteenth century, a mythical spot, and it was this sense of history, legend and a connection to the most famous English king that attracted Richard. Towards the end of the previous century, the French poem *Tristan and Iseult* had told the tragic love story of a Cornish knight, Tristan, who falls in love with Iseult, the wife of his uncle King Mark of Cornwall. Much of the story is set at Tintagel, King Mark's castle, but of even more interest was the burgeoning Arthurian legend, particularly as told by Gerald of Wales, also during the previous century, in his *History of the Kings of Britain*. In Gerald's tale of Uther's lust and Arthur's heroism, Uther pursues Ygerna, a married woman, to her husband's castle at Tintagel, described as 'built high above the sea, which surrounds it on all sides, and there is no way in except that offered by a narrow isthmus of rock. Three armed soldiers could hold it against you, even if you stood there with the whole kingdom of Britain at your side.' When Ygerna's husband was absent, the mystical Merlin transformed Uther into the likeness of her husband so that he could lie with Ygerna, and 'that night she conceived Arthur, the most famous of men, who subsequently won great renown by his outstanding bravery'. King Arthur was supposedly conceived on the very spot Richard had acquired and built his castle on. He was not buying a rocky crag clinging to the Cornish coast, he was buying a piece of history in the hope that it would rub off on him and leave an aura of chivalric heroism. It also served to ingratiate the earl to his county by promoting its part in one of Britain's greatest stories.

Away from loftier ideals, politics did not stop for long in Henry's England. On 24 June 1233 a council was scheduled to meet at

Oxford but virtually all of the barons, under the leadership of Richard Marshal, refused to attend. A Dominican friar named Robert Bacon explained to the king that there could be no peace in England whilst the Bishop of Winchester was the senior figure in Henry's government and was importing foreign men to key offices. On 5 July, most stayed away again. When a new meeting was arranged for 1 August, attendance at which was required on pain of identification as a traitor, the barons told Henry that he must expel all of the foreigners in his government or they would call a Great Council and elect a new king for themselves. This was a shocking development that harked back to the Anglo-Saxon principle of the Witan, or Witenagemot, which was a council of all the great magnates, empowered to appoint a king at a time when inheritance was not a guarantee.

The pressure was ramped up when Marshal, who had not attended because his sister had got a message to him on the road that des Roches was planning a trap for him, was declared a traitor and a date set for his trial. The barons retaliated in Marshal's support, citing the illegality of such a move when Marshal was entitled to trial by his peers. Peter des Roches displayed a flagrant lack of tact when he told the barons that there were no peers in England in the true sense, as there were in France – his inflammatory comment drew a threat of excommunication from his fellow bishops as a disturber of the peace. On 17 August, Henry was at Gloucester gathering a force to march against Marshal's Welsh lands. Usk Castle fell quickly, and peace seemed to have been enforced by September. When council was called for 9 October, Marshal appeared to vanish en route. The barons accused des Roches of kidnapping him, insisting again that he was entitled to trial by his peers, but Marshal was not the bishop's prisoner.

In the midst of this ugly dispute, Edmund Rich was elected Archbishop of Canterbury. The See had been vacant since the death of Archbishop le Grand in 1231, and there had been intense conflict in attempts to appoint a successor which Henry would approve. The election of Ralph Neville, Bishop of Chichester, was quashed by Pope Gregory, as were subsequent elections of John of Sittingbourne and John Blund. Edmund was a learned man who loved his studies at Salisbury. One anonymous chronicler records that when a servant rushed in hoping to be the first to break the news of his election to Edmund he was told abruptly, 'Go away, you ass, and close the door behind you. See that nobody interrupts my studies.' Edmund was later canonised, and Matthew Paris wrote one of several histories of his life in which the monk-chronicler records that Edmund's protests of unworthiness went so far beyond what was traditional that eventually his friends and brother monks pleaded with him:

> Unless you consent and are installed without delay, the king's council will procure the substitution of some alien, and have him intruded into the place where God has ordained so many saints. An unwillingness to assent to just requests is a kind of folly. Do not refuse to be moved by the entreaties of good men. If you are not careful, your pusillanimous resistance will be the cause of great confusion in the most noble church of Canterbury.

The words inserted into the mouths of these men by Matthew Paris carry his usual distaste for foreign interlopers and, whilst he cannot resist the kind of grand moralising statements that abbey chronicles all ring with, it demonstrates a sentiment, at least in Matthew's circles, that they needed an Englishman at Canterbury to fight against the wave of Poitevin appointments being made by Henry.

It was also during this period that Hubert broke out of his custody, as mentioned in the articles against him. On 29 September, a group of Hubert's men sprang him from Devizes Castle and he fled into a local church, where he claimed sanctuary. He was swiftly removed by force, returned to Devizes Castle and given a beating for his troubles. On 1 October news of the escape and removal reached Henry, and the Bishop of London protested vehemently against Hubert's removal from sanctuary. The king acquiesced and Hubert was returned to the small church, which was however put under siege by Henry's forces. In spite of this, Hubert slipped out and vanished into Wales.

The year had been a hard and harsh one in any quarters. There had been a famine so devastating that Roger of Wendover lamented, 'It was a wretched sight for travellers in that region to see on the highways innumerable dead bodies lying naked and unburied, to be devoured by birds of prey, and so polluting the air that they infected healthy men with mortal disease.' Roger also wrote expansively and in damning terms of Henry's domination by Peter des Roches and the policies the king pursued as a result of it. The Bishop of Winchester, Roger complained, 'in order to gain the King's favour more completely, associated with himself Stephen de Segrave, a yielding man, and Robert Passelewe, who kept the King's treasury under Peter de Rivaulx; and he entirely ruled the kingdom with the advice and assistance of those men'. Henry apparently imported large numbers of men from Brittany and Poitou and gave them castles and positions of authority across the kingdom, so that 'these men used their utmost endeavours to oppress the natural English subjects and nobles, calling them traitors, and accusing them of treachery to the King' and gave them control over 'all the youths of the nobility, both male and female, who were foully degraded by ignoble marriages'. Roger summed up the year by explaining that,

In short, judgment was entrusted to the unjust, laws to outlaws, the preservation of peace to the quarrelsome, and justice to those who were themselves full of injury, and when the nobles of the kingdom laid complaints before the King of the oppression they endured, the said Bishop interfered and there was no one to grant them justice.

It was during his summation of this year that Roger used a phrase in his description of the king that is frustratingly unclear. It is translated as 'he, simple man that he was, believed their lies', but the Latin word used for and translated as 'simple' was '*simplex*' and, although this could have a connotation that implied a lack of intelligence or even what might be considered learning difficulties, it is the only mention of something that might have drawn far more attention, particularly in a king who had been referred to as a good pupil in his youth, though it might also explain the ease with which he was dominated by powerful men and the way in which his policy often flip-flopped and lacked an overarching plan. *Simplex*, though, has several other meanings, including being open or straightforward, lacking in guile, being unsophisticated or naïve. It is even a word that was frequently used to describe saints as being above worldly corruption. It seems unlikely that either extreme of the word was what Roger meant. If Henry had been unintelligent it would surely have attracted more mentions in the chronicles of educated monks and there is no other suggestion of it or sign of it during his career. Neither is it likely that Roger was imbuing the king with saintly characteristics whilst decrying his policies. What Roger probably meant was that Henry was naïve and easily led, perhaps a mechanism to excuse the king from the criticism he was attracting and to focus attention more fully on Peter des Roches.

In November 1233, Henry gathered an army at Gloucester and marched north along the Marcher borders, only to be driven back to Gloucester by a surprise attack during the night. On 25 November, Richard Marshal was ambushed by a much larger royal force near Monmouth as he tried to slip past the castle. Henry was outraged at the earl's victory, but as Christmas approached he tried to open negotiations with Richard. At Marshal's refusal to come to terms with his king, Henry swore that he would never be reconciled with the Marshal, who might have remembered the fate of the garrison at Bedford. Undeterred, Richard Marshal continued his rampage into the New Year, capturing and burning Shrewsbury. When council met at Westminster on 2 February 1234, Marshal was present and listed his grievances at the course Henry was taking in placing himself and the country so entirely in the hands of foreigners. Supported by several bishops, Richard reminded Henry that it had been precisely the same policy that had brought his father to civil war, and further that it was by the counsel of Peter des Roches that Normandy had been lost, the people alienated and the country's wealth squandered so that England had ended up being sold to the Pope to save the crown. On 6 March a truce was sealed between Henry and Richard after hard negotiation by the bishops of Coventry and Rochester. In stepping back from his previous oath never to be reconciled to Marshal, Henry demonstrated that, although his temper might burn white hot as quickly as his father's and his other Plantagenet forebears, he lacked the insidious malice and ability to hold a grudge that John held tight to.

Edmund Rich was consecrated as Archbishop of Canterbury on 2 April. The month was to prove a testing one for a man nearly sixty years of age and required to hit the ground running. The two and a half years without a head of the English Church had left a vacuum that Edmund set about filling quickly. On 9 April Edmund presented another long list of grievances against Henry's policies and threatened the king with excommunication if he did not listen and mend his ways, ignoring the papal ruling that Henry and his brother could only be excommunicated by direct written order of the Pope himself. Astonishingly, Henry capitulated. He immediately ordered Peter des Roches to restrict himself to the business of the See of Winchester and to no longer involve himself in the government of the realm. Peter de Rievaulx was instructed to provide a full account of his term as Treasurer and to consider himself dismissed from that office. Poitevins throughout England were deprived of their offices and ordered to remove themselves from the realm. Stephen de Seagrave was relieved of his position as Justiciar, and the post remained empty in a clear signal that Henry now meant to rule entirely himself with no favourite to guide him – which also meant no one to hide behind if things went wrong.

The difficulties inherent in this conflict of internal politics is shown by a letter from Pope Gregory penned on 3 April, which must have arrived after Henry's momentous decision in which the Pope describes his purpose as the delivery of peace and harmony wherever there is disunion. In it, Gregory wrote:

> It is, therefore, necessary that you sedulously exhort and warn those born in England not to take it amiss if strangers living amongst them obtain honours and benefices in the country, since with God there is no acceptance of persons, and he who lives according to justice in any nation, finds favour in His sight.

He further instructed Edmund to

> earnestly exhort others to show their trust and devotion to him. In this way, and in this way only, the new archbishop will be able to prove that the good reports upon which the pope had appointed him to his high office were well founded.

The letter arrived too late, but demonstrates the meddling impact of Rome when England was struggling with foreign influence which can only have inflamed passions. It also shows a lack of tact on the part of the Pope, though he had his reasons for such an insistence: many of the foreigners filling clerical posts in England were Roman and Gregory did not want that source of patronage and income cut off to him.

Richard Marshal died on 16 April whilst defending his lands in Ireland. He never saw the fulfilment of his desire to see England freed from the Poitevins. *The Annals of Dunstable* recorded that, in spite of their differences, Henry 'mourned for his friend as David had lamented Saul and Jonathan'. When council met on 28 May at Gloucester, the expulsion of the Poitevin faction was confirmed and Gilbert Marshal, the fourth of William Marshal's five sons, was knighted and received his heirless brother's lands and titles. On 21 June, Edmund, Archbishop of Canterbury, negotiated a two-year truce with the perennially troublesome Llywelyn. England appeared to be settling once again after another period of turmoil and upheaval that had brought its beginnings and endings. One thorn that continued to twist in Henry's side was his stepfather, Hugh de Lusignan, who was doing all that he could to scupper peace negotiations between Henry and Louis IX.

Peace with Scotland was on Henry's mind at the beginning of 1235, though there was no fresh outbreak of hostilities with his brother-in-law. Rather, Henry seems to have become interested in the terms of the peace, and it marked a fresh effort to clarify and press his rights. Gregory wrote to Alexander II to explain that he was 'bound to the English king by a special bond of love' and that Henry had asked him to mediate in an effort to make the peace enjoyed between the two kings permanent. Gregory explained that Henry had forwarded a copy of the agreement made by Alexander's father, William I 'the Lion', with King John in 1212 and asked him to confirm its measures. It had been made when William was nearly seventy and John was at the head of an army, so whilst England might have liked its terms, Scotland was less keen. Gregory, though, told Alexander he would consider the peace that existed and how it might be made to last, though nothing more was done on the matter.

At the same time, Henry asked Gregory to intervene in Brittany to use his power to cause that region to return to its allegiance to the English Crown and to threaten them with sanctions if they were not willing. In February an embassy from Frederick II, the Holy Roman Emperor, arrived in England to negotiate a marriage for the Emperor to Henry's sister Isabella, who was turning twenty-one. The union was approved by the Pope in spite of the troubles between the two men, and on 27 February Henry gave his approval to the match. It was a prestigious match and represented a powerful family alliance for Henry which would mean he could add the Holy Roman Emperor to the King of Scotland as his brothers-in-law. The downside was the need to raise a dowry of £20,000. Henry wrote to the Pope of the settlement, assuring Gregory he 'wished in this and all other matters to carry out humbly and devotedly what you advise to be done according to your good will and pleasure, as becomes one who is the most devoted son of the Holy Roman Church' and asking Gregory to act as guarantor to Frederick for the prompt payment of the dowry. Henry offered to submit to any ecclesiastical punishment the Pope saw fit if he failed to pay the money on time. On 6 May the agreement was solemnised and celebrated at Westminster Abbey, and five days later Isabella sailed to meet her new husband. The couple were married on 30 July, and a delighted Frederick sent Henry a gift of three leopards to add to the royal menagerie.

Having taken the reigns of his realm more firmly and independently than at any other point in his nearly twenty years on the throne, Henry found himself in the middle of a calm and settled year. There was peace with France, in spite of Hugh de Lusignan's efforts, with Scotland, with the Holy Roman Empire, with the Pope and even within England and Wales. In order to enjoy this rare achievement, Henry toured his kingdom.

It might also have been this peace that allowed his mind to wonder to another important matter. Seeing Isabella had perhaps also helped turn the king's mind to thoughts of his own marriage. Henry was nearly twenty-eight and had no known mistresses. The second half of 1235 was dominated by his decision to seek a wife. His first approach was for the hand of Joan, daughter of the Count of Poitou, and Henry encouraged her to apply to Gregory for permission for the match. Quickly, though, Henry's attention turned to Eleanor, the second daughter of Raymond of Provence. Eleanor was the niece of the Count of Savoy and her sister Margaret was the Queen of France, so the match would give Henry the King of France as another brother-in-law.

Christmas 1235 was celebrated at Winchester amid the excitement of the impending arrival of Henry's intended bride. In January 1236, Eleanor was escorted to England by her uncle William, bishop-elect of Valence, and immediately, on 14 January, Henry and Eleanor were married at Canterbury Cathedral. Just six days later, on 20 January, Eleanor was crowned at Westminster Abbey. Although her date of birth is not known, Matthew Paris describes her as being twelve years old at her wedding. Plenty of detail from the ceremony is recorded in the Red Book of the Exchequer that paints a scene which must have been overwhelming to a young girl. There appears to have been much squabbling over the right to key offices during the ceremony, which led to the Court of Claims being established as the disputes were set aside to be resolved on a fixed date. The Court of Claims would later sit regularly prior to the coronation of a new monarch to judge and settle matters of precedence and right to perform certain key duties at the ceremony. Simon de Montfort, who had arrived in England in 1229 to make his fortune, was key amongst the arguments. He claimed the right to the earldom of Leicester, to which his grandmother had been a senior co-heir and which Simon's crusading father had claimed. John had denied it to de Montfort and given it instead to Ranulf, but Simon, displaying an uncanny knack that he possessed, persuaded Ranulf to cede the earldom when Henry refused to order him to give it up. At the coronation Simon, not yet invested with his earldom formally, defended his right to act as hereditary steward against Roger Bigod, Earl of Norfolk. He won the dispute, though it was just one of many as young noblemen jostled for prominent and prestigious positions.

The king attended the coronation wearing his own crown, and Eleanor walked with her husband on ray cloth laid on the floor between the chamber where they began and the altar of Westminster Abbey. The cloth was laid by William de Beauchamp of Bedford, the king's almoner, and after the ceremony any part of the cloth that was inside the abbey was given to the sacristy of the abbey and any part that was outside was cut up by the almoner and distributed amongst the poor as a valuable thing to sell or a memento of a glorious day (if they could afford to keep it). Henry walked ahead of Eleanor beneath a square canopy of 'cloth of purple silk on four silvered lances, with four silver-gilt bells', carried above the king by 'barons of the Cinque Ports, four to each lance, by reason of the number of the ports, so that no port should seem to be preferred above another'. 'In like manner the same people carried a silken cloth over the queen coming after the king', and the cloth seems to have been another subject of dispute as the barons of the Cinque Ports claimed it as theirs whilst the wardens of the Marches believed they had a right to it. Few argued for posts in the queen's retinue, though Gilbert de Sandford claimed a hereditary right to act as her chamberlain, which gave him a right to claim the bed and basins of the queen's chamber. He also insisted that he was entitled to place a clerk in the queen's household, to be paid sixpence a day from queen's gold income. Queen's gold, or *aurum reginae*, was a portion of fines that the queen was entitled to claim as her income which, although a subject of some discussion, probably constituted 1 per cent of any fine over one hundred marks.

When council dispersed from Merton after the coronation, it was a tetchy parting. The barons complained that foreigners had already begun to appear back in roles from which they had been expelled and the barons were disturbed to learn that Henry had appointed twelve councillors about him, led by Eleanor's uncle William, bishop-elect of Valance, without whose approval he intended to do nothing. As always, Henry's finances were in dire straits and he was alienating his magnates. In his distress, he turned to the Pope and wrote to Gregory IX asking him to appoint a legate – more than a decade after the last one left England. When Gregory replied on 2 August he told Henry that he considered the English king 'as a special son and watched over his welfare like a mother, since by so doing it was consulting not any foreign interests, but its very own'. The Pope and the cardinals of the Curia had debated the request and decided that they should wait a little longer to see how events developed before offering an opinion, since 'previously he had urged the same request for a legate, and that when one had actually been appointed, then he had changed his mind and had asked to have the appointment revoked'.

When council met on 13 January 1237 in London, William de Raleigh requested a tax be levied for the king. The motion was met with outrage by the barons, who saw no reason to give the king more money and complained loudly about the increased influence of foreigners again. At their protests, Henry declared himself willing to make reforms, including replacing the council of twelve with three magnates elected for him by the barons and authorising excommunication for anyone acting against the Charters. On this basis, a tax of a thirteenth was granted which included the Church. On 28 January, Edmund, Archbishop of Canterbury, absolved Henry for his own frequent breaches of the Charters as the king reaffirmed his commitment to the liberties they provided. In St Catherine's Chapel at Westminster, Edmund and the gathered bishops each held a burning candle as Henry took a lit taper in his left hand, placed his right hand on the Gospels and recited the oath Edmund led him through. Matthew Paris records that Edmund declared anyone breaking the Charters subject to excommunication at which, according to custom, the bishops called 'Amen, Amen', extinguished their candles and threw them to the floor still smoking, as Edmund proclaimed, 'Thus, let those who violate or wrongfully interpret these charters, be destroyed and their condemned souls smoke and stink in their place of punishment.' According to Matthew Paris, Henry's voice was heard above all others in replying 'Amen' to this curse.

On 13 February, Gregory wrote to Henry granting him the legate he had requested and appointing Otto, the former nuncio, to the post. Cardinal Otto arrived in England on 29 June 1237 to, Matthew Paris insists, shocked dismay amongst the barons because 'the nobles of the country were unaware of his coming'. Paris has the nobles decrying the king's duplicity in damning terms:

Our king perverts all things. In every way he sets at nought our laws and disregards his plighted faith and promises. At one time, by the advice of his followers, and without even the knowledge of his friends and natural subjects, he contracted a marriage; now he has secretly called a legate into the country, who will change the whole face of the land; now he gives and now at will he takes back what he has given.

Richard, the king's brother, voiced the common concern that Henry had placed his faith back in foreigners and summoned a legate in secret. Otto's arrival seems to have had a profound effect on Henry, who Matthew Paris claimed,

Seemed to worship his very footsteps, and declared in public, as well as in private, that without the consent either of the lord pope, or of his legate, he was unable to do anything in the kingdom, or to change or to alienate anything in it, since he was really not so much king as feudatory of the pope.

Whether Henry was slightly in awe of Otto or simply looking to delegate some of his responsibility, or blame, for what was happening is uncertain.

Gregory wrote to Henry on hearing of the promises made at the January council to voice his irritation at Henry's actions:

We were greatly moved, on hearing that, acting under the advice of some indiscreet people, you have, with improvident liberality, surrendered to prelates and nobles, etc., certain liberties, possessions, and dignities, as well as many other privileges which belong to the rights and dignity of the Crown, to the great prejudice of the Roman Church, to which the kingdom of England is known to belong, and to the great injury of the kingdom itself. You have, moreover, bound yourself by oaths and charters not to recall these grants. Seeing, therefore, that by the said alienation this Holy See, the rights of which you may not in any way prejudice, is injured in no small degree and the kingdom itself is damaged, we order you, notwithstanding your oaths, to recall the said grants and charters.

This was perhaps the toughest line a pope had taken with Henry to date and offers a reminder that papal coffers were gaping in anticipation still of English coin.

Gregory also penned several letter in the spring of 1237 on the subject of Scotland. On 27 March he told Henry that Otto had been tasked with resolving the peace with Scotland that Gregory felt Alexander II was failing to keep properly, perhaps in response to Henry's previous submission of copies of the treaty his father had made with William the Lion, and on 7 May he appointed Otto legate to Scotland as well as England. On 14 September Henry and his brother-in-law Alexander met at York, with several English lords in attendance, to see Alexander renew his homage to Henry for his English lands.

In November, Otto summoned a synod to meet at St Paul's. On 18 November all of the archbishops, bishops, abbots and many other clerics of England gathered. When the first session opened on the following day, Otto absented himself to allow his proposals to be discussed by all those gathered without having to worry about his presence. The next day, 20 November, Otto attended the meeting with an armed guard of 200 men that he requested of Henry, demonstrating a genuine fear of a backlash to his measures aimed at expanding Stephen Langton's definitions of the rules governing clerical life. The constitution of Cardinal Otto was to be a powerful force in English church life and law for centuries to follow, though Henry had sent letters forbidding the creation of any statute that would infringe upon the rights of the Crown. The focus of Otto's reforms were the establishment of qualifications required for appointment to posts, to prevent unqualified but well-connected men obtaining positions they were not able to fulfil and thus diminishing the Church; the prohibition of marriage for members of the clergy, which had for some time been a grey area that had not been definitively settled; and the prevention of sons succeeding their fathers in clerical posts, since they were not meant to be hereditary.

The main complaint recorded came from the Bishop of Worcester against a ban on pluralism. He argued that some parishes in England were so poor that they could not support a clergyman and that more than one such office had to be held to make them viable and to allow the poor to be properly supported. He also disagreed with a prohibition on the eating of meat, which he said might prove dangerous to frail nuns. In response, Otto offered to write to the

Pope and ask him to reconsider these matters if they were felt to be of such great concern. When the meeting closed on 21 November, Matthew Paris wrote that those leaving were 'not too well satisfied with their experiences' but they had trouble dissenting in any major way with the legate's proposals.

During December 1237, Archbishop Edmund left to visit Rome. Shortly after he left England, Henry made another monumental decision. Henry's sister Eleanor, the widow of William Marshal the Younger, had taken a vow of celibacy after his death six years earlier. Early in the New Year of 1238, Henry presided over a quiet and secretive ceremony to marry his twenty-two-year-old sister to Simon de Montfort, Earl of Leicester, who was around thirty. When news of the marriage seeped out, the magnates were outraged. The most vocal amongst them was Eleanor's other brother, Richard. Simon was French and amongst the foreigners constantly riding high in Henry's estimation. He was also of unsuitable stock to marry an English princess. Henry's other sisters had married the King of Scotland and the Holy Roman Emperor in matches considered suitable, and even Eleanor's first husband had been the Earl of Pembroke, the second most senior noble in the country and a member of the Marshal family who had preserved Henry's throne for him. There were rumours that Simon had been conducting a secret affair with Eleanor against her vow of celibacy and that this caused Henry to agree to, or perhaps even insist upon, the match.

Otto contacted Richard to plead with him to support his brother, but the earl began to gather a force at Kingston and Henry retreated into the Tower. The legate tried to win Richard over with promises of land and money to compensate his wounded pride, but Richard snapped that Otto well knew that such gifts were not within his power or even the Pope's. Nevertheless, Henry managed to reach a settlement worth around £6,000 that mollified his brother and drew the sting from his anger. It was to prove Otto's last contribution in England. The Archbishop of Canterbury had taken the country's concerns about the influence of foreigners and the appointment of a legate in secret to Gregory who, swayed by Edmund's petitioning, recalled Otto. The legate was not pleased by the ending of his term and eventually returned to Rome carrying letters from Henry, Richard and, surprisingly, the bishops explaining the good work he had done and the positive contribution he had made. For the moment, though, the king encouraged him to delay his departure.

During the spring Henry was visited by Baldwin II, Emperor of Constantinople to discuss the problems in his empire and the Holy Land. The meeting was also dominated by the need to find a resolution to renewed hostilities between the Pope and Frederick, Henry's brother-in-law. The dispute between the Pope and the Holy Roman Emperor destabilised much of southern Europe and drew attention away from the Holy Land so that no concerted effort could be made to regain it. The positions of both Pope and Holy Roman Emperor had become intractable, though, and Henry was not really well placed to solve the problem. The English court was also visited by an embassy of Muslims from farther east who sought help against the terrifying and lightening quick expansion of Genghis Khan and his Mongol horde. The crusading warrior-bishop of Winchester Peter des Roches was scathing in his assessment of the request, saying, 'Let these dogs devour one another,' so that it would be easier for Christians to retake the Holy Land when they had worn each other down.

Shortly after this visit, on 9 June 1238, Peter des Roches died. His date of birth is not known, not even roughly, but he had been Bishop of Winchester for thirty-two years. A key pillar of John's resistance to the barons, Peter had been Henry's tutor from his early childhood and had been reappointed to that role when Henry became king. In spite of a period in the cold, which he had used to visit the Holy Land on crusade, Peter had returned to re-enter Henry's high affection, and probably orchestrated the downfall of Hubert de Burgh after a twenty-year feud, only placed on hold for Henry's benefit. *The Annals of Tewkesbury* recorded that 'Peter des Roches was as hard as rocks', playing on his name in an unsubtle, monkish joke. At a time when clerics were becoming discouraged from the arena of war, Peter was a shining example of a dying breed, and disapproving ecclesiastical commentators sneered that he was more at home on the battlefield than in the pulpit. According to the *Lannercost Chronicle* Peter had become known as the 'Butterfly Bishop' because of a story that when out hunting, he had met King Arthur and the two had dined together. When Peter asked for a token of their meeting to prove it to others, King Arthur told him to close his eyes and close his hand, then open his eyes and his hand. When he did, a butterfly flew out of his palm. Peter could reportedly repeat this miracle on demand and earned the nickname from this feat. Trouble quickly followed Peter's death as the wealthy and influential See of Winchester became vacant for the first time in thirty-two years. Henry tried to insert William, bishop-elect of Valance, into the post, but the monks elected Ralph de Neville, the Chancellor and Bishop of Chichester. Henry refused to accept the election and asked Gregory to quash it. Henry tried again to have William elected, but the monks instead chose William de Raleigh, who was roundly rejected by Henry.

9

Papal Exactions

Henry began one of his most ambitious and impactful building projects during 1238, ordering a new curtain wall containing eight towers to encircle the Tower of London; but there was a disturbing event in September of that year. Whilst staying at the royal palace at Woodstock, Henry was asleep in his chamber one night when he was woken by a sudden sound. The noise had been caused by an armed intruder, but Henry appears not to have equated any danger with the situation and began to talk to the man. This conversation woke Eleanor, who was sharing her husband's bed that night (which was by no means normal for a medieval king and queen), and she raised the alarm so that guards rushed in and arrested the man. The intruder admitted that he had entered Henry's chamber with the intention of assassinating the king and that he had been hired by several of Henry's enemies. Matthew Paris recorded the man's terrible punishment, writing, 'In the first place he was dragged asunder, then beheaded, and his body divided into three parts, and each was then dragged through one of the principal cities of England, and was afterwards hung on a gibbet used for robbers.' As Henry celebrated Christmas at Winchester, doubtless to keep the pressure on the monks there to bend to his will, he managed to upset Gilbert Marshal, who was refused entry to see the king. The following day, Gilbert returned to ask why he had been treated so rudely and to offer to clear his name against anyone who impugned him to the king, perhaps even implicating him in the assassination attempt. Henry flew into a rage, according to Matthew Paris, bellowing, 'Whence has Earl Gilbert got his horns? How is it that he threateningly raises his heel upon me, against whom it is hard for him to kick?' Henry continued to rant about the treachery of Gilbert's brother Richard Marshal and decry the advice of the Archbishop of Canterbury to allow Gilbert his inheritance. In stunned shock Gilbert withdrew into the north. He and his remaining brother Walter were never again involved at the heart of government.

June brought happier news that was to delight the kingdom. In the early hours of 17 June 1239 Queen Eleanor delivered a son, the couple's first child. Henry was a father at last, at the age of thirty-one and after twenty-three years on the throne. London, where the child was born, celebrated wildly according to Matthew Paris: 'They assembled bands of dancers, with drums and tambourines, and at night illuminated the streets with large lanterns.' Four days after his birth, the child was baptised and given the name Edward, doubtless for Henry's favourite saint-king. Otto performed the baptism, Paris noting that the Archbishop of Canterbury had to confirm it because Otto was not a priest, and the baby's uncles Richard, Earl of Cornwall, and Simon de Montfort, Earl of Leicester, stood as godparents. As gifts poured into the capital from well-wishers, Henry took the ungallant step of asking who had sent each gift and, if he did not deem it of suitable value for the worth of the sender, he ordered it returned and replaced by a better one. The news dismayed Matthew Paris, who wrote that 'the king deeply clouded his magnificence as a king'; one joke doing the rounds was that 'God gave us this child, but the king sells him to us'.

Trouble erupted once more on 9 August when Queen Eleanor underwent her churching ceremony to allow her to re-enter the world of high society following her period in isolation in the run up to and period of rest immediately after the birth of a baby. As everyone arrived for the ceremony, Henry barred his brother-in-law Simon and his sister Eleanor from entering, warning Simon that he had been excommunicated and was not welcome. In spite of repeated pleading from Simon and Eleanor, Henry would not be moved. When Simon and his wife left and returned to the Bishop of Winchester's palace, which Henry had loaned them to stay in, the king sent men to eject them. When they came again before the king and begged his forgiveness with 'tears and lamentations', Henry's temper boiled over again. Paris reports this rant as the cause of the rumour about Simon and Eleanor's pre-marital relationship. Henry bawled, 'You seduced my sister before marriage, and when I found it out, I gave her to you in marriage, although against my will, in order to avoid scandal.' Henry continued that Simon had sought to have Eleanor's vow of chastity quashed in Rome by the payment of heavy bribes and expressed his anger that Simon had not only defaulted on the debts, leading to his excommunication, but had 'named me as your security, without consulting me, and when I knew nothing of the matter'. Simon was overcome by embarrassment and shame at the charges and he and his wife immediately sought out a ship to give them passage to France.

At the end of July Otto attended a meeting with all of the bishops of England, who complained that Rome was bleeding England dry as the legate claimed procurations on top of other exactions. The bishops, according to Matthew Paris, angrily told Otto, 'Let him supply you, who has summoned you without consulting any one on the matter', making it clear to Otto that if he wanted money he should see Henry for it, since none of them wanted him there. The bishops may have arrived at the meeting ready for a fight. Throughout July a fresh wave of foreigners arrived in England and they were showered with extravagant gifts by the king. Queen Eleanor's family, known as the Savoyards, began to arrive and land prime offices and rich posts from Henry. Prominent amongst the new arrivals was Peter of Savoy, Eleanor's uncle, who Henry would make Earl of Richmond in 1241 along with a grant of land alongside the Thames near the Strand. Here Peter would build a magnificence palace, the Savoy Palace, which would eventually become the property of John of Gaunt and, thanks to his ownership, be burned to the ground during the Peasants' Revolt of 1381 (the Savoy Hotel today stands on the same spot as Peter's luxurious palace). Another uncle, Peter's older brother Thomas, Count of Flanders, also appeared with a third brother, Boniface. The appeal to Henry perhaps lay in the loyalty he could expect from these men due to the ties of family and patronage, something he was continually unable to find in the English barons, but if he thought the answer was to replace the despised Poitevins with a Savoyard faction and that the barons would welcome such a turn of events, he was very wrong.

Letters began to pour into England from the Pope and the Holy Roman Emperor again, marking a fresh wave of hostility between them that had seen Frederick excommunicated. The language from both sides as they sought Henry's understanding and support for their position grew more heightened as the summer slipped into autumn. Frederick began one letter to Richard, Earl of Cornwall, with the thunderous words, 'Cast your eyes around you: attend, ye sons of men, and grieve over the scandal of the world, the quarrels of the nations, and the universal banishment of justice.' On learning that Frederick had sent copies of the same letter across Europe to try and justify his position, Gregory sent his own letters in equally bellicose terms:

There has risen from the sea a beast, full of words of blasphemy, which, formed with the feet of a bear, the mouth of a raging lion, and, as it were, a panther in its other limbs, opens its mouth in blasphemies against God's name, and continually attacks with similar weapons his tabernacle, and the saints who dwell in heaven.

Just in case there was any doubt to whom Gregory referred, he later instructed the readers:

Consider how the said Frederick, by his letters, sent throughout the various countries of the world, has endeavoured to stain the sincerity of the Apostolic See and our own by his polluted statements; a worker of falsehoods; ignorant of all modesty, and untinged by the blush of shame.

The dispute was a long-running one centred, as so much was for the papacy in this time, on crusading. Gregory constantly lambasted Frederick's failure to fulfil his crusading vow, and when he finally did the Pope took exception to Frederick's apparent admiration of the Muslim faith and their mosques. By now, it was an intractable battle of personalities. Frederick was

used to being excommunicated and simply used it as an excuse
to take an army to Rome.

With the Pope distracted, Henry stepped up his efforts to get his
wife's uncle, William of Valence, elected as Bishop of Winchester.
The king installed a foreigner in his service named Andrew as
prior of the monks at Winchester, but on 1 November William
was poisoned and died at Viterbo. Shortly afterwards, Robert
Grosseteste, Bishop of Lincoln, a well-respected churchman and
politician, wrote to the Archbishop of Canterbury to complain
about interference with the free election to clerical positions. He
asserted that the constant interference of the Crown would damage
the Church and was also in contravention of the Charters, which
clearly promised the freedom of the Church. The letter seems to
have spurred Edmund into action and he began to petition the Pope
on the matter.

On 17 January, tragedy struck Henry's brother Richard. Matthew
Paris records that Isabella Marshal 'was taken dangerously ill of
the yellow jaundice' in the final stages of a pregnancy. Her hair
was cut to try and stave off a fever, and she delivered a boy, who
was quickly baptised Nicholas, before both mother and son died.
Richard was in Cornwall at the time, but on hearing the news 'he
broke out into the most sorrowful lamentations, and mourned
inconsolably'. He rushed to his dead wife and had her buried
at Beaulieu Abbey, his father's foundation. Matthew Paris also
records, somewhat mysteriously, that 'about this time a terrible
sound was heard, as if a huge mountain had been thrown forth
with great violence and fallen in the middle of the sea; and this
was heard in a great many places at a distance from each other, to
the great terror of the multitudes'. Perhaps it was an earthquake,
but just maybe it was the sound of the Earl of Cornwall's grief.
Gilbert Marshal's sorrow at the passing of his sister was added to
when Henry focussed his gaze upon the earl again, accusing Gilbert
of what Paris describes as 'certain particulars, of which I think
it better to be silent than to make mention'. A date was set after
Easter for Gilbert to answer the charges.

Messengers arrived from the Holy Roman Emperor during
January, too, bringing Frederick's furious complaint that Henry
had allowed the papal excommunication against him to be

published in England. He insisted that Henry should send Otto back to Rome, since he had been brought to England in secret and, as a servant of the Pope, was an enemy to Frederick. Henry responded that, as a feudal vassal of the Pope, he was obliged to obey papal orders, but offered to write to Gregory on Frederick's behalf. When he received little by way of response, Henry conceded that it was perhaps time to send Otto out of the country and told Gregory as much. Otto insisted that he would not leave without a safe conduct from Henry. In May, Edmund received notification that the Pope had approved his scheme to allow archbishops of Canterbury to appoint to sees vacant for more than six months rather than waiting on the king and allowing him to pocket the income. Henry immediately appealed against the decision, and by 28 July had secured Gregory's confirmation of a reversal of the decision. Flexing newly found muscles, Henry immediately appointed his wife's uncle Boniface of Savoy as Bishop of Winchester, though it should be mentioned that, probably with the help of Prior Andrew, Boniface had been properly elected by the monks.

Matthew of Westminster recorded that at this time, perhaps as a result of renewed and expensive war against Frederick, a papal tax collector named Peter Rubeus appeared in England, sweeping across the country and collecting a twentieth tax. Simultaneously, Peter de Supion went into Ireland 'like a genuine inquisitor of the Pope' and extracted 1,500 marks, though Peter Rubeus had managed to gather twice that amount from Scotland. On his way back through England, Rubeus 'exacted money for the use of the Pope with exceeding strictness' from all religious houses. Matthew of Westminster scathingly recorded that in this manner, and by forcing those who paid to swear an oath to keep the tax secret for six months, Gregory and his collectors 'turned aside the hearts of the faithful from any devotion and affection towards the Church of Rome'. In October, Otto finally left England to return to Rome, and on 16 November, whilst abroad in a self-imposed exile in protest at papal exactions from the Church in England, Edmund, Archbishop of Canterbury, who was later to be sainted, died at the age of about sixty-five in Pontigny. The See of Canterbury was vacant again – always a recipe for disaster.

On 1 April, Simon de Montfort had arrived back in England and been welcomed by the king, whose pregnant sister had remained on the Continent. Simon set about selling some of the woods on his lands to the Knights Hospitaller and other religious houses, raising at least £1,000 to prepare himself to go on crusade. On 11 April, Llywelyn the Great, later known affectionately as Ein Llyw Olaf, 'Our Last Leader', passed away having left much of Wales subdued to his authority. Welsh inheritance did not follow primogeniture as the English traditionally did, and illegitimate sons were every bit as able to inherit as legitimate sons. Llywelyn appointed his second son Dafydd as his heir in preference to the oldest, Gruffydd, who was in agreement with the plan. When Dafydd summoned his brother to a council meeting he had Gruffydd seized and thrown into prison. Henry's brother Richard also gave his son Henry and all of his possessions into the king's care and, after asking the monks at St Albans for their prayers, departed on crusade. Simon's planned trip to the Holy Land and the infighting in Wales were good news for Henry, and on 2 October 1240 there was more pleasure as he celebrated the birth of a daughter, baptised Margaret. Around the same time, Henry caused the citizens of London, the wardens of the Cinque Ports and any others near the capital at the time to swear fealty to Prince Edward as his heir. The dispute on the Continent between Gregory and Frederick, though, was spreading like a disease. Queen Eleanor's uncle Thomas, Count of Flanders, declared war on Frederick, and Louis IX in France came out on the side of the Pope. Henry wrote letters, but England must have begun to wonder how long it would be before the king was dragged in and forced to choose a side.

Christmas 1240 was celebrated at Westminster. During the feast Henry caused something of a stir by encouraging Otto to sit in the king's seat, no doubt as a final demonstration of his belief in the legate's worth and as a protest at his imminent departure. On 7 January 1241, Henry personally escorted Otto to the coast and watched him sail away, ending three years as legate. Matthew Paris records that Henry bid Otto farewell with 'an embrace and kisses', but also complains that 'there was not left in England so much money … as he, the said legate, had extorted from the kingdom'. This was not, however, the end of papal requests for money.

As the war in the Holy Land gathered pace, so Gregory continued to send demands to England. In April the Pope, perhaps to smooth the reception of his constant requests, agreed to a request from the monks of Canterbury to absolve Boniface of Savoy and approve his translation to the See of Canterbury. Henry had wanted his wife's uncle promoted to the position even though he was only a subdeacon and had not long become Bishop of Winchester. The monks seem to have lacked the will or the energy to argue the point, and Gregory willingly approved the appointment.

Tragedy was to strike at the sons of William Marshal once more in June 1241. Gilbert, having been reconciled to the king, nevertheless attended a tournament just outside Bedford, an activity prohibited by the king and the Pope on several occasions. Matthew Paris records the terrible events as the earl, keen to display his military prowess (he had originally been intended for holy orders), donned his armour and sat astride a powerful Italian warhorse. As the knights dispersed to begin the tourney proper – after the earl had excelled himself in the early knightly displays – Gilbert was putting his horse through its paces when, at a full gallop, the reins snapped. The horse flung its head up and smashed Gilbert squarely in the chest, leaving him dazed and unable to control the horse in the dusty heat of the summer day. He eventually fainted as the horse bucked and bolted, falling, 'with one foot, however, fixed in the stirrup; and in this manner he was dragged some distance over the field, by which he suffered some internal injuries'. On 27 June, Gilbert passed away. When his body was opened, 'his liver was discovered to be black and broken, from the force of the blows he had received'. Gilbert was buried in London near to his father. He had been due to leave for the crusades the following month, having made all of the preparations and arranged his passage. The earldom passed to William's fourthson, Walter, since none of the preceding three earls had sired any sons.

In Wales, Dafydd was asserting his new-found authority. The Bishop of Bangor petitioned the king to secure the release of Dafydd's brother, Gruffydd, pointing out that news of such behaviour within his kingdom would shame Henry if it spread. The king ordered his nephew Dafydd to release Gruffydd, but the prince refused, asserting that if Gruffydd were free, Wales would never be at peace. News of this reached the captive Gruffydd, and he managed to get word to Henry that if the king would free him Gruffydd was take Dafydd's lands and, in future, hold them from the English king, paying him two hundred marks a year and doing homage for them, further offering to subdue the parts of Wales Henry had not reached. This, Dafydd's belligerence and an additional offer from another chieftain named Gruffydd to aid the king in response to Dafydd's unjust rule, was enough for Henry to gather an army. Once the muster had been completed at Gloucester, Henry marched north along the border, as appears to have been traditional, no doubt reluctant to enter Wales without a pressing need since it offered difficult and little-known terrain. At Shrewsbury Henry held a council, but in spite of several demands, Dafydd obstinately refused to come before the king or to free Gruffydd. When the king arrived at Chester and made preparations to plunge west into Dafydd's heartland, the Welsh prince's fear got the better of him. There had been drought and baking heat for four months so that the advantage Dafydd might have found in local waterways and marshes was withdrawn; he was faced by the full threat of an English army bearing down on him. Suddenly, Dafydd agreed to Henry's terms and released Gruffydd and other hostages into the king's care. To avoid the threat, Dafydd insisted his brother was installed at the Tower of London. On 7 October, Dafydd arrived in London to pay homage to Henry. Matthew Paris was effusive in his praise, writing, 'Henry thus, under God's favour, triumphed over his enemies, and subdued Wales without bloodshed, and without having to tempt the doubtful chances of war.'

The avoidance of a Welsh rebellion was good news indeed, but before Dafydd had travelled to London news had arrived that Pope Gregory IX had died on 22 August 1241, at the age of almost one hundred, hounded into his grave by the constant disputes and wars with Frederick, a man half his age. Gregory was well aware that Frederick was not above attacking the Pope's family and so had used crusader money to build a magnificent fortress in Campagna to protect his nephew and other relatives. Frederick laid siege to the palace and smashed it down, leaving only a broken tower as a reminder of what had been there, and hanged everyone he found inside. Matthew Paris blames this shock, as well as the Pope's age, for hastening Gregory to the grave.

Pope Celestine IV was elected on 25 October but died just over a fortnight later on 10 November. As Frederick stepped up his campaign, Rome came under such pressure that it was eighteen months before another election could be held. Suddenly, the Roman Church was without a leader. Innocent, Honorius and Gregory had been vigorous administrators dedicated to extending the influence of the Church and to regaining the Holy Land. With no firm hand on the rudder, it remained to be seen how far and in what direction the Church would drift, and who would take advantage of the situation.

The discovery of vast quantities of tin in Germany served to depress the English economy. Until this find it had been believed that tin existed nowhere else in the world but Cornwall; the monopoly was shattered by the flood of German tin into the market. Personal bad news also reached Henry before the end of the year. His twenty-seven-year-old sister Isabella, wife to Frederick, had died in childbirth on 1 December in Italy. Her marriage was perhaps not a happy one, since Frederick kept something akin to a harem of which Isabella was only a part, but the union had been a prestigious one for England and for the Emperor. Joan, who had been married to Alexander, had died in 1238, and only Eleanor, Simon de Montfort's wife, remained of Henry's three sisters. With his brother Richard and remaining brother-in-law Simon undergoing the risks of the crusade, it must have been a sharp reminder to the thirty-four-year-old Henry how quickly people could be lost. Henry ordered a thousand of the poor to be fed at a feast in his sister's honour.

This year also saw a string of arguments with the Church. Bishop Grosseteste of Lincoln complained vehemently to Henry when the king gifted a church in Grosseteste's diocese to one of his own clerks, John Mansel, since the bishop had already assigned it to another and it lay in the bishop's gift, not the king's. A confrontation seemed likely, with Henry unable to back down to one of his bishops, but Mansel himself graciously withdrew and avoided the trouble. The Bishop of Norwich, who had originally been nominated to the See of Winchester on the death of Peter des Roches, also attracted

Henry's indignation by refusing to give up his claim even though the king did not want him there. William, Bishop of Norwich, was required by the king to sign papers swearing that he would never agree to a translation to Winchester but the bishop refused. As a result, clerics and monks at Winchester were ruthlessly hounded and even, according to Matthew Paris's report, beaten to try and force them to do as the king wished, but they would not be cowed. In stark contrast to this friction with the Church, Henry took delivery in 1241 of a stunning shrine for the relics of St Edward the Confessor, made, according to Paris, 'of the purest gold and costly jewels' and 'constructed at London by picked workmen'; Matthew quotes a poet, who wrote that in spite of the stunning gold and jewels employed, '*Materiam superbat opus*' ('The workmanship did far indeed, The rude material exceed').

The lack of a Pope to act as a restraining figure saw the swift disintegration of a quarter of a century of peace between England and France. Perhaps unsurprisingly, Hugh de Lusignan was at the core of the troubles, along with Henry's mother who, Matthew of Westminster wrote, 'the French call the most impious Jezebel'. Hugh wrote to his stepson and told him that Poitou was ready to rise against the French king and return to loyalty to England. Hugh insisted that the scheme would need no great army from England but only some coin to fund it. Excitedly, Henry called a council at London to discuss the matter but was furious when his nobles refused to travel to France with him whilst a truce remained in place, and also declined to grant him funds for the expedition on the basis that he had enjoyed the vacant sees of Winchester and Canterbury recently and so should have plenty of his own money. Having recently lavished a fortune on the shrine for St Edward, it is easy to see where the nobles were coming from, but also easy to understand why Henry was constantly short of funds.

During the discussions, Richard, Earl of Cornwall, returned from the Holy Land to a rapturous reception. Matthew Paris records that, on hearing of his brother landing at Dover, Henry and his queen rushed to the south coast 'and on seeing him, rushed into his arms and received him with every mark of joy, fraternal blood arousing the affections on both sides; and the king and almost all the nobles loaded him with various presents'. When they arrived in London, 'the city was decorated with banners and hangings, as if for a festival' and Henry threw a huge banquet in his brother's honour.

Richard's return as a famous soldier spurred on Poitevin calls for English help but the barons would not budge. On 15 May 1242, Henry took ship to sail across the Channel, only to be forced to return to Portsmouth when the wind failed. Richard had tried to dissuade his brother from the venture but, unable to convince him, had agreed to join the expedition. This encouraged a further seven earls and three hundred knights to join the king and queen and, with the kingdom left in the care of the Archbishop of York, Henry made a longed-for attempt to regain his inheritance. Henry landed first at St Matthew de Finisterre in Brittany, writing to the Archbishop of York that he should ensure 'of the five hundred poor people whom the king had been wont to feed daily', that his almoner, Brother John, continues to feed 'the greater part of that number, namely, three hundred and fifty'. From Brittany, Henry moved on to Royan in Gascony where he disembarked and took several days to rest and prepare. From there, he marched to Pons where he was welcomed by a group of barons. On hearing of his brother-in-law's arrival, Louis IX immediately offered generous terms for peace, which Henry, full of blustering confidence, flatly refused. Matthew of Westminster reported that 'the King of France repented of having humbled himself to the King of England, and unfolding the oriflamme, he made vigorous attack on all the territories which belonged to the Count de la Marche [i.e. Hugh de Lusignan]'. The oriflamme was a sacred banner of the medieval Kings of France, originating, according to legend, with Charlemagne who took it to the Holy Land atop a golden lance. It showed a burning sun with streamers and obtained an almost mythical position in the imagination of the French. When raised on the field of battle it was a signal that no quarter was to be given, in an attempt to drive fear into the enemy, especially those nobles who would expect to be captured for ransom. It stood as a powerful emblem from Louis VI's first use of it in 1124 until the last time it was raised at the Battle of Agincourt in 1415. Bringing it out of its spiritual home at the Abbey of St Denis was a demonstration of Louis' resolve.

On 8 June, Henry formally declared war on Louis. Although he made some early gains as he was welcomed into Gascony and Poitou, Louis quickly amassed an army to press back. In the midst of this war, Queen Eleanor delivered another daughter, who was given the name Beatrice. In a lightning campaign, Louis took the fortress at Frontignac, which Matthew of Westminster claims 'appeared to the Poitevins to be impregnable', followed quickly by Movent Castle and a series of others that fell swiftly. When Louis came to the town of Taillebourg on the Tarente River, Henry presented his own army in battle order on the opposite bank, so close that Matthew of Westminster, continuing, says 'they could see one another's flags and standards'. Richard apparently had to force his brother to withdraw from a battle they were unlikely to win, and the English fell back to Saintonges. Louis, though, pursued his foe into a fierce but inconclusive battle outside the town after which, Matthew of Westminster asserts, the French 'against their will, were forced to confess that the English gained the most honour'. As Louis's army grew and grew, Henry seems to have panicked and retreated once more to Blaye, where he fell ill. This was enough for Hugh de Lusignan to abandon his stepson again. He asked the Count of Brittany to mediate and eventually won harsh terms from Louis. The French king, buoyed by his gains and the abandonments Henry suffered, decided to drive Henry out of France once and for all. Louis's success, though, proved his downfall. His army had grown out of all management and as Henry moved backwards he was giving alms and asking for prayers at religious houses on his route. Many of the towns, possibly still keen to see Henry as their master rather than Louis, poisoned their wells and took all of their supplies into hiding so that when Louis's army passed through they could find no food and when they drank from the wells they were struck ill. Matthew of Westminster recorded that eighty French nobles of sufficient rank to display their own banner died and 20,000 men-at-arms perished. When Louis himself was struck ill, the French panicked, since Louis was a weaker man than many of those who had already been killed by the illness.

In desperation to return to a better climate and better medical care, Louis asked Henry for a five-year truce, which Henry gladly accepted. Louis made sure to receive the homage of the

Poitevin lords whose lands he had taken before returning to France and making a swift recovery. Hugh de Lusignan appears to have played his games one too many times. As Matthew of Westminster noted:

> He was with difficulty saved from the infliction of an ignominious death. But he became a sort of prodigy in the eyes of all men; a sign that is to be pointed at and ridiculed, and hissed at by all men, because he had so wickedly betrayed the King of England, who rashly trusted in him.

But he also stressed that the final loss of these lands lifted a weight from Henry:

> The prodigal anxiety of the King of England was released from its burdens, though before that time he was accustomed foolishly to distribute amongst the Poitevins seven thousand marks every year, for their shadow of homage and useless service.

It is doubtful that Henry felt any relief at the loss, not least because he would have to return to England and explain the loss of money and honour to his barons. Simon de Montfort had returned from the Holy Land and joined Henry's forces in Poitou. With the loss of the campaign, Simon railed that Henry was useless, comparing him to Charles the Simple, a Carolingian King of France from 879 to 929 who was blamed for the loss of much of Charlemagne's land, and suggesting Henry deserved to share his fate of being locked up by his nobles. Charles was a famous example of a bad, weak king, and even if Simon was attempting to joke with his brother-in-law it was a cutting insult to Henry's kingship. Early in 1243, Henry pardoned around £2,000 of Simon's debts in an effort to help his sister and brother-in-law, perhaps demonstrating that no lasting offence was taken but also acknowledging that Henry needed a man like Simon. The king's military reputation was in tatters, whilst Simon's crusading adventures made him a respected military figure much as his father had been.

The journey home from Gascony offers an odd insight into Henry's personality. The Fine Rolls record what appears to be a practical joke played on a man travelling with the king named Peter the Poitevin, one of the king's long-term servants who was not quite of the rank of knight but who is noted as being in Henry's service as early as 1229. The entry in the Fine Rolls reads:

> Memorandum that Peter the Poitevin owes the king 3 m., which he received from the abbot of Margam and which the same abbot ought to have rendered to the king. Item, he owes five dozen capons for a trespass onboard ship. Item, he owes the king 34 tuns of wine for the arrears of wines which he bought to the king's use at Mussak where he dreamed he had seen the Emperor Otto. Item, he owes the king the £100 which he promised him onboard ship on the morrow of the octave of the Nativity of the Blessed Mary. Memorandum that Peter the Poitevin is in arrears of £71 for the 71 tuns of wine that cost £142, which wines he sold by order of the king, each tun for 60s, and he ought to pay to the wine merchant all of the aforesaid money beyond the aforesaid £71, which he is to pay to the king.

The rolls were left out so that Peter could read the entry relating to him, and he was sent into a panic at the size of the debts that he knew nothing about. Once Peter had seen the entries, Henry and the others who were in on the joke kept up the pretence, presumably asking Peter at regular intervals all the way home what he proposed to do about the debts and how he was going to pay them off. The crux of the episode is that once Peter had read the entries on the Rolls, Henry ordered them to be immediately struck through and cancelled. He was only too aware that if left, they might well be executed by the machinery of his government at a later date, which shows the understanding Henry possessed of the workings of his government. Whereas his father might have left the entries in place and even perhaps tried to collect them, Henry was at pains to ensure they were cancelled straightaway even though the joke continued. There are few extant examples of a medieval king's sense of humour, but the practical joke played on Peter the Poitevin shows a fun, down to earth side of Henry that is endearing, all the more so because he made very sure that the joke could not go too far.

In May 1243, Hubert de Burgh passed away having lived out the last decade of his life in quiet retirement. He had been a huge influence, for good or ill, on Henry, contributing to the salvation of the realm in 1216–17 and representing the final pinnacle of the role of Justiciar in England. The following month, Innocent IV was elected as Pope after a year and a half without a head of the Roman Church. This opened up fresh wounds between Henry and his bishops. Although Innocent wrote to Henry to confirm the appointment of Boniface as Archbishop of Canterbury, he also wrote to William de Raleigh, Bishop of Norwich, to formally translate him to Winchester as the monks there had wished. Henry was incensed. He penned letters to Oxford and Rome accusing William of obtaining the papal confirmation by trickery and bribery and he forbade anyone in Winchester to allow William to enter the town or to give him any support or aide. William, his patience exhausted with the matter, placed Winchester under interdict. William's case was energetically championed by the self-appointed guardian of Church freedom Robert Grosseteste, Bishop of Lincoln, who wrote to Boniface to protest that Henry had no grounds for opposing the move 'since in thus acting he clearly was going against the action of the lord pope'. 'As it belongs to you above others to protect ecclesiastical liberty, and to see that the determination of the lord pope is rightly carried out', the bishop continued, Boniface was obliged to do all within his power to convince the king to drop his opposition to William's translation, advising him to call on the queen's influence on her husband if necessary.

Grosseteste, along with the bishops of Worcester and Hereford, travelled to Reading to confront Henry on this matter, but the king heard of the approach and immediately despatched two messengers to Rome with large quantities of cash and permission to make whatever promises it took in Henry's name to have Innocent overturn his decision. Henry moved to Westminster, but the bishops would not be deterred and followed him. When they finally obtained an audience they scolded Henry for his tyranny and threatened to place all the royal chapels under interdict. This was a very real and potent threat to a man as pious as Henry, and he did not refuse them but merely asked for time to await

1. The text of Magna Carta, the prelude to Henry's reign and a document that would obtain its mythical status during his rule.

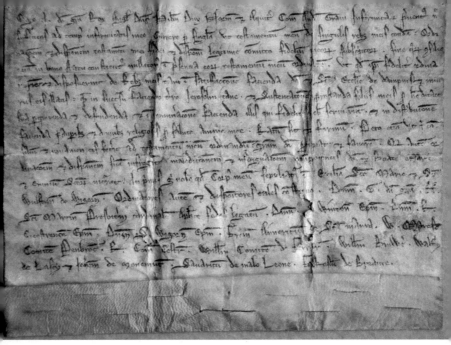

Above: 2. The will of King John, preserved at Worcester Cathedral.

Below: 3. Gloucester Cathedral, the scene of Henry's first, rushed coronation at the age of nine on 28 October 1216. (Author's collection)

Right: 4. The cloisters of Gloucester Cathedral, also used as parts of Hogwarts in the Harry Potter films. (Author's collection)

Below: 5. The High Altar at Gloucester Cathedral. (Author's collection)

6. Pope Innocent III dreams of Francis of Assisi. This superior pope was a huge influence on young Henry. (From Giotto's *Legend of St Francis*)

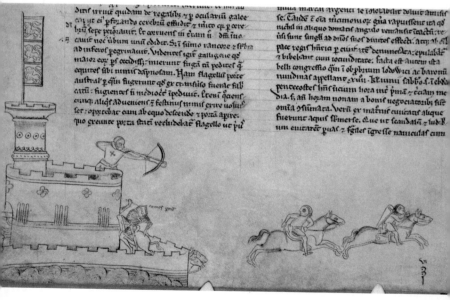

7. Manuscript illustration of the Battle of Lincoln, 1217. From Matthew Paris's *Chronica Maiora*. (Courtesy of the British Library)

Above left: 8. Carvings believed to be Henry's parents King John and Queen Isabella at Worcester Cathedral. (Author's collection)

Above right: 9. Carvings believed to represent King Henry III and Queen Eleanor at Worcester Cathedral. (Author's collection)

Below: 10. The tomb of King John before the altar and the chantry of Prince Arthur Tudor at Worcester Cathedral, commissioned by Henry. (Author's collection)

Above: 11. The Tower of London, a stunning fortress that owes much of its appearance today to the building work of Henry III. (Author's collection)

Below: 12. The White Tower was the original Norman fortress in which Henry took refuge several times during his turbulent reign. (Author's collection)

Above: 13. The tower now known as the Bloody Tower is also a testament to Henry's energetic building. (Author's collection)

Below: 14. Wakefield Tower dates from the rule of Henry III. (Author's collection)

Above left: 15. Manuscript illustration of the marriage of Henry III and Queen Eleanor of Provence. (Courtesy of the British Library)

Above right: 16. Bishop Robert Grosseteste, a towering figure in the English Church during Henry's rule. (Courtesy of the British Library)

Below: 17. Edward the Confessor, the Anglo-Saxon saint-king who Henry hero worshipped throughout his life. (Courtesy of the British Library)

18. The Gothic façade of Westminster Abbey, the epic building project begun by Henry to replace the abbey built by Edward the Confessor. (Author's collection)

19. An illustration of Edward the Confessor's shrine, erected by Henry as the centrepiece of his new abbey. (Courtesy of British Library)

20. A Gothic feature on the front of Westminster Abbey. Henry sent masons to France to learn the Gothic style. (Author's collection)

na vers lour au roy maugieterre

L · De la bataille au roy de france contre

21. Illustration of the meeting of Henry III and Louis IX meeting in France. Their friendship was a golden period in Anglo-French relations. (Courtesy of British Library)

22. Prince Edward's horse prepared for the re-enactment of the 1265 Battle of Evesham in 2015. (Author's collection)

Above: 23. Prince Edward rides to the rescue of his father against Simon de Montfort. (Author's collection)

Below: 24. Father and son are reunited after Edward's victory at the Battle of Evesham. (Author's collection)

Above: 25. King Henry is freed from captivity at the 750th anniversary re-enactment of the Battle of Evesham in 2015. (Author's collection)

Below: 26. A plaque that now commemorates Simon de Montfort, often romantically remembered as the father of parliamentary democracy. (Author's collection)

HERE WERE BURIED THE REMAINS OF
SIMON DE MONTFORT, EARL OF LEICESTER
PIONEER OF REPRESENTATIVE GOVERNMENT WHO WAS
KILLED IN THE BATTLE OF EVESHAM ON AUGUST 4th 1265.

THIS STONE BROUGHT FROM HIS BIRTHPLACE THE
CASTLE OF MONTFORT-LAMAURY IN FRANCE WAS
ERECTED TO COMMEMORATE THE SEVEN HUNDREDTH
ANNIVERSARY OF HIS DEATH.

UNVEILED BY THE SPEAKER OF THE HOUSE OF COMMONS
AND DEDICATED BY
HIS GRACE THE ARCHBISHOP OF CANTERBURY
ON THE 18th DAY OF JULY 1965.

27. The keep of Kenilworth Castle, where Montfortian rebels continued to hold out after Evesham in a long, gruelling siege. (Author's collection)

Above left: 28. Manuscript illustration of King Henry III. (Courtesy of the British Library)

Above right: 29. Illustration of King Henry III holding a church, representing his enduring reputation as a builder. (Courtesy of the British Library)

Below: 30. Tomb of King Henry III at Westminster Abbey, next to the shrine of his idol, Edward the Confessor.

31. Tomb effigy of King Henry III.

Innocent's reply. The bishops were forced to agree to this delay, though neither of Henry's messengers ever reached Rome. One refused to be part of something so sordid and returned to England; the other disappeared with the king's gold. William, for his part, was forced to flee to France for his own safety.

In November 1243 Henry was at Dover to meet his mother-in-law, Beatrice, Countess of Provence. Beatrice had brought another of her daughters, Sanchia, to be married to Henry's widowed brother Richard and the English king paid for Beatrice and Sanchia's journey, welcoming them at Dover and escorting them into London. The city had been cleaned and decorated to make a good impression, according to Matthew Paris, 'with hangings, curtains, and divers other ornaments, from the bridge to Westminster', whilst the citizens were instructed 'that they should put out of the sight of those who passed through the city, blocks of wood, mud, dirt, and all obstacles'. Richard could now also count himself brother-in-law to the King of France – it was a good match for the earl and also brought him even closer to Henry.

On 20 February 1244, Innocent delivered a scathing upbraiding to the English king on the matter of William de Raleigh's translation. The Pope rebuked Henry because 'as we are grieved to hear, you have been pleased not only to pay no attention to our requests, but what is more grave, you have given expression to words in no way showing fitting modesty or filial reverence'. He continued,

You have asserted that, if you were unwilling, no postulation in the kingdom of England either ought or indeed could be made by the Apostolic See. You have declared that you had the same power in temporals as we had in spirituals [so that] no one, appointed to a See without your consent, could obtain possession of his temporalities. Further, you added that you would hold the translation of this bishop ... as invalid, as if obtained from us by false information. Certainly, beloved son, such expressions as these do not redound to the honour of God, the Church, or your Highness; they are not suggestive of justice nor manifest equity, especially when the received belief of all the faithful is that the Apostolic See by God's providence possesses full power and authority in all Churches, and is not so bound to the will of princes as to be obliged to ask their assent to their elections and postulations.

Henry was hamstrung and left with no option but to agree to the translation, though William did not finally enter Winchester until 29 August. As if to reinforce the punishment of Henry's obstinacy, Innocent also sent a new man named Martin to England with the task to extract money once again. Matthew of Westminster described how Martin took up residence at the New Temple in London and set about dragging every mark he could from the English Church. Matthew complained that Master Martin had been given 'power of excommunicating, suspending, and punishing in various ways, and just as he pleased, all who resisted his will, though it might have been a mere hasty action; just as if on that very day he had, according to established custom, produced authentic Bulls, drawn up in the papal chancery', and even heard a rumour that 'he had brought over a great many papers sealed with a Bull, but not filled up, for him to fill up himself as he pleased', adding 'but I would hope that this was not the case'. Martin searched out vacancies across England and filled them with the Pope's relatives – 'of whom there was an astonishing number' – selecting one lucrative prebend at Salisbury belonging to the gift of the bishop and, in spite of the bishop's protests, gave the office to one of Innocent's nephews.

When council met the mood was mutinous. Matthew Paris recorded that amongst the complaints of papal exactions grew an increasing desire to be free from Roman control. The bishops were dismayed at the poverty the Church had been left in so that it could not perform its social duties, and the barons began to complain that since most of the money was destined for a war against Frederick, and since Frederick had a daughter by Henry's sister, then the money they were forced to send was for the purpose of waging war on an English lady. It was perhaps convoluted rhetoric but it summed up the mood of a nation baulking under the yoke placed across its shoulders by Rome. As a result of the protests, Henry penned a letter to Innocent that was stripped of his usual subtle requests. 'The more that the son submits himself to the pleasure of his father,' he began, 'and the readier and more devoted he shows himself to his commands, the more deserving is he of obtaining his father's protection, and of reaping the advantages of his devotion and service.' Henry had clearly forgotten the troubles over the Bishop of Winchester. Nevertheless, he went on to complain about the heavy exaction taken from England to Rome so that 'many works of charity are given up'. As a result of the loud complaints now disturbing his kingdom as a result of all of this, Henry 'considered it our duty to pray to your holiness to abstain from granting provisions of this kind, at least for a time'. The plea, according to Matthew Paris, fell on ears as deaf as all of Henry's other attempts.

The reason that Henry was unlikely to succeed was that the war with Frederick was going badly. The Pope was driven out of Rome and forced to set up court in France. Whilst Innocent languished there, Dafydd took the opportunity to visit the Pope and make a daring request. He offered Wales to the Pope, as John had done with England. Dafydd offered to pay homage and an annual tribute to Rome in return for a letter barring Henry from action against Wales. It was a startling move for Welsh independence, at least from neighbouring England, and Innocent's interest was pricked. The Pope authorised the bishops of Aberconwy and Cumhyre to look into the oath Llywelyn had given Henry and to establish whether it had been extracted under duress or by force. The bishops summoned Henry to be questioned and he, unsurprisingly, utterly refused. Earlier in the year, on 1 March, Gruffydd had died trying to escape the Tower of London. He reportedly made a rope from sheets but found, once out of the window, that he was too heavy. The makeshift rope snapped and Gruffydd plummeted to his death. It was perhaps freedom from this worry that caused Dafydd to make a bid for more power. Christmas was celebrated at Wallingford at the invitation of Richard, Earl of Cornwall, and most of the nobility of England attended. The trouble with Rome was perhaps forging a new sense of unity.

10

The Seneschal of Gascony

On 16 January 1245, King Henry and Queen Eleanor had a second son, named Edmund. It was a welcome addition to the thirty-eight-year-old king's family, providing him with a valuable backup should anything happen to Edward and promising Edward the kind of support Henry had enjoyed from his own brother, Richard.

During June the suggestion was mooted of inviting the Pope, still in France, to England to visit. Several cardinals wrote to Henry that,

> It would be a great honour and immortal glory if the lord pope, who is the father of fathers, should personally visit your country, which no pope has ever done. We remember, indeed, that he himself said, and we were very glad to hear it, that he would rejoice to see the delights of Westminster and the riches of London.

Although Henry was apparently keen on the idea, he was reminded by those around him that with the Pope would come a trail of hangers-on, moneylenders and Romans looking for a lucrative post in England. Given the troubles of the previous year, the notion was quickly forgotten. Henry did, however, send representatives to the Pope to try and get Dafydd's actions overturned, and secured the Pope's recognition that 'from time immemorial' princes of Wales had owed homage to the king of England and that Dafydd had tricked the Pope into believing his representations. When Henry led a campaign into Wales to subdue Dafydd once more, it was financed by his wealthy brother Richard, who took the crown jewels as security. A truce was put in place for the winter, but the campaign was rendered unnecessary when Dafydd died unexpectedly on 25 February 1246, in his mid-thirties.

1245 was also to see the beginning of what Henry might have viewed as his real life's work. His interest in building and architecture stretched back many years and he had left his mark on cathedrals and castles around England, most notably the Tower of London and most ominously the mighty fortress at Kenilworth that he improved. This year saw the first mention of a throne standing on the dais in Westminster Hall, designed to be used on state occasions but to represent the king's ceremonial presence when he was not physically there. The realisation of one of Henry's dreams came with the engagement of Henry de Reynes as architect with a group of master masons. They were sent to Reims, Chartres, Bourges, Amiens and Saint-Chapelle to see, assess and learn the new Gothic technique in which Henry now planned to completely rebuild Westminster Abbey. All that remains today of Edward the Confessor's Abbey is the foundations and crypt: everything above that people have marvelled at for seven and a half centuries was created by the sheer will, and willingness to find money for this project when there was none for any other, of Henry III.

Isabella of Angoulême, Henry's troublesome mother, died on 4 June 1246, at the age of nearly sixty. She was buried at Fontevraud Abbey, and, in a move that courted trouble, Henry offered a home to the three half-brothers and one half-sister that his mother had borne Hugh de Lusignan – the thorn that would persist for another thirteen years. Isabella and Hugh had nine surviving children; four made their way to England. The country doubtless sagged its shoulders at the thought of another foreign faction upon whom the king might pour favours the country could ill afford.

The following year began with a meeting of the council at which Henry again criticised Innocent's constant demands for money to fund the crusade and the defence of Constantinople, though the barons eventually conceded and the Church was required to find 11,000 marks to send to the Pope. In April 1247, Henry sealed the Treaty of Woodstock with Llywelyn and Owain, the sons of Gruffydd. In return for recognition as princes of Gwynedd and Snowden respectively, they submitted to Henry as his vassals. Shortly after this victory, on 1 May 1247 Simon de Montfort was appointed Seneschal of Gascony. The region clung to its English allegiance but was in need of a champion. Henry clearly saw Simon as the perfect man for the job, perhaps with the added benefit of removing him from England for a while, too. Simon was given wide-ranging powers and appointed for a seven-year term with protection against dismissal, meaning the only way that he could be removed was by his own resignation.

When council met at the beginning of 1248, Henry asked for money once again, pleading his financial difficulties. He opened a floodgate of criticism that must have been building pressure for some time. The barons utterly refused to grant a tax when Henry was not in real need of one, meaning that there was no threat to the kingdom. They reminded Henry that he had promised the last time they made such a grant, at great difficulty to themselves, that he would not ask for another, yet here he was, asking. According to Matthew Paris, the barons proceeded to list a tirade of complaints against Henry's rule, beginning with 'the indiscreet way in which he summoned foreigners into the kingdom, and for lavishly and indiscreetly scattering the property of the kingdom amongst them, and also for marrying the nobles of the kingdom to ignoble foreigners, thus despising and putting aside his native and natural subjects'. Henry was blamed for the depression in trade in England because of his tendency to seize 'by force on whatever he used in the way of meat and drink', taking 'especially wine, and even clothes' without payment so that merchants packed up their wares and hid so traders from abroad saw no profit in risking a trip to England. They complained at length that the king 'in order that he may bestow alms indiscreetly, and may make immoderate illuminations, forcibly seizes wax, silk stuffs, and other things, without making any terms of pacification; thus bringing scandal on himself, his kingdom, and all who inhabit it', since gifts given to God that are the result of theft are abhorred by God. Henry's tyranny, for that is what Matthew Paris called it, reached so far that herring fishermen on the coast were too scared to land with their catches, 'nor do they dare to appear in the places adjoining the sea-coast or in the cities, for fear of being robbed; so that they consider it safer to trust themselves to the stormy billows and to seek the further shore'.

The breaches of the king's coronation oath to protect the Church were cited because of the money he allowed to be extracted by Rome, though given that the Pope was his feudal lord, this was perhaps a little unfair. It might however also have reflected a growing sense, exposed years earlier, that the time had come to rid themselves of such an exacting master. Matthew Paris recorded a further complaint, 'and it was no slight one', that Henry had not employed the services of a Justiciar, a Chancellor or a Treasurer in years, 'unlike his noble predecessors', and instead surrounded himself with 'only such persons as obeyed his pleasure in everything, provided that it was advantageous to himself, and such as did not seek the advancement of the common weal, but their own especial benefit, by collecting money and obtaining wardships and revenues for themselves'. It was a damning summation of Henry's kingship that must have chafed at the king. Whether he wanted the love of his subjects or simply their money, it was clear he was getting neither.

In January 1249, Simon returned to England to report on his success, but Henry raised concerns that he had been hearing tales of heavy-handed actions on Simon's part that displeased the barons of Gascony. Doubtless Simon was able to make the point that such a firm grip was precisely the reason Henry had appointed him. In November, the ten-year-old Prince Edward was given Gascony as an estate of his own, though Simon was retained as seneschal.

In March 1250, with his financial problems mounting and his nobles unsupportive, Henry took a step reminiscent of his father, though not in the worst vein. At the age of forty-three, Henry took the Cross and promised to go on crusade. At the same time, he asked the Pope to help him raise the money he would need for such an important venture, and Innocent granted Henry a tenth of all ecclesiastical revenue for three years, the term provided for a crusader to make preparations and leave for the Holy Land. It must be questioned whether Henry really meant to make a pilgrimage to the Holy Land and take part in a crusade or whether this was nothing more than a cynical, short-term ploy to gain access to funds that he needed desperately but could not get a grant from the barons or the Church for.

September that year saw the death of William de Raleigh, six years after he had finally gained access to the diocese he was to serve. Henry immediately set about trying to have his half-brother Aymer de Valence, one of Hugh and Isabella's sons who had been invited to England, appointed to the vacancy. As was by now usual, the monks resisted. Before the end of the year Henry extended the truce with France for another five years, perhaps in recognition that he was in no position to defend what remained to him if push came to shove, never mind to go on the offensive overseas. Christmas was kept at Winchester, most likely to once more keep pressure on the monks there by the menacing weight of his presence to give in and appoint his candidate as their bishop. On 6 January 1251, Simon de Montfort again returned to England in what Matthew Paris describes as 'inglorious haste', bringing only three squires and dire news on 'horses worn out with hunger and work'.

Gascony was in open uprising and many of the nobles were threatening to throw off their allegiance to Henry. Simon requested money and men urgently to prevent the complete loss of the territory. Henry willingly gave the assistance but also took the opportunity to question Simon once more on the steady stream of reports reaching the court from Gascony of his unjust, high-handed style of governing. Indeed, it may well have been Simon's presence that was driving the barons and towns there to make their threats and shuffle their feet in protest. 'By God's head,' Henry reportedly told Simon, 'thou speakest truth, sir earl; and since thou servest me so doughtily I will not deny thee effectual aid. But loud cries of complaint reach me that thou hast improperly thrown into prison or even put to death men who came to thee in peace, or whom thou hadst thyself summoned.' Simon steadfastly replied to the king, 'My lord, their treachery which thou knowest and hast experienced makes them unworthy of belief,' and the response must have satisfied the king as Simon returned to Gascony to put down the threat of rebellion. By November, though, Simon was back in England once more having been driven out of Gascony altogether. Henry's hardest man, an experienced soldier, a crusader no less and someone not lacking in personal charisma, had failed to hold the last English possession on the Continent. He was sent back to undo his disgrace.

Christmas was celebrated at York so that on 26 December 1251 Henry could witness the marriage of his eleven-year-old daughter Margaret to the new nine-year-old King Alexander III of Scotland. Alexander was the son of his father's second wife, Marie de Coucy, having had no children with Henry's sister Joan. The union would put back in place the ties that had ensured a long period of peace and friendship with the Scottish. Matthew Paris describes a lavishly celebrated moment that was well attended, explaining,

> Because of the dense unruly crowds, who rushed together to witness the ceremonial of such a marriage, the ceremony was performed secretly in the early morning before the expected time. There were assembled there so many various peoples, such a number of English, French and Scottish nobles, such hosts of knights decked in elegant robes and glorying in their varied silk attire, that a full description of that wanton and worldly vanity would excite wonder and weariness in the ears of my hearers.

On 14 April 1252, Henry set the date that he planned to leave on crusade as 24 June 1256, four years ahead and a full six after he had taken his crusading vow. In May, Simon was recalled to England and Henry threatened to put him on trial for his misgovernment in Gascony following another deluge of complaints. When the king told Simon that he was considering removing him from the post, the earl reminded Henry that he was protected from such a dismissal. As tempers frayed, Henry told his brother-in-law that he did not consider himself bound by a promise made to a traitor. The accusation was too much for Simon, who erupted at the king, warning him, 'Were thou not my king it would be an ill hour for thou would thou dared to utter it.' Matthew Paris continues to put words in the mouths of his protagonists, as Henry throws Simon's own father's reputation and achievements in the earl's face, petulantly ordering, 'Return to Gascony, that thou, who art so fond and such a fomenter of wars, mayst there find enough of them, and bring back with thee therefrom thy merited reward, as did thy father.' Simon's father had died during the Albigensian Crusade in the south of France, and this sounds an awful lot like Henry suggesting that Simon follow suit in Gascony. With an irreverence that seems to have been a hallmark of

Simon's relationship with his king, he replied, 'And I will go there willingly. Nor as I believe shall I return until, ungrateful though thou art, I make these rebels subject to thee, and thine enemies thy footstools beneath thy feet.' In September, the fraying relationship snapped once more as Henry paid Simon off to quit his post as seneschal. The earl stalked into France to brood on his treatment, though only after handing the castles of Fronsac, Renauges and La Réole over to the very dissidents he had been sent to subdue.

During a meeting of the council on 18 October 1252 Henry produced a copy of the papal requirement that the Church pay him a tenth of all ecclesiastical income for three years. He was, of course, low on funds, and the barons were adopting their now traditional stance of refusing to grant an aid. They could perhaps point to Henry's spending on his building projects and on failed ventures such as supporting Simon, who then had to be paid off with even more crown money, as reasons why they did not feel Henry could be trusted with additional funds – funds that they would have to find from their own pockets, simply to watch him fritter them away. Led by the Bishop of Lincoln, the formidable Robert Grosseteste, the bishops refused to grant the order, their ringleader storming, 'By our Lady, what does this mean? You are arguing on premises that have not been granted. Do you think that we shall consent to this accursed contribution? Heaven forbid that we should thus bend our knees to Baal.' Matthew Paris's account continues with a reply from the bishop-elect of Winchester, Henry's half-brother, who insisted, 'Father, how can we resist the will of the pope and of the king? The one drives us, the other drags us.' Aymer also pointed out that the bishops of France had agreed to such a provision for their king, to which Grosseteste sharply replied, 'For the very reason that the French contributed, must we resist. For the repetition of an act creates a custom.' The bishops' logic was frustratingly sound and Henry could not force them to agree. They were, however, set on a dangerous collision course.

In January 1253, as a synod of the Canterbury archdiocese met in London, the Church took the opportunity to press the king into addressing their complaints. The meeting began on 13 January, and the early exchanges were dominated by a need to resolve a bitter disagreement between the queen's uncle Boniface and Henry's half-brother Aymer. Henry, reaching his fingers into a strictly ecclesiastical matter, ordered that the bishops should not leave London until the dispute was settled and told them that he would not come to them until it had been. Matthew Paris recorded that this was done quickly in order to get on with the more pressing business of the king's demand, backed by the Pope, for his tax of a tenth, on which matter the bishops resolved to seek concessions from the king in return for agreeing to hand over the money. When Henry arrived around 23 January, he was, Matthew Paris noted, in a conciliatory mood. When presented with the offer, the king asked the bishops to submit all of their grievances in writing to him for consideration. This was duly done and, according to the *Annals of Burton*, Grosseteste was key to compiling the list of reforms the Church wanted. The Bishop of Lincoln asserted that Henry broke almost every clause of the Great Charter on a regular basis, particularly the first article regarding the freedom of the Church, since the king constantly interfered in appointments.

It will be remembered that the status of Magna Carta as it stood at this point was the final 1225 version, last reissued in 1237, which was becoming deeply embedded as a measuring stick for good governance and could also be used to prod the king back into line. The flaw of the Charter by 1253 was that many of its very specific provisions dealt with issues that had ceased to vex the country and had really been the specific complaints of a moment in time, which necessarily change. The Church, in being able to cite Archbishop Langton's prominent and general first clause, were both fortunate and ultimately undone. The clause was general enough to remain relevant and to be able to encompass most issues that would ever arise that might impact the freedom of the English Church. However, it was so vague that enforcing it became more and more problematic. What exactly was the scope of the freedom? Was a specific issue covered or not? Who should decide such questions? What was the remedy for any breach? Where many clauses had been so specific they had pared themselves from relevance, in its attempt to avoid such a fate, clause one had proven so general as to be impossible to apply.

Nevertheless, by 10 February Henry must have received the rolls (suggesting a rather long list) of complaints because on that date he wrote to the barons of the Exchequer to seek their advice on what was being asked of him:

> Writ of the lord king on behalf of the king.
>
> King to the barons.
>
> We are sending you the rolls which the venerable father B[oniface] archbishop of Canterbury and his suffragans lately delivered to us inscribed. Although to several of the things there, we could have replied by ourselves, and have expedited several of their contents without injury to anyone, however, wishing to have discussion on these things with our beloved brother, Richard earl of Cornwall, and certain other of our magnates, and with you, and to enjoy in this matter their and your counsel, we have fixed for the foresaid archbishop and his suffragans a day on the quindene of Easter next coming at Westminster to reply to them on the foresaid things and do what will be just and reasonable by means of your counsel and that of the foresaid magnates.
>
> Wherefore, we order you that, since there are many things contained in them [the rolls] which specially touch our state and that of our kingdom and our subjects, having diligently inspected and understood these things, you should meanwhile give us careful counsel as to what to do on these matters.
>
> Witness myself at Merton, on the tenth day of February, in the year of our reign thirty seven.

The original roll does not survive but can perhaps be suggested to be in line with Grosseteste's complaints recorded in the *Annals of Burton*. The quindene of Easter was an official judicial court return date, beginning fifteen days after Easter Sunday and falling on 4 May in 1253. It was an important statement that Henry believed any reforms the Church wanted required lay approval from him and his magnates. No doubt Henry was happy to consult on a matter the nobles were only ever likely to side with the king on. It is tempting to try and see in the exchanges an almost concerted effort to put the Church in a position beneath the king, where Henry wanted it and the bishops denied it should be. Either that, or Henry was simply being spiteful because of their refusal to give him money the Pope had instructed them to.

Henry appears from the records to be almost enjoying the experience of toying with the most powerful men in the English Church, who had for so long used the Pope every bit as much as Henry had to try and get their way. The concessions mentioned in his letter to the barons of the Exchequer may include a move against the Jewish population that did not, for once, centre on their financial activities but was aimed at protecting the Christian faith from the influence of Judaism. The move might have reflected Henry's increasing zeal in the face of a crusading adventure but might also have been a jab at an easy target that would mollify the bishops. Towards the end of January an odd series of posturing undermined the Bishop of Lincoln's reforming ardour, though he perhaps saw that as a group they were not going to get their way. The bishop still owed a fine of £100, a traditional imposition when a bishop or magnate failed to produce someone under their authority at a judicial hearing. The fine was frequently imposed and almost as often pardoned after a time on record. Grosseteste had been handed such a fine when one John de la Lade had failed to appear before Henry's justices. Taking the moment of this illustrious gathering to quietly complain to the king about the fine, the bishop found himself in possession of not one but two pardons expunging the fine on 26 January, the second a longer-winded account of the matter than the first. Either Henry was trying to split the unity of the bishops or Grosseteste saw an opportunity to obtain something for himself, though it was perhaps a more mutual arrangement.

There was more mischief from the king in April as the matter lumbered on. The Archbishop of Canterbury and the bishops of Winchester, Salisbury and Carlisle decided to confront the king about his appointment of favourites to key positions in the Church, and they challenged him to allow completely free elections. Matthew Paris recorded Henry's response, and it is easy to picture a poker-faced Henry trying not to smirk as he feigned shocked agreement with the four men:

> It is true, and I grieve for it, and repent me greatly for having so acted. We ought therefore to arrange forthwith for the remedying of what has been done, and to prevent its occurrence in the future. And in this you should be my coadjutors; for remember it is I who

advanced Boniface of Canterbury here to his high dignity, and thee, William of Salisbury, who art the writer of my briefs, I raised from the lowest position; and thee Silvester of Carlisle, who wert long a petty clerk in my chancery, how have I raised thee over the heads of many reverend men to be a bishop? And my brother Aymer, it is well known how I raised thee against the wish of the monks to be head of the noble church of Winchester, though from thy age and learning thou wert still in need of a teacher. First and chiefly therefore is it expedient for me and for you, that you, being guided by my repentance, should resign offices you have unjustly acquired, lest you incur eternal condemnation. And I being justified and chastened by such an example will take care for the future to promote no man who is not worthy.

The king must have revelled in the stunned confusion and fear of the four men, who eventually gathered their wits enough to reply, 'Lord king, we make no mention of the past, but direct our speech to the future.' Unsurprisingly, the matter was dropped. Henry had cast another large stone that sent ripples through the unity of the prelates. If there was an overarching plan in the opening months of 1253 to dismantle the unity and defiance of the Church and the bishops, then it succeeded spectacularly – though successful plans with clear means to reach an identified end were never really Henry's forte. Henry knew that he had the backing of his nobles against the complaints and pressure for reform, not least because one of Grosseteste's demands was reportedly that every baron should swear an oath to allow the clergy freely to investigate the moral failings of the barons. This was perhaps the final consequence of Rome's heavy-handed involvement in England over the last four decades. As much as the barons might have sympathised with the Church's view of Henry, the one thing they didn't want was more authority handed to clerics, and they were forced to unite behind the king in order to avoid this outcome.

Henry agreed to a reissue of the Charters in return for the Church's agreement to give him the tax of a tenth for the next three years and he also agreed that the money was to be used to fund a pilgrimage and would only be spent at the direction of the barons. As in 1237, the reissue that was confirmed on 13 May 1253 was accompanied by a sentence of excommunication on those who opposed or broke the Charters. As the bishops threw down their extinguished candles and intoned, 'So let all who incur this sentence, be extinguished and stink in hell,' Matthew Paris reported that Henry could be heard clearly and loudly swearing, with his hand pressed to his chest, 'All these will I faithfully observe unimpaired, as I am a man, a Christian, a knight and a crowned and anointed king. So help me God.' Is there a hint here of Henry revelling in what amounted to a victory over the Church? With the Charters confirmed in their 1225 form, including the ambiguous first clause relating to the freedom of the Church, nothing at all was changed, none of the grievances formally addressed; and Henry had his tax.

The only concession that the bishops did obtain related to the excommunication sentence. It was a shallow victory which the king quickly sought to completely undo. Grosseteste and his colleagues sought to make the most of their small attainment by having the sentence publicised as widely as possible. The Church published a copy of the sentence that would be applied to anyone who violated the rights and privileges of the Church, but included legislators and lay judges within its remit as they sought to restrict the impact of judicial law on members of the clergy and rights of the Church. Anyone threatened with excommunication was to be given fifteen days to mend their ways or the sentence would be delivered 'at the decision of the ordinary'. Crucially, this version of the sentence was never entered into the Chancery Rolls because Henry issued his own version under letters patent. This version made no mention of the ecclesiastical right to excommunicate after fifteen days but insisted that the sentence would only be passed 'by consideration of his court'. Henry's version also omitted many of the reasons the Church specified for excommunication, primarily ignoring the limitations the clergy had sought to place on legislators and judges, mentioning those who infringed the liberties of the Church only alongside those who sought to harm those of the king and kingdom.

Henry clearly knew what he was doing, since his letters patent included the following provision:

It is to be known that if in writings on this same sentence, made by anybody, or to be made, anything is placed, or any other articles are found, the king and all the aforesaid magnates and the community of the people, protest publicly in the presence of Boniface Archbishop of Canterbury and all the bishops in the same colloquium, that they never consented to those things, but plainly contradicted them.

What the king meant was that his version was the only one to be considered legal and binding. Even the small measure of success the bishops departed London trying to claim was snatched away from them in a move reminiscent of Henry's grandfather's disputes with the Church before and during the term on the throne of Canterbury of Thomas Becket. That Henry felt able, willing and free to re-examine the relationship between Church and State that had so vexed the Angevin kings for decades speaks to a level of security that had been missing in England for a long time but which appeared to be returning. The question was whether Henry would heed the lessons of his forebears or bring the peace clattering down about his ears.

During June, the month following the confirmation of the reissue of the Charters, letters arrived in England from Bordeaux pleading with the king to send urgent assistance. The lords who Simon had handed the three key castles to were, according to *The Chronicle of Thomas Wyke*, 'intolerably oppressing the nobles and people of the said province by undue extortions'. Flushed with his success and the peace he was finally enjoying at home, Henry began preparations to lead an expedition to Gascony himself. On 6 August 1253 he sailed out of Portsmouth to Bordeaux in ships laden with soldiers. The kingdom was left in the hands of his brother Richard and the Archbishop of York, 'at their general desire', and when Henry landed the people of Gascony came out in demonstrative support of the king who, Thomas Wyke continued, 'relying on the assistance of the people of the country and the soldiers whom he had brought with him, he laid siege to the castles so deceitfully occupied, assaulted them with engines of war, captured and held them'. Stephen Longsword, a man described by Thomas as 'of great vigour', was appointed seneschal, and the region was completely subdued in the shortest possible time. It was a rare military success for Henry, whose confidence must have been riding high.

On 9 October, Bishop Grosseteste of Lincoln died. He was in the midst of a dispute with the Pope over reforms the bishop insisted were needed. The Bishop of London, at what was later adduced to be the very moment of Grosseteste's passing, was travelling on the road and heard a loud bell tolling which no one else in his party had heard. When it was later discovered that Bishop Grosseteste had died at the same moment, the Bishop of London was shocked to discover that there were no churches or religious houses or anywhere else possessing a bell within hearing distance of the spot where he had heard the chime. The story should, perhaps, be taken with a pinch of salt, as Bishop Grosseteste's ardent campaigning met with widespread approval amongst the monkish commentators who supply us with much of our understanding of this period. Matthew Paris effused of the bishop:

> He had been an open rebuker of pope and king, the corrector of bishops, the reformer of monks, the instructor of the clergy, the support of scholars, the preacher of the people, the persecutor of the incontinent, a careful reader of the scriptures, the hammer of the Romans whom he despised. At the table of bodily food he was liberal, plentiful, courteous, cheerful, affable; at the table of spiritual food devout, tearful, penitent; as a prelate sedulous, venerable, indefatigable.

On 25 November Queen Eleanor gave birth to another daughter, who was named Katherine and whose birth completed Henry and Eleanor's family of two sons and three daughters. Margaret was already married to Alexander III of Scotland, and the success of the campaign in Gascony seems to have given Henry the idea that an alliance with Castile, Gascony's neighbour to the south-west, who also tentatively coveted the territory, would serve to help better secure the region. Whilst abroad he began negotiations for a match between his oldest son, Edward, now fourteen, and Eleanor of Castile, the sister of Alfonso, King of Castile. When council met in January 1254 under Richard's leadership, a tax was refused once more, although many gave oaths of support to the king should Alfonso of Castile invade Gascony, some promising to cross and join the king in person in that event. Interestingly, Richard pointed out to the gathering that there could be no general tax extracted from them without a confirmation of the Charters to accompany it, showing that a strong connection had already become entrenched between the good government required by a reissue of the Charters and a granting of an extraordinary tax to the Crown.

On 14 February, whilst still in Gascony and perhaps to improve his son's marital prospects, Henry made provision for Prince Edward to increase his role and his power. He was created Duke of Aquitaine, a title that came to the Angevins through Henry II's marriage to Eleanor of Aquitaine and which Richard I had held previously. Edward was also given the county of Chester, several castles in Wales, Peak, Stamford, Grantham, Bristol, the Channel Islands, Gascony and the Isle of Oleron (which had long been disputed with Hugh de Lusignan). Edward was also given the Lordship of Ireland, initially excluding Dublin and Limerick, though later in the year Henry wrote to officials in Ireland to advise them that he had now included those towns so that Edward held the whole of Ireland, albeit that Henry insisted 'the allegiance of the land remain to us for our lifetime' so that 'the land of Ireland be never separated from the crown of England'. It is noteworthy that Henry increased his son's role willingly and began to give him authority during his lifetime, in stark contrast to the problems that dogged Henry II for his unwillingness to relax his own grip on his sprawling empire. Henry III's moves might reflect a lesson learned from that episode of history and might also be an acknowledgment by the king of the impact his own lack of experience had on him, at least in his early reign, if indeed he ever shook it off.

Henry had achieved a rare and rarefied victory. His campaign to Gascony had been an unmitigated success and had led to negotiations toward an advantageous marriage for his oldest son. Simon had caused his mischief but it had been corrected and the Earl of Leicester had fled into France. He had been forced to retake lands given away by an officer of the Crown but Henry must have revelled in a real, tangible military success. It perhaps went to his head, because there can be little else to explain what Henry did next.

11

The Sicilian Affair

Two years earlier, on 21 May 1252, Pope Innocent IV had written to Henry to offer him the crown of Sicily. The Pope had fallen into dispute with Conrad, King of Sicily, and by May 1252 the task of replacing Conrad had already been offered to the Count of Anjou and even to Richard, Earl of Cornwall, who had apparently quipped at the offer, 'You may as well say: I will sell or give you the moon; now climb up and take it.' It was perhaps more correct to say that Innocent offered to sell the Kingdom of Sicily to Henry rather than give it. On 24 May 1254, in the full flush of his victory in Gascony, Henry penned a letter to Pope Innocent IV in which he gleefully accepted the offer on behalf of his second son, Edmund. For all that Henry appeared to have learned a lesson from history regarding the slow introduction to power of his son, his military success in Gascony seems to have blinded him to the massive challenges of the scheme he now sought to embark upon. Henry was perennially poor and the scheme required vast sums, not only to buy the crown from the Pope but to raise an army and transport it to make good the claim. The logistics of moving an army across Europe, through less than friendly French lands, or even of taking the dangerous sea route around the Iberian Peninsula, should have rung alarm bells, as should the persistent unwillingness of the barons to support him overseas. The son of Frederick and Henry's sister Isabella, a famous youth also named Henry, was killed in Sicily in May, and rumours abounded that it was Conrad's doing, though the two had been firm friends. This desire for familial revenge, given his sister's death, might also have fuelled Henry's desire and affected the timing of his acceptance. Henry perhaps believed this initiative was sufficiently disconnected from issues at home or in the old Angevin Empire to circumvent the issues that had dogged him there. If nothing else made an impact on the king, the way his brother had laughed the idea off should have rung alarm bells.

For the moment, Henry still made the most of his time in the old Angevin territories. During the summer he visited his mother's tomb at Fontevraud and commissioned a mausoleum to be erected over it. In November he witnessed the marriage of his son Edward to Eleanor of Castile and heard her brother Alfonso renounce any claim on Gascony, securing one border of that territory. There was a shock on 7 December when Pope Innocent IV died before reaching the age of sixty. In a rage, according to Matthew Paris, the Pope had ordered the bones of Robert Grosseteste, Bishop of Lincoln, to be exhumed and treated as those of a heathen. On the night of writing to Henry to order it,

> A vision appeared to the pope whilst lying restless in his bed, in which the said bishop of Lincoln, clad in his pontifical robes, with a severe and grim look approached him, and addressed him with a terrible voice, at the same time poking him in the side with the point of a shepherd's staff which he carried.

Grosseteste berated the Pope for his behaviour, booming, 'The Lord will not suffer you henceforth to have any power over me.' Grosseteste had written to Innocent in good faith to encourage reform but was mistreated for his care. Innocent awoke with a stabbing pain in his side and did not eat for the whole day, an episode that was later said to have contributed to his death. It may have been the first manifestation of an illness exposed in a manner drawn out by a guilty conscience. With the death of Innocent IV, Alexander IV was elected to wear the papal tiara.

Henry applied to King Louis for permission to travel home through France and, during December, the brothers-in-law met in person for the first time. On 9 December the two kings entered Paris, where Henry was installed at the Old Temple. To show his gratitude for Paris' hospitality, Henry ordered that as many poor people as could fit inside the Old Temple should be feasted the following day. The kings visited Saint-Chappelle, built by Louis as a museum to house his vast collection of invaluable relics. Louis, like Henry, was immensely pious and would in fact be made a saint after his death. He sank a fortune into purchasing holy relics from Baldwin II, Emperor of Constantinople, which included the crown of thorns, a fragment of The True Cross, the lance used to pierce Christ on the cross, the sponge used to apply vinegar to the wound, the Image of Edessa (a cloth thought to show the first ever likeness of Christ which appeared on the cloth before King Abgar of Edessa after he was healed by one of Jesus' disciples) and a selection or relics of the Virgin Mary. After the visit, Louis threw a huge banquet at the Old Temple for Henry, and the palace overflowed with nobles and a rich variety of foods. Henry gave gifts to all those who came, an act of generosity that Matthew Paris believed was only fit and proper of a king in another king's land.

The two kings seemed to become fast friends, spending a great deal of time in each other's company and enjoying long conversations together during the days of Henry's stay. Henry, his brother Richard, Louis, and his brother Charles were all married to four sisters, – Raymond Berenguer, Count of Provence, having made an extraordinary set of matches for his four daughters. Matthew Paris noted that Louis spoke to Henry of the closeness he felt and how pleased he was that all of their children would be like brothers and sisters. When the time came for Henry to leave, Paris reported that Louis 'said with a sigh' how much he wished his nobles and Henry's could also be friends, since 'our disagreement gives cause of rejoicing and pride to the Romans'. They parted with embraces and kisses and Henry moved on the coast, where he was forced to wait longer than he wished for a favourable wind to return to England. The meeting represented the end of a golden year and must have created a hope of lasting peace between kings with so much in common.

As a parting gift, Louis gave Henry an elephant to add to his growing menagerie, the first to be recorded in England and perhaps the first brought north of the Alps. Henry also had a polar bear in the Tower's menagerie by this point, a gift from King Haakon IV of Norway in 1252. At the end of October 1252, Henry had issued an order that stated, 'Let the Keeper of the King's White Bear, which was lately sent to him from Norway, and is now at the Tower of London, have a muzzle and an iron chain ... and a long and strong cord to hold it when fishing in the Thames.' The sight of a polar bear out fishing in the River Thames became something of a tourist attraction and a thing of fascination to the people of London. Clearly Henry was concerned that it might escape the Tower; how its keeper felt, attached to the great animal by a long cord, is not recorded.

Richard and the nobles met the king on his landing and showered him with gifts, though Matthew Paris insisted, 'With these the king might have raised a large sum of money, but all together would not suffice to pay all the debts he had contracted, even though it were multiplied a hundred-fold.' When the king returned to London in triumph he was given a gift by the citizens of £100. As he had done when Edward had been born, Henry displayed a startling lack of grace by telling the citizens that their gift was not enough. In a bemused panic they set about trying to correct the offence they had inadvertently caused, and the king was only satisfied when they produced a cup valued at £200 to add to the previous gift. This was an odd repeat of a strange piece of behaviour that defies explanation. Either Henry had a very clear value in mind for the worth of his triumph and the gifts rich men should offer at the birth of his son as a proportion of their wealth, or he deliberately caused offence and panic to keep them on their toes and remind them precisely who was boss and how difficult he could be to please. Otherwise, the explanation is more obscure. Henry then further demanded 300 marks from the city as talliage and punishment for the escape of a suspected murderer.

Finding himself once more in dire need of cash, Henry borrowed a large sum from his brother, providing some of the gold in the royal treasury as security. When a proclamation was issued reaffirming the Charters once more and insisting that they should be 'observed inviolate', Matthew Paris complained that Henry himself ignored them, taking property from the Church without permission, and then complained that his nobles did not enforce the Charters against their liegemen. Henry was apparently reminded that he was required to set an example for all his subjects in observing the Charters with a quote from a poem that read *'Mobile versatur semper cum principe vulgas'* ('Wherever the prince his footsteps bends, There too the fickle mob attends').

In April 1255, Pope Alexander IV wrote to Henry to confirm the final details of Edmund's acquisition of the Sicilian crown. Edmund was to rule as king but as a vassal of the Pope in the same way that England was held by Henry. A tribute of 2,000 ounces of gold per year was to be paid and an army from Sicily was to be put at the disposal of the Pope for three months of every year. When Edmund was invested as King of Sicily on 18 October, it was amid mounting concern amongst the barons that Henry had taken a poison chalice and didn't even realise it. He still owed the Pope an initial payment of £4,000 which he did not have. Richard, probably the wealthiest man in England, had refused to lend his brother another 40,000 marks toward the cause, and Henry owed Jewish moneylenders in excess of 300,000 marks. The king appeared to still have no concept of the consequences of what he was doing or of the financial burden he was placing on himself for a venture that seemed so unlikely to ever succeed.

The Church, too, was feeling the strain of financial mismanagement and the exactions from Rome. Matthew Paris saw the 4,000 marks of debt dogging Canterbury as just punishment for their election of foreigners from amongst the king's favourites instead of more deserving Englishmen. He cites similar financial problems at Rochester, Winchester and York amongst many others, blaming their troubles on 'the accumulation of their sins'. When a papal collector named Rustand arrived in England and demanded money from a gathering of the prelates, Fulk, Bishop of London, told him, 'Rather than willingly subject our great church to slavery, wrong, and intolerable oppression, I will lose my head,' and Walter, Bishop of Worcester, added, 'And I will be hung rather than see holy Church so ruined.'

Henry also received word from Scotland that his daughter and her fourteen-year-old husband were being mistreated by the guardians of the kingdom during Alexander's minority. News reached him that Robert Ross and John Baliol were mishandling the government and were keeping the king and queen as prisoners, even denying them each other's company. Henry resolved to gather an army and march north to confront Ross and Baliol, but he sent the Earl of Gloucester and one of his own clerks, John Mansell, on ahead with a force to find out the truth of the reports. Earl Richard and Mansell managed to pose as Ross's men to gain entry to the castle, where the queen confirmed what they had heard. The two men immediately arranged for the king and queen to share a bed and spend time together, and when they sent word to Henry that his daughter considered herself to have been imprisoned the king angrily summoned Robert Ross to his court to answer for his actions. Ross initially refused to attend, perhaps in fear, and although he eventually agreed to come to Henry, the king ordered all of Ross's property to be seized and him to be taken into custody. John Baliol, whose father had been an ally of King John and who himself had been loyal to Henry, offered the cash-strapped king funds by way of an apology – that is, a bribe – to excuse his actions, a clear sale of justice prohibited by the Charters. Henry and Eleanor spent some time with their daughter and son-in-law before travelling back south, visiting religious houses and, Matthew Paris complained, relieving them of money as he passed. As they returned to the south, Prince Edward's new wife, Eleanor of Provence, finally arrived in England to a rapturous welcome.

In February 1256, Pope Alexander IV wrote to Henry to demand the full payment of his debts relating to Sicily, now standing at an astounding 135,000 marks. Henry confirmed the Charters once more on 12 February but was unable to secure any money for it, forcing him to write to the Pope on 27 March to explain his pecuniary difficulties. Papal representatives were also given greatly increased powers to collect money from the Church. In June, Alexander wrote back urging Henry to launch a campaign to take Sicily, allowing him the proceeds of vacant benefices and granting an extension to his debts to entice Henry. The continual appearance of episodes such of this drew out once more the question of the wealth of England as perceived from Rome. Successive popes had spoken of their belief that England was a rich country, and they had repeatedly sent their representatives to collect more money than the English Church insisted it could afford. In over forty years as a papal fiefdom England had continued to be bled but was yet to provide the kind of bountiful and steady income Rome wanted. As an extension of this endeavour, the Pope had induced Henry to agree to buy a kingdom that he then had to take an army to win, only to have to pay rent for the Crown to the Pope if he managed it. The Sicilian Affair has long dogged the reputation of Henry III, such as it is, because it is viewed as a frivolous whim, an utter waste of money that Henry did not have to disburse. But it should be remembered that Henry had grown up in an England that belonged to the Pope and that, since the moment the crown was placed on his head at Gloucester in 1216, Henry was a king with a feudal lord whose commands he was bound to obey. The offer of Sicily might have at least appeared, if not in fact have been, more of an instruction that an invitation, and the Pope might have believed that it was a method by which he could finally tease out some hidden wealth that he believed was secreted somewhere in England.

In August 1256, there was another family reunion as the king and queen of Scotland travelled south to visit Margaret's parents and to tour England. There was such a huge gathering of nobles congregating wherever they went that the town of Oxford overflowed and the royal palace of Woodstock could not accommodate all those who sought to join in the festivities and meet the two kings and two queens. At the beginning of November, the Welsh, perhaps seeking to take advantage of the distraction of all the English barons, gathered in force and began to strike at Prince Edward's possessions in Wales. Edward, aware of his father's money troubles, immediately went to his uncle Richard and borrowed 4,000 marks to raise a force to defend his lands. In the wet, wintry Welsh weather the money was quickly spent without a scent of a victory. When the weather finally improved, Edward's retainers went on a violent rampage in pursuit of the rebels, but the Welsh kept ahead of their English pursuers all the way to Chester, where they turned back into Wales and disappeared into the mists with their booty. This episode marked the recommencement of uprisings by the Welsh and represented a personal slight to Edward, and it is entirely possible that he began to harbour a grudge which would define many of the years of his kingship.

On 26 November 1256, Richard, Earl of Cornwall, accepted a nomination for the election of the next King of the Germans, a role that also brought with it the title of Holy Roman Emperor. At a gathering to hear him accept the nomination Richard announced, 'I, trusting in the mercy of God, though I am incompetent and unworthy, gratefully accept this honour and burden, conferred on me as I hope by heaven, and this I do that I may not be called timid and weak-hearted.' He continued:

> If I do this from ambition or courteousness, may I be consumed by hell-fire, and die by a sudden death before leaving this chapel. My desire is to restore the condition of that kingdom, which may God grant, and to have strength to govern those, who of their own free will have chosen me to lord with all modesty and honour.

In January 1257 the forty-eight-year-old Richard was brought news of his election. 'They declared that no one had ever been elected to that dignity so spontaneously, so unanimously, and with such few obstacles,' wrote Matthew Paris, explaining their election of an Englishman as being because 'the nobles of Germany ... hated the pride of the French and they annoyed one another', but added that 'they elected Earl Richard, I say, on account of his fidelity, firmness, and wisdom, as also on account of his wealth'. On the subject of Richard's famous wealth, Matthew noted 'a valuation was made of Earl Richard's wealth, and it was found to amount to such a large sum of money that he could furnish a hundred marks daily for ten years, without including his daily increasing profits arising from his revenues in England and Germany'. Richard's main rival for the election had been Alfonso, King of Castile, Prince Edward's brother-in-law, and Alfonso was not pleased at missing out on probably the most prestigious and powerful position in Europe.

Around this time, during some repair work at the Abbey of St Albans, workmen found a stone coffin buried under the ground that was declared to be the mortal remains of St Alban himself. Nobles, prelates and pilgrims flocked to the site, and an indulgence of fifteen days was granted to any who visited in recognition of the discovery. King Henry himself visited St Albans and stayed in the town for several days, during which Matthew Paris spent time in the royal company and indulged himself in the sin of pride as he wrote about his time talking with the king. He noted that the king was able to recite a list of all of the German electors and all of the English saint-kings. Matthew seemed to enjoy his time with the king, though he left at that point no physical description of Henry or comment on his character or personality.

At Lent, Edmund appeared before Parliament as King of Sicily in spite of Henry's earlier admission to the Pope that he was struggling to raise any money toward the venture. Henry had also written to his representatives in Rome to prime them with preparations to drop the claim altogether. At the gathering, the Church agreed to grant Henry 52,000 marks, which Matthew Paris complained was 'to the irretrievable injury of the English church'. Matthew continued his complaints about the financial state to the country when he noted at the end of April 1257 that Richard had set sail to his new kingdom, appointing the Bishop of London as 'his absolute agent'. As Richard left, Matthew grumbled that

> there were carried away with him, never to return, seven hundred thousand pounds, which were bloodstained by many crimes, besides his daily increasing revenues in England, which were daily carried off. By such means was England despoiled of these and many other good things, especially money, and reduced to a state of pitiable want.

The coronation of Richard on 27 May marked the creation of another important foreign ally for Henry, albeit one willing to criticise Henry when he was wrong. The relationship with Frederick had been good, but made awkward by the Emperor's constant wars with the Pope. It remained to be seen how much Richard's influence would be missed at home if he had been a check on his brother, mediating with the nobles and preventing disputes.

This juncture perhaps represents something of a golden age of European peace, at least for England. Henry's brother was Holy Roman Emperor; he was on good personal terms with the King of France, his brother-in-law; his eldest son was married to the King of Castile's sister; and his other son was (at least on paper) King of Sicily. As a favoured son of the Pope, Henry had managed a calm in international relations that many before and after might envy, with the exception of those who went out of their way to wage war.

On 3 May, Henry and Eleanor suffered their first personal tragedy when their youngest daughter, Katherine, died at the age of just three. Matthew Paris recorded that 'the queen was so overcome with grief that it brought on a disease, which was thought to be incurable', and Henry, who had ordered the rebuilding of the walls of London as they had become dilapidated, received no peace as the Welsh continued to hound Prince Edward's lands and run riot through the Marches. Paris noted that 'the king was overcome with grief at the frequent successes of the Welsh' and that the 'accumulation of sorrows brought on a tertian fever, which detained him for a long time at London, whilst at the same time the queen was confined to her bed at Windsor by an attack of pleurisy'. In the midst of all this sorrow, Prince Edward came to his father to ask for assistance against the Welsh. His timing was perhaps poor, and Henry snapped that it was Edward's problem to deal with, telling his son, again according to Matthew Paris, 'What is it to me? The land is yours by my gift. Exert your powers for the first time, and arouse fame in your youth, that your enemies may fear you for the future; as for me, I am occupied with other business.' The king's reaction may have reflected the personal anguish he was feeling, but it might also have been the kind of tough love that he felt Edward would need if he were ever going to succeed. Henry was nearing fifty and Edward just reaching eighteen in mid-June, so it is possible that Henry felt his son needed to stand firmly on his own two feet and not rely on others in times of need – indeed as Henry had been forced to do (and the effects of which he had perhaps failed to shake off).

During this year, Matthew Paris also recorded the outbreak of a problem with the king's half-brother William de Valence, who had been married on one of William Marshal's granddaughters in the female line, a match which had, with the death of all of her uncles without issue, brought William the Earldom of Pembroke. William had set about aggravating other nobles by seizing property with seeming impunity. He met his match when he tried to snatch Simon de Montfort's goods. The Earl of Leicester made sure that he got every single piece of gold back: 'These matters of complaint having been brought before the king and nobles, the two parties mutually reproached one another, and almost came to blows.' It was perhaps here that further seeds of discontent were sown, as Matthew Paris notes, 'The dregs of enmity produced by this quarrel between the two parties, could never afterwards be entirely got rid of.'

In September, Henry was perhaps feeling revived, or realised that he had been too harsh on Edward, as he gathered an army and marched to Chester. Llywelyn had no taste for a confrontation with an English army and, if the truth were known, Henry lacked the funds for a prolonged campaign that would involve paying men into a winter notoriously hard to endure in Wales. A truce was hastily agreed that allowed Llywelyn to keep the lands that he had taken so far, provided he stopped attacking any more lands of Edward or the Marcher Lords. At the same time, Pope Alexander IV wrote to Henry again to insist on payment of his debts: this time the demand was accompanied by a threat of excommunication if he failed to pay. Henry had been protected from the ultimate sanction of the Church all his reign as Rome had always insisted that he and his brother Richard could only be excommunicated by direct order of the Pope. Now, Henry stood under threat of something that, to such a pious man, would have been genuinely frightening. The Church at this time had a tendency to overuse excommunication, one English earl having been excommunicated for trying to stop a bishop's dogs hunting on his lands, and some, like Frederick II and even Henry's father, became so used to it that it lost any sting, but to Henry it was most likely a very serious and frightening moment. Matthew Paris recorded that Henry, 'being in a state of mental confusion, paid five thousand marks to the pope to appease his anger, and to put off the sentence for a time'. The 'mental confusion' may well have been a genuine panic at the threat.

Pope Alexander wrote to Henry early in 1258 once more to demand payment in spite of the fact that Manfred had now been crowned King of Sicily and Edmund's prospects lay in tatters. The affair had cost Henry huge amounts of money, brought him to verge of excommunication and made him look a gullible fool to his nobles. 1258 was to prove another year of reckoning for Henry.

12

The Road to War

England was wracked by famine as winter came to an end. Matthew Paris lamented, 'The dead lay about, swollen and rotting, on dunghills, and in the dirt of the streets, and there was scarcely anyone to bury them.' At Easter 1258, England received some relief from one of her foreign allies as 'fifty large ships arrived there from the continent, having been sent by Richard, King of Germany, laden with corn, wheat, and bread'. The truce with Llywelyn expired and Henry was forced to try and gather men once more as the Welsh began to buck against the English again, with his barons refusing financial support to help with his debts to the Pope. It may have been seen as a sign that amidst this pestilence and horror another papal nuncio named Herlot arrived in England.

The *Tewkesbury Chronicle* recorded that in April Henry was confronted in his own chamber by a group of his barons in full armour, though they had all left their weapons outside. The king asked whether he was their prisoner and was told that he was not, but the threat was perfectly clear. They had left their weapons outside this time, but the next time they may be pushed to armed revolt. Their primary concerns revolved around the constant requests for money and Henry's failure to observe the Charters. On 11 June a parliament met at Oxford, and the nobles, appearing fearful that civil war was imminent, asked Henry to reaffirm the Charters once more and appoint a Justiciar to moderate the worst excesses of his financial mismanagement. Henry and Prince Edward agreed to put new measures in place, though William de Valence, Henry's half-brother, and John de Warenne, Earl of Surrey, who was married to Alice de Lusignan, Henry's half-sister, opposed the measures.

The result of the negotiations was a document sealed by the king and known as the Provisions of Oxford. The original document has not survived but the stipulations were recorded by chroniclers and can be assumed to be accurate. Hugh Bigod, the younger brother of the Earl of Norfolk, was appointed the first Justiciar in England for over twenty years. The Provisions began by insisting that four knights from each county should convene whilst the county's court is in session to hear any complaints against the sheriff, bailiffs or other Crown officials and to refer any that required investigation to the new Justiciar. The knights were not permitted to buy their way out of service on these juries, nor could the king exempt them by charter. The most shocking measure put in place was the creation of a twenty-four-member panel, half selected by the king and half by the barons, to act as a check on the king and to effectively control the government on his behalf. It was a return to a measure so completely unacceptable in 1215 that it almost broke Magna Carta on its own. The important difference in 1258 was that the council mooted in 1215 had the permission to make war on the king if they felt he deserved it, meaning that the provision opened the door to civil war rather than preventing it. In 1258, there was no mention of such a mechanism and the Council was simply designed to help the king be a better ruler. Still, it was a restriction of royal authority that had previously been vehemently resisted.

The king chose Fulk, Bishop of London, Aymer, Bishop-Elect of Winchester, Henry of Almain (son of Richard, Earl of Cornwall), John de Warenne, Guy de Lusignan, William de Valence, the Earl of Warwick, John Mansell, Brother John of Darlington, the abbot of Westminster and Lord Henry of Hengham. The barons selected Walter, Bishop of Worcester, Simon de Montfort, Richard, Earl of Gloucester, Humphrey, Earl of Hereford, Lords Roger Marshal, Roger de Mortimer, John Fitz-Geoffrey, Hugh Bigod, Richard de

Gray, William Bardulf, Peter de Montfort and Hugh Despenser. All twenty-four swore an oath as follows:

> We make known to all people that we have sworn on the holy gospels and are held together by this oath, and promise in good faith, that each one of us and all of us together will help each other, both ourselves and those belonging to us against all people, doing right and taking nothing that we cannot take without doing wrong, saving faith to the king and crown. And we promise on the same oath that none of us will ever take anything of land or movables whereby this oath can be disturbed or in any way impaired. And if any one so acts contrary to this, we will hold him as a mortal enemy.

Each of the twenty-four swore their oath on the gospels and dedicated themselves to the king and the kingdom. Hugh Bigod committed to 'dispensing justice to all men and for the profit of the king and the kingdom'. The Chancellor, Henry Wingham, next swore that he 'will not seal any writ except a writ of course without the order of the king and of the councillors who are present' and 'he will not seal anything that is contrary to what has been and will be ordained by the twenty four or by the greater part of them'. The wardens of royal castles next took their oath to 'keep the king's castles loyally and in good faith for the use of the king and his heirs' and 'give them up to the king or his heirs and to no other and through his council and in no other way' with their promise to bind them for the next twelve years.

The Church also had its concerns catered for with the statement that 'the state of Holy Church is to be amended by the twenty-four chosen to reform the state of the kingdom of England'. It is telling that no other mention of the Church is made and that this brief mention allows for the reform of the Church by a lay council which, although it included a few bishops, was essentially temporal. It represents an exertion of control by the State over the Church that marks another signal of a sea change and the perception that Roman interference was problematical. The battle between Henry II and Thomas Becket was being resurrected, perhaps tentatively, but nevertheless in earnest. The full extent of the council's temporal powers can be seen in the provision that the Chancellor, insisting 'merely by the king's will he shall seal nothing out of course, but shall do so by the council that surrounds the king'. At the end of each year, the Chancellor, the Treasurer and a Chief Justice were to provide an account of the year to the king and the council, with the Chief Justice permitted to serve for only a year and required also to render his account of the year before his appointed successor. According to the document, the Chief Justice 'has power to redress the misdeeds of all other justices, of bailiffs, of earls, of barons, and of all other people, according to the rightful law of the land', a sweeping role aimed squarely at controlling the worst excesses of injustice at the top of society.

All of the twenty-four and the officers appointed were required to refuse any gifts beyond bread and wine, so that 'no bailiff, by virtue of his office or of some plea, shall take any fee, either by his own hand or in any manner through another person' in order to avoid the suspicion of bribery and corruption. In order to facilitate this freedom, 'the king, if it is suitable, shall give fees to his justices and to his people who serve him, so that they shall have no need of taking anything from others'. Sheriffs were also required to serve for only one year and render their accounts without taking fees. Escheators, those responsible for dealing with property transferred to the crown by virtue of death without heirs, were to be similarly prevented from indulging in corruption. The rights of cities were to be upheld and the households of the king and queen were to be reformed.

One of the most significant of the requirements related to the defining of the meetings of Parliament, as it was noted that 'the twenty-four have ordained that there are to be three parliaments a year: the first on the octave of St. Michael, the second on the morrow of Candlemas, and the third on the first day of June, that is to say, three weeks before St. John'. The twenty-four were to be entitled to attend these gatherings whether they were summoned or not, for the first time removing the composition of Parliament from the sole hands of the king. Henry issued a proclamation confirming that 'we shall observe inviolably whatsoever shall be ordained by the twenty-four chosen from both sides and put under an oath for this special purpose, or by the greater part of them; and we wish and strictly enjoin that their decisions be observed inviolably by all,' in order to give force to the measures, and also stated that Prince Edward 'having taken an oath on his body, has granted by his letters that, so far as in him lies, he will faithfully and inviolably observe and cause to be for ever observed everything above set down and conceded'.

According to the *Annals of Waverley*, the first major outcome of the Provisions of Oxford was the expulsion of Poitevins from England again, led across the Channel by the king's half-brothers. The chronicler reported rumours that the foreigners around the king despised the English and were even planning to kill English barons, maybe even the king, and replace them with Poitevins, though 'they were not the only guilty ones, but – a yet greater matter for sorrow – Englishmen rose against Englishmen, majors against minors, all aflame with the lust of gain, and by means of pleas and amercements, talliages, exactions, and divers other abuses, strove to take from each man what was his own'. The annalist clearly approved of the measures set out at Oxford, noting 'the Earls and Barons, Archbishops and Bishops, and other nobles of England, as though aroused from sleep by a divine touch, seeing the miserable state of the kingdom, banded themselves together, and boldly assumed the strength and courage of a lion which fears the attack of no one'.

As summer progressed in July, Matthew Paris compared the mood of the nation to the summer storms that might rage overhead as he wrote that 'fears and anxieties of the barons were increased by the coming of the month of July with its pestilence-bearing lion and scorching dog-star, whose deadly barking usually disturbs the atmosphere. More than by all else were they alarmed at the fickleness and inscrutable duplicity of the king.' He was already openly suggesting that Henry's unwillingness to be bound by his own word was the greatest enemy and he goes on to report a prophetic incident during one of July's storms. Henry was on his barge on the Thames when a great storm broke with thunder and lightning. The king was frightened by such storms, and his barge was immediately put in at the nearest available place, which happened to be the Bishop of Durham's palace where Simon de

Montfort was staying. Simon welcomed the king but was disturbed by the way the king reacted to him. Simon asked Henry why he was acting so terrified when the storm was already subsiding. The king replied, 'I fear thunder and lightning greatly, but by God's head I fear you more than all the thunder and lightning in the world.' Simon reportedly took offence and indignantly replied, 'My lord, it is unjust and incredible that you should fear me your firm friend, who am ever faithful to you and yours, and to the kingdom of England; it is your enemies, your destroyers, and false flatterers that you ought to fear.'

On 15 August 1258 Herlot returned home, 'seeing', according to Matthew Paris, 'the disturbed state of the kingdom, he wisely took his departure quietly, until a gale of peace and unity, and more favourable for him, should blow'. In October the Provisions of Oxford were confirmed in proclamations issued throughout the kingdom in Latin, French and, for the only time during Henry's reign, in English. The Provisions of Oxford represent another Magna Carta moment in English history. Reform was no longer a bargain but a weapon once more to be suspended above the head of a king viewed as unpopular and tyrannical. Feudal government at all levels relied on the absolute control of a larger number of people by a narrowing class of political, military and financial elites. There was no political mechanism for dealing with weakness and unpopularity anywhere within the system and it is at this issue that the Provisions were squarely aimed. There was no mention of the resort to violence that Magna Carta had tried to authorise in 1215, but it must be remembered that the prelude to this agreement was the unsubtle threat by the barons of armed revolt so that, although the Provisions didn't refer explicitly to violence, the shadow of its threat hung over the negotiations. The Provisions represented an attempt to force reform on the king by restricting his power, with violence as the likely outcome of failure. It was 1215 all over again. This was to be a big test of whether both Henry and the barons had learned any lessons in the forty-three years since Runnymede.

During January 1259, Richard, Earl of Cornwall, was travelling back to England from Germany when he was intercepted by representatives of the barons and told that he would only be permitted to enter England if he accepted and pledged to uphold the Provisions of Oxford. Richard appeared shocked and slammed the messengers, according to Matthew Paris, by offering them an oath 'by God's throat' that

> I will not take the oath which you require, not inform you of the period of my stay in England. I have no peer in England, seeing I am son of the late and brother of the present king, and earl of Cornwall. If therefore the nobles of England wished to reform the state of the realm, they ought to have summoned me, and should not in impetuous daring have approached so difficult a matter without my knowledge or presence.

Henry met his brother at Dover, and on 2 February Richard swore to uphold the Provisions, suggesting that he was not so much opposed to reforms as he was to his own exclusion from the process.

By October, Prince Edward was in Parliament to hear loud complaints that the barons, rather than his father, were failing to uphold their side of the Provisions of Oxford. Given Edward's later flair for using Parliament to control his nobles it is possible that this was something of a set-up, as the prince began to test the shackles placed on the king which would one day be transferred to him. The result of the wrangling that followed was the Provisions of Westminster, a set of proposals that left aside constitutional matters to deal with the barons' other complaints and requests for reform. What was produced was something far more palatable to Henry and Edward than the Provision of Oxford, but it must also be seen as a royalist attempt to damp down the authority of those measures, much as the 1217 reissue of Magna Carta altered the 1215 Charter into a form more acceptable to the Crown.

The Provisions of Westminster began by limiting the authority and reach of the courts run by magnates so that, with few exceptions, 'no one who is enfeoffed by charter shall henceforth be distrained to perform suit to his lord's court' and so that any breach of this provision should result in 'quick justice' in the king's courts. This was clearly an attempt to reassert the primacy of royal justice against the power of the magnates, and it is important to consider that for all they demanded ever-increasing control over the king's prerogative, the magnates jealously protected their own. What they were doing was the equivalent of the tenants of their land telling them how they may run their estates, and few, if any, of the great lords would have taken kindly to such a challenge, so there was a genuine hypocrisy in their position that Henry and Edward perhaps saw as a chink in their armour. There were several other measures relating to court actions designed to appeal also to magnates with ongoing cases to allow swifter resolution.

Archbishops, bishops, abbots, priors, earls and barons were significantly not to be required to attend the sheriff's returns 'unless their presence is specially demanded', eroding the notion that the twenty-four had a right to be present at such important moments. The eleventh provision stated that, 'No one except the king is in future to levy a distress outside his own fee or on the king's highway where everybody can come and go,' and the twelfth that lords were required to make reparation to tenants underage heirs if they withheld the inheritance on the majority of that heir. It was also enacted that 'no man of religion can buy any land without the agreement of the lord'. There were forty-seven provisions in all, dealing with matters ranging from inheritance to the appointment of sheriffs; all carefully avoided mentioning wider constitutional affairs whilst increasing the king's authority again without making the measures unacceptable. It was a carefully balanced counter-bid to the Provisions of Oxford, and Henry might well have been harking back to his old guardian's successes of 1217. If that was his plan, it worked.

That November, Henry and Eleanor travelled to France as the king sought a final resolution to the lingering issue of the possession of Angevin lands. This is telling in that Henry felt free enough from troubles at home to look across the Channel once more, something he only usually did after a victory that brought calm at home. On 24 November the king and queen arrived in Paris, and although Henry's predictable starting point was a demand for the return of every piece of land, this was most likely to have been an opening gambit aimed to allow room for negotiation. On 4 December a treaty was sealed and published between Henry and Louis IX which was judged a victory, though that might be surprising given the terms agreed. Henry officially gave up his claim to all French dukedoms except Aquitaine and kept Gascony as a fiefdom of the King of France. He was granted several minor towns and lordships around France in compensation but without creating a solid and cohesive power base for him. The speed, the ease and indeed the fact of this final settlement are perhaps a testament to the close personal relationship and shared piety of Henry and Louis. Despite giving up so much, the treaty was judged a positive success. The Pope was pleased with the peace and the end of a dispute that had lasted the entire century thus far; at home the English nobles, who by now considered their links to Normandy and any other French lands well and truly severed, had begun to cultivate a novel idea of an English national identity that did not rely on possession of French lands. The constant pursuit of the Angevin Empire had become like chasing a shadow. It had eluded John and Henry, cost fortunes that the country could barely afford while the papacy made its own demands, brought nothing but dishonourable failure and driven an almost constant wedge between the king and his nobles. Henry had achieved occasional success, but it had always been fleeting and its cost had always outweighed its benefit. They seemed to welcome Henry's final realisation that it was over. Gascony was the rich, wine-producing territory – and that remained in Henry's hands. The notion of holding it as a vassal of Louis can hardly have been repugnant to a man who had only ever been king on those terms. The unsolvable distraction of trying to win back long-lost lands was lifted from Henry's shoulders and by extension those of the country.

Henry and Eleanor celebrated Christmas in Paris and enjoyed watching the wedding of their seventeen-year-old second daughter, Beatrice, to John, Duke of Brittany. It was another valuable alliance with a powerful figure on the Continent. At fifty-two, Henry could reflect on strong ties to the most powerful men in a Europe at peace. He had no need to try and assuage some abstract notion of the honour he might gain by retaking lands his father had lost, and his free quitting of his claims surely reflects a realistic, though overdue, acceptance that Philip Augustus had done his work even before Henry had become king. Two kings later it was becoming difficult to justify the continuance of a paper claim to lands it was proving impossible to take.

The end of this year also marked another crucial moment. Matthew Paris, the St Albans monk-chronicler, passed away. His work was continued by another writer whose identity is uncertain. The continuator is often identified as William Rishanger, another monk at St Albans, though a Brother Balaeus has also been suggested. There is a definite change of tone and style at this point, with the chronicle becoming far more a list of dates and events and far less an expansive oratory that reflected Matthew's personal views and monkish prejudices. Even with all of its inherent bias, which can be seen in the frequent moral judgements offered, it is one of the most invaluable sources for a complex period of English history. Matthew's writing was entertaining in a way many dry abbey chronicles avoided but which gives such rich insight into events in England and abroad. I have continued to refer to the evidence from this source as coming from Matthew Paris for simplicity's sake and because the identity of the continuator is not definitively known.

Henry returned to England in April 1260 to find problems that caused him real distress. Simon de Montfort had been stirring up the barons in the name of reform once more, but the real heartache came when Henry learned that Prince Edward had chosen to join his uncle and godfather in fomenting the unrest. Simon had been squabbling with the Earl of Gloucester, and only the presence of Henry's brother Richard had kept the peace and prevented an outbreak of hostilities in Henry's absence. The king began gathering men against the threat: a long standoff ensued, during which Henry was reported to lament, 'Let not my son come before me, for if I see him, I shall not be able to refrain from kissing him.' The betrayal he felt seems to have been very real and very painful.

There was a year of cold war and posturing until Parliament met in June 1261. Alexander IV had died on 25 May 1261 and been succeeded by Pope Urban IV, a former patriarch of Jerusalem who was likely to continue the crusading focus of Rome. In June, Henry produced a letter sent by Alexander before his death which absolved Henry of his oath to uphold the Provisions of Oxford. Matthew of Westminster recorded the king's repudiation of the Provisions before the gathering with the following speech:

All of you laboured perseveringly on behalf of the general advantage and benefit (as you asserted) of the King, and for the sake of increasing my treasures, and diminishing my debts; and you unanimously agreed to a promise which was to be observed upon oath, to the observance of which you also bound me and my son by a similar oath. But now I have experienced beyond a doubt that you are desirous not so much of the advantage of the King and of his kingdom as of your own, and that you are altogether receding from your arrangements, and that you have reduced me not as your lord, but as your servant under your authority. Moreover, my treasury is exhausted to an unusual degree; my debt increases in every direction, and the liberality and power of the King is almost overthrown and put down. On which account I desire you not to wonder if I do not walk any more by your counsel, but leave you to yourselves for the future, and allow myself to seek a remedy for the existing state of affairs.

Henry wrote to Louis and to Prince Edward to request their urgent assistance to free him from the restraints placed on him by the barons. Louis promised to furnish Henry with a large army for seven years if it should prove necessary and offered to fund it himself. Edward, according to Matthew of Westminster, began to work hard to bring men to his father's side. The king is described as 'no longer a youth, but a veteran', so that he had begun to rely on his oldest son to provide the energy for his efforts. Edward appears to have abandoned his allegiance to his war-hero uncle in favour of supporting his father when push came to shove. Buoyed, Henry entered the Tower of London and broke into the treasure room, taking everything that he could find into his custody. He used the money to have the Tower further fortified and the locks on London's gates replaced and reinforced. Every man and boy over the age of twelve was called to serve the king and swear allegiance to him as proclamations were sent out insisting all 'who were willing to serve the King should come to receive pay from him'. When the nobles heard news of what Henry was doing they brought their own armed retinues to London but could not gain entrance 'since all entertainment within was entirely denied to them'.

Henry's action in obtaining papal authority to break an oath made to his barons was startlingly close to his father's ignition of civil war, though Henry was perhaps more measured and less combative in his tone. The king may have judged that, with everything settled abroad, the time was right to push back against the reforms imposed upon him. His speech makes it clear that he felt the barons were still not delivering their end of the bargain and were using their newly acquired powers to enrich themselves, and whilst this may have been a convenient pretence for denying his own liability to observe the Provisions, the figure of Simon de Montfort had a reputation for ruthlessly snatching all that he could for himself and his sons which gave the accusation the ring of truth it needed. Henry perhaps also felt the need to show that there was a limit to how far he would bend and that the barons, in failing to fulfil their portion of the deal, had reached that limit. As he headed toward his mid-fifties, Henry may have also begun to feel a heightened sense of his own mortality and developed a concern for what he would leave to his son. Matthew of Westminster closes his account of the repudiation of the Provisions of Oxford with the prophetic and ominous assertion that 'a deadly war was expected on every side, which, indeed, had never been so near in past years'.

During February 1262, Pope Urban IV wrote to England to confirm the validity of the bulls of absolution provided to Henry by his predecessor. Prince Edward chose to take a stand and insisted that he did not want to be absolved from his oath. It is hard to see whether this is a noble willingness to see his father restrained and for himself in turn to be similarly restricted, or whether the twenty-two-year-old had fallen under the bewitching influence of Simon de Montfort again. The barons pleaded with the king to remain true to his oath in spite of the papal absolution and eventually the parties managed to arrange mediation, with a representative of the king and two representatives of the barons hearing the complaints of both sides. Matthew Paris recorded that 'by the intervention of the queen, they made their peace with some of the nobles, although with some difficulty, and the kiss of peace was exchanged'. It was a year of fragile amity in which both sides waited for the other to make a decisive move.

In January 1263, Henry agreed to be bound by the Provisions of Oxford again. It is not recorded what persuaded him to sign back up to the restraining reforms but it may have been a combination of his son's attitude, Simon's increasing influence and power, and the unwillingness of the barons to back down from the brink. It might be seen as a mark of weakness that the king instead decided to step back, but it is to be noted that his father has been roundly condemned for centuries for failing to do precisely that. It was a difficult position for Henry to find himself in. The choice was to act with power and authority and undoubtedly spark war, or avoid conflict by appearing weak before his nobles. There was no right course of action, but Henry selected the one that avoided civil war. Simon seems to have been unwilling to be appeased, or perhaps no longer believed in Henry's oft-reversed promises. The earl began to assemble an army, with bases around Hereford, Gloucester and Bristol. Prince Edward in turn gathered mercenaries to Windsor to protect the king and queen from Simon's threatened aggression.

As summer approached, Simon made his move. He took his army into the capital and seized control of it. London was not pleased with the king, in the main because of his constant financial exactions but also perhaps because of his jarring ingratitude to them when they tried to give him gifts. Simon was welcomed as an antidote to Henry's presence. The king and queen were installed at the Tower when Simon arrived, and although Henry continued to insist that he would be bound by the Provision of Oxford, Matthew Paris reported that 'the Queen, impelled by woman's malice, opposed the Barons as far as she could'. She decided to take a barge along the Thames to Windsor where her son and his men could protect her but found herself unable to pass the wrath of the crowds. Eleanor was attacked in an episode that was to become infamous, Paris recording,

When she had embarked in a boat on the Thames for the purpose of proceeding by water to the castle at Windsor, a mob of townspeople gathered at the bridge under which she had to pass, loaded her with abuse and execrations, and, by throwing stones and mud, compelled her to return to the Tower.

Prince Edward appears to have held a grudge against the citizens of London for the outrageous treatment of his mother and, like the violent vengeance he would later exact on Wales, London was to suffer a fractious relationship with Edward during his reign.

On 15 July a truce was negotiated between Henry and Simon by Richard, Earl of Cornwall. In the same month, Pope Urban gave Henry four months to either press or renounce Edmund's claim to Sicily, a matter surely as far distant from the king's mind as it was from his means. A papal representative named Mansuetus arrived in England with instructions to complain that the country had not provided sufficient support to the papacy and to find the money the Pope wanted from his vassal state. Mansuetus was reportedly shocked at the state of the country when he arrived. The tension continued until September, when Henry and Simon, who had clearly emerged as a leader of the reforming barons with an agenda to press, travelled to France to submit their dispute to the arbitration of Louis. This move can only have been at Henry's instigation since the outcome seems a foregone conclusion. If Louis were to approve the curtailing of royal authority by a baron, he would not only let down an ally and risk the peace that had been achieved but would also create a risk within his own kingdom of setting a precedent for dissent.

When the two parties met before Louis to make their cases every nobleman in Burgundy, Spain and Champagne attended, no doubt keen to witness the spectacle of the English king submitting a dispute with one of his nobles to the mediation of the French king. Simon would have been relying on his natural charm and powers of persuasion to try and carry his case, though even in his supreme self-confidence and carrying the crusading renown of himself and his father he must have known that he could not expect a king to rule in his favour against another king. Some of Henry's allies who had been driven from England – including Peter of Savoy and Boniface of Savoy, Archbishop of Canterbury – appeared at the meeting to demand justice against Simon's party, but, as the

Chronicle of Dover recorded, the reformers were in no mood to mollify the foreigners they blamed and despised, insisting 'the barons of England were not bound to account for their actions in the court of the French king nor to undergo judgement anywhere save in the court of the king of England, and this by their peers'.

Henry had pledged to return to England by 6 October to attend a meeting of Parliament that would settle matters. He had been compelled before leaving to write letters to Louis urging the French king not to allow his English counterpart to become distracted whilst in France and to compel him to return by 6 October if he looked unlikely to do so. The odd request probably had more to do with fears that Henry might try and establish a base of operations in France from which to gather support from his Poitevin friends and family and launch some kind of invasion to drive the baronial faction, who had not renounced their fealty to Henry and so were treading a line precariously close to treason, out of power. The king's return to England on 7 October was perhaps a sideswipe at the restrictions he had been placed under which would not quite break the peace. Henry was accompanied by Prince Edward, but the queen had remained in France with her family. This may well have been the strongest indication yet that Henry recognised both the height of the danger surrounding him and also the need for a reliable ally free from the coming turmoil who could orchestrate help should it be required.

Louis informed Pope Urban of the troubles Henry was facing, and in short order a papal legate named Gui Faucoi was appointed to travel to France – though not across to England – with powers to summon anyone, including kings and princes, to him for their case to be heard and judgement to be passed. Letters reached Henry and the barons informing them of the appointment: within them, Simon de Montfort was marked out as 'the chief disturber of the realm', a serious accusation since those disturbing the realm contrary to the Charters were liable to excommunication and temporal punishment. It appears to be an attempt to not only warn Simon and his allies of the consequences of the road they were taking but to move them into a legally compromised position, too, by setting them up as rebels in breach of the Charters rather than those championing the reforms. When the session for which Henry had returned opened it immediately fell into disarray under the guise of a disagreement over appointments to Henry's household. It is not clear who started this argument but it seems likely that it was a deliberate falling out that had little to do with household appointments in reality. As soon as the meeting broke up, Henry and Edward rode to Windsor leaving Simon in control of the Tower. Although unable to agree over the simplest of things, neither side was really ready for a fight, either. Simon and his reforming allies were royalists because there was nothing else for them to be without denouncing allegiance to Henry, and war was a huge step that had caused chaos fifty years earlier. Henry lacked the manpower and money to launch a military campaign and also risked exposing his desire to undo the Provisions of Oxford, and perhaps even the Charters, again. Henry called several barons, including the Earl of Gloucester, to hear him issue letters patent, recorded in the Patent Rolls, assuring them that he 'did not propose in any way to infringe the provisions lately made at Oxford'.

The barons agreed to the appointment of Richard, Earl of Cornwall, as chief mediator between the king and his nobles. It must be assumed Henry began with Richard's knowledge and consent, if not at his instruction, to take back control of his finances through the Exchequer. Simon moved out of London and took up residence at Kenilworth Castle, a huge fortress that Henry had given to Simon as part of a financial settlement between them a decade earlier. When Henry had owned it, much money had been spent to improve the castle and make it all but impregnable, with an artificial lake protecting it and thick, high walls around the keep. It was a rich prize for Simon, so recently refurbished, and he had adopted it as the centre of his Midlands powerbase. With arbitration from Louis due, the well-respected Richard steering the peace and the Provisions of Oxford reconfirmed, Simon might well have felt his task was complete. The observance of a reformed model of government was what he had been arguing for and it appeared to have been delivered, meaning that a failure to withdraw at that point could only have seemed like a bid for power that might have driven his allies away and brought any hope of reform crashing down around his ears, perhaps just as Henry hoped, if it was he who began the squabble that ended the sitting of Parliament.

As those who had gathered behind Simon began to return to the king, Henry overplayed his hand. In demanding the immediate return of castles and attempting to take control of the Cinque Ports, Henry sparked fear that he was about to bring over a force of mercenaries from France, making those who had returned to his side because of his compromises instantly nervous again. Henry went to Dover to order the castellan to hand the fortress over but was unable to secure the castle. When he returned to London he found Simon had darted south with the Earl of Derby and set up a camp at Southwark. During the ride, Simon had been thrown from his horse and had sustained a broken leg, though he still slipped through London whilst Henry was on the south coast. In spite of Henry's assurances, written from Croydon, that he was not up to anything and deploring the disturbances caused by Simon, he had reignited suspicion of his motives that never lay too far beneath the surface. Henry managed to convince four of the leading citizens of London to close the bridge behind Simon as Henry approached his camp. Although they did this, on 11 December the gates were reopened to the earl. As violence threatened the capital once more, both sides stepped back from the brink again. On 13 December, Simon agreed to a settlement. On 16 December Henry also agreed to the same deal and on 20 December the king issued a clear statement of his position by proclamation, stating, 'We are and always will be ready firmly to observe the oath made at Oxford to the honour of God, to our fealty and to the well-being of the realm, and to defend and protect you as our good and faithful men in your rights and liberties, against any men whatsoever.' It was a clear statement and Simon's input into the wording, so that the king had no room for manoeuvre, seems likely; a later repudiation based on any ruling Louis might offer would at least seem a breach of this promise.

When Henry left for France to hear King Louis' verdict, arriving in Amiens on 12 January 1264, he must have counted himself lucky that the persuasive Simon could not travel. The earl's broken leg made the journey impossible and he was forced to delegate his attendance to others, including his son Henry and the Earl of Hereford's son Humphrey de Bohun. It was a fairly low-impact gathering of sons and minor relatives that lacked the impact of

King Henry's attendance and the charisma Simon surely would have brought. The King of England was banking on getting the answer he needed from his brother-in-law the King of France against his other brother-in-law Simon. The meeting took on the flavour of a court of law rather than informal arbitration, and Henry almost immediately laid his cards on the table. He demanded the right to select his own Justiciar and to have no Justiciar at all if he so wished. The barons were accused of taking upon themselves the king's authority to make appointments and decisions relating to his own household, his castles and the whole kingdom, and he cited the Pope's decision that the Provisions of Oxford were not to be upheld and that those adhering to them were to be excommunicated as reasons that he was unable to do as the barons demanded. He had a good case, but coming so hard on the heels of a promise to be bound by the Provisions, made long after the papal annulment, it was a bitter blow to the barons which not only exposed Henry once and for all as duplicitous and untrustworthy in the barons' eyes, but also made Louis' job easy.

On 23 January, only eleven days after Henry's arrival, Louis gave his judgement, recorded within Rymer's *Foedera* in a document known as the Mise of Amiens. The document is simultaneously unsurprising and astonishing. Louis utterly overturned the Provisions of Oxford and declared them null and void:

> The obligations resulting from them and brought about by them, have been of exceeding great hurt to the King's rights and honour, and have occasioned disturbances in the kingdom, depression and damage to the Church, and much loss to other persons – laymen and churchmen, natives and aliens – in the kingdom; believing, also, that even more serious results may reasonably be feared in the future; and bearing in mind, especially, that the lord Pope has already by his letters declared them null and void.

Louis went on to declare that no one was permitted to enact new measures based on the Provisions, to enforce anything already in place because of the Provisions or force anyone to swear to uphold them. Louis ordered the barons to return any letters or grants obtained under the Provisions to Henry along with the custody of any castles taken as surety for the king's observance of them. Louis next declared that Henry 'may, freely and of his own will, elect, dismiss, and remove from office, the Chief Justice, the Chancellor, the Treasurer, counsellors, lesser justices, sheriffs, and all other officials and servants of his kingdom and household, as he did and was allowed to do before the time of the aforesaid provisions', adding also that anti-alien measures in the Provisions were to be overturned since 'we ordain that aliens may freely dwell in the said kingdom; and that the King may freely call whomsoever he pleases, both aliens and natives, to his council'. The document ended, just to dispel any lingering doubt, by stating that 'the said King shall have full power to govern freely in his kingdom and its dependencies, and shall be in the state and in the enjoyment of plenary power, in and through everything'.

The result can hardly have come as a surprise to anyone. Louis was never likely to uphold the cause of a baronial class when it infringed on the authority of a king. The barons' hope lay only in the faint possibility that Henry might choose to observe at least some of the reforms in order to keep the peace. The judgement left them little cause to believe that he would. In this respect, the Mise of Amiens was utterly predictable and unsurprising. The astonishing aspect was the tone of the judicial type of authority given to a Capetian king of France over the internal politics of the Angevin kingdom of England. The unity displayed between two nations who had spent and would spend far more time fighting each other than cooperating on matters of legal technicality is perhaps to be applauded, and had it continued medieval Europe might have been a very different place, but it lays bare Henry's willingness to submit to the authority of others he considered his peers or superiors. This may come as little surprise in a man who had, from the age of nine until his current age of fifty-six, been a king who owed feudal allegiance to a greater power. The issue of his odd, awkward position may have lain at the heart of many of Henry's problems as he struggled to attain supremacy over a Church and kingdom that could always appeal to a power higher than him and having always to consider the rights and authority of the Pope when he tried to impose himself on his barons. John had lived under that strange form of kingship only briefly and for a short enough time to see only the advantages of saving his crown. Henry had lived every day of his life trying to balance the power of a king with the limitations of having a feudal master. The effects of this can be seen in submitting an internal political dispute to the courts of the King of France. No previous Norman or Angevin king and no later Plantagenet of the medieval period would have countenanced such a thing.

For all Henry had kept the plates spinning with only relatively minor hiccups for the forty-seven years of his rule, the victory he won from the King of France would bring them all crashing down in a spectacular and terrible cacophony.

13

The Second Barons' War

King Henry III returned to England on 8 February 1264 with the intention of regaining control of his castles, but any triumph he felt was short lived. During his absence in France, Simon had not been idle as he nursed his injured leg, a wound many thought might kill him. To Simon, the Mise of Amiens could only mean a stepping up of, not an end to, the dispute. He was not a man to give in, and the further Henry pushed the more Simon dug his heels in. The first flashpoint came in the perennially unsettled Marches of Wales where Roger Mortimer, Lord of Wigmore and Radnor, was no friend to Simon. When Roger got wind that Simon's sons Simon the Younger and Henry were in alliance with Llywelyn and were planning an attack on Radnor, he prepared himself for war.

On 4 February, Richard, Earl of Cornwall, received news of the plot and ordered the destruction of all the bridges over the River Severn except the one at Gloucester before moving personally to Hereford. Richard did nothing to confront the de Montfort brothers and was most likely to have been laying the ground for his nephew to take decisive action aimed at displaying royal authority, because when Henry and Edward landed on 8 February, the prince tore across England like an arrow aimed squarely at the throat of the rebellious brothers and Llywelyn, who again rose within Edward's heartlands to embarrass him. Edward seized all of the lands of Humphrey de Bohun around Brecon and tried to push the de Montforts back against the now almost impassable Severn. Henry de Montfort managed to take control of the town of Gloucester, though the castle held for the king, and their ally, Robert de Ferrers, Earl of Derby, had ploughed south to take Worcester, intent on joining up with the de Montforts.

During this episode Prince Edward was to display the kind of political and military astuteness that would define his own reign and which seems completely lacking in his father. Edward seemed to sense that although the uprising appeared a serious threat the cause underlying it was not strong and could be disrupted. On 5 March, Edward was inside Gloucester Castle when he used the Bishop of Worcester to mediate a truce with the de Montfort brothers, which he alluded would be the beginning of a more thorough negotiation to deal with their complaints. As the brothers withdrew, they lost all advantage they had gained in the Severn Valley and irritated both Llewelyn and the Earl of Derby, who had risked much to come out in their support. Edward took a slow journey to meet his father at Oxford, where a parliament had been summoned and a muster ordered for 30 March. Most of the widespread unrest was disjointed and reflected local concerns and outrage at the Mise of Amiens, manifested in a resurgence of anti-Semitism and the resurrection of petty local disputes. The majority of the baronage, whatever they may have thought of the results of the king's trip to France, were with Henry rather than Simon. This was not a cohesive movement and on top of that, those churchmen that supported Simon's position all wanted peace to avoid war. This was what Edward perceived and seized upon.

Henry ordered his royal standard, a dragon on a red samite background, to be brought from Westminster to Oxford in a clear signal that his preparations had a military edge, but, although Simon was calling men to him at Northampton, Henry was not to be hurried. A parliament was held at Oxford at which four prominent bishops who supported Simon, those of Worcester, Winchester, Coventry and Chichester, were courted in a fairly disingenuous way. An agent of Louis, John de Valenciennes, was in England at the time and agreed to oversee discussions at Brackley between the two parties. By the end of the negotiations the bishops appeared willing to concede to all of Louis' judgement if only Henry would refrain from reintroducing his foreign favourites to the government. The cracks in the opposition's unity had been well and truly exposed, and the king and his son were ready to act. Leaving Oxford on 3 April, Edward stormed Northampton four days later and ransacked the town for its support of the rebels. High-profile prisoners, the highest being Simon the Younger, were despatched to Marcher fortresses to be held safely out of the way.

The next decision was to prove a decisive one. Earl Simon had been in London when Northampton was attacked and had ridden out too late to try and aide his force there, turning back to London when news reached him of Edward's victory. Henry led a large part of the royal army north to Nottingham while Edward turned west, and he and his men set about attacking the properties of the Earl of Derby into Staffordshire. Had they plunged south, they might have snuffed out Simon's cause with ease, but the time their foray north bought the earl was well used. Simon began to gather a fresh army in London, allowing the city's worst excesses of anti-Semitic violence to run free and fan the flames of an uprising in his support. Men fell over themselves to pledge allegiance to his reforming cause. Simon could count figures such as Robert de Vere, Earl of Oxford, and John de Burgh, the grandson of the Justiciar Hubert, amongst those who answered his call. His cause was buoyed by news that Gilbert de Clare, the previously uncommitted Earl of Gloucester, had decided from his castle at Tonbridge in Kent to support Simon, who now moved east from London as Gilbert set out north-east from Tonbridge to join together and attack Rochester, the siege of which had led to King John's downfall. They took the town on Good Friday, 18 April, and broke into the outer parts of the castle, preparing to lay siege to the keep but when news arrived that the king was thundering south, the earls abandoned their preparations and returned to London. Henry and Edward knew that they could not afford to allow Simon control of the ports in the south and south-east, as he undoubtedly planned to cut them off from support from Eleanor and Louis in France.

As Henry and Edward sought to take control of the Cinque Ports, Simon saw his chance to strike. On 11 May, Henry's force arrived at Lewes, in the keeping of the loyal John de Warenne. Dover Castle was holding out against the king, the men of the Weald of Kent – who two generations earlier had been so effective in their guerrilla war against Prince Louis – were harassing the royal army, and the men within London had been whipped up into a frenzy in support of Simon's cause, which seemed to be taking on the characteristics of a crusading mission for reform, perhaps because Simon knew how to operate such a campaign and the effect it could have on those who followed him. The next two days were spent trying to find a route to peace. Simon sent the Bishop of Chichester to ask whether the king would be bound by the Provisions of Oxford in a form modified and approved by a set of theologians and canons, adding to the religious, crusading feel of the dispute. Henry flatly refused as Prince Edward and Richard, Earl of Cornwall, offered the earl challenges.

Mathew Paris noted an exchange of letters which derive from this period of negotiation. Simon and Gilbert sealed a letter to Henry on behalf of a number of barons claiming that 'it is clear, from several proofs, that some people who are about your person have heaped lies upon lies concerning us', protesting that their aim was only to protect the person of the king against his true enemies and assuring Henry that 'we shall always be found faithful subjects of yours'. Henry's reply was utterly uncompromising, faced as he was by a large army gathered against him: 'It is clearly evident, by the warlike proceedings and general commotion excited in our kingdom by you, as also by acts of incendiarism, and other enormities perpetrated by you, that you do not observe towards us the fealty due to us.' The king then initiated the renouncing of allegiance that was a formal prelude to war with one of his noble, announcing 'we do not care either for your fidelity or your love'.

Richard and Prince Edward also sent their own, equally bellicose, letter to the barons. They explain that they understood they were defied by the barons, 'though this verbal defiance was not necessary, having long ere this been made manifest to us by your hostile acts', warning Simon and Gilbert that 'we defy each and all of you as public enemies, and inform you that henceforth we will use all our endeavours to do you injury, both in person and property, wherever we can find the means to do so'. They also offered a safe conduct for Simon, Gilbert or both to bring their case before the king's court, to be heard by a judge 'your equal in birth and dignity', a sideswipe at the fact that they would find no others of Edward and Richard's birth and dignity since it was so far above that of the barons. The bishops of London and Worcester returned from the baronial camp to offer a settlement of £30,000 in reparation for damages caused around the kingdom only if Henry would agree to be bound by the Provisions of Oxford. It was Richard who, in a fury at the barons' nerve, rejected the offer outright so that the bishops returned to Simon 'to announce that the adverse party were fully and finally bent on war'.

Simon spent the night awake in prayer, and the Bishop of Worcester gave absolution to all, promising entry to Heaven to anyone who died for such a noble cause. Both sides had effectively issued notices of *diffidatio* (defiance) which constituted a formal renouncement of allegiance and oaths of fealty on both sides as described in the letters. Open rebellion against a liege lord risked lands, titles and properties in the event of a loss. In theory, at least, a notice of *diffidatio*, served and accepted by both sides, absolved any tie of fealty and permitted armed revolt against one who was no longer a liege lord. The real message was startlingly clear as Simon's army approached Lewes on the evening of 13 May. It was to be war.

Henry and Richard were lodged at the Priory of St Pancras, with Edward installed at Lewes Castle. Matthew Paris gives the king around 60,000 men against around 50,000 in Simon's army, but the numbers in such accounts are rarely accurate. The point would seem to have been that there were a large number of men on both sides, with Henry having a numerical advantage. The royal army was arrayed outside the town at the bottom of a slope, and Henry sat in his centre, with Richard on his left flank and Edward leading the right. Simon was still incapacitated by his injured leg and had been forced to travel everywhere in a covered carriage; the carriage was set at the top of the slope amongst the London contingent on his left flank. When the fighting began, Edward charged furiously into the Londoners, aiming for Simon. The prince was furious when he reached the carriage to find that Simon was not there, as the earl had, in fact, managed to mount a horse and was controlling the battle from his right flank, unseen. The sleight of hand enraged Edward and his men fell upon the Londoners in fury. The citizens were not really fighting men and their resolve quickly broke and they fell into a shambolic retreat. It has been suggested that

Edward's pursuit of the Londoners for miles from the field was an act of revenge for their treatment of his mother the previous year, pelting her with stones, mud and refuse as she tried to leave the Tower. If he found it satisfying, his contentment didn't last long. By the time his men made it back to the field the battle was lost.

King Henry had been driven back into the priory and Richard and his son Henry of Almain had been forced to take refuge in a windmill. Edward realised his wild mistake too late as he saw fighting had spilled into the streets of Lewes and Simon's army had taken the field. The king was forced to surrender, handing over his sword to the Earl of Gloucester. The *Chronicle of Melrose* recorded that Simon's men taunted Richard, Earl of Cornwall, King of the Germans and Holy Roman Emperor for hiding in the windmill, shouting 'Come down, come down, you wretched miller! Come out unlucky master of the mill, come out!' and 'It is a great pity for you that you must be made a miller – you who so lately defied us poor barons to battle; and when you defied us no less glorious title would serve you than king of the Romans and ever Augustus.' The king was taken into what William de Nangis described as 'honourable captivity' along with Edward, Richard, his son Henry, Roger Mortimer, Roger Clifford and other Marcher Lords – even some Scots barons were amongst those taken from Henry's side, such as John Baliol, John Comyn and Robert Bruce. William de Valence, Guy de Lusignan, Hugh Bigod and others managed to escape to Pevensey and to secure transport across the Channel.

Letters were sent out from Rochester in Henry's name, though clearly by Simon's hand, explaining to the realm the settlement known as the Mise of Lewes. The Marcher Lords and their Scots counterparts were to be set free to return to administering their manors in what amounted to an admission by Simon that he needed them. In order to keep them under control, Edward and Henry of Almain were to be prisoners as security for the peace. Simon the Younger and other prisoners taken at Northampton were to be freed, as were prisoners that the baronial force had taken. The king was effectively being required to swear to uphold Magna Carta, the Charter of the Forests and the Provisions of Oxford. In Henry's own mould, Simon offered to submit some of the disputed matters to a list of French barons and bishops for arbitration, and on 25 May a copy of the Mise of Lewes was sent to King Louis in the hopes of his approval of the terms. This might have been a fine and noble action but may equally have been Simon's polite equivalent of two fingers stuck up to the interference of the French king, who had sent the Mise of Amiens into England to be observed by the English. Simon explained that now the king was a captive, they had their own settlement, thank you very much. The letter was written in Henry's name and did express a desire that Louis might bring the foreigners who lingered menacingly at his court with Queen Eleanor to peace, but Simon also used Henry's hand to add an important caveat that, 'If any shorter way of peace, more suitable to us and our realm can be found, we propose to pursue it.' Louis' help would be appreciated but not needed; nothing was off the table in Simon's pursuit of his aims.

Those aims were neatly but expansively summed up in a Latin poem entitled the *Song of Lewes*, believed to have been composed by a monk around the time of Simon's victory. The long poem deals in the first half with the glorious victory at Lewes and in the second with Simon's ideas on the government of the realm, explaining and denying Henry's notion that a king was above the law and that the barons were separately responsible to the king for the good government of their piece of his land. Rather, the composer explains, the barons form a community with joint responsibilities and a power when acting as one far in excess of that of the king. The *Song* listed the demands of the barons in poetic form, encapsulating the use of English advisors, the banning of gifts of wardships to foreigners, the appointment of a Justiciar, Chancellor and Treasurer by a council rather than the king and the freedom of justice from corruption. The poem is epic but offers an interesting insight into the Montfortian notion of government. It ends with an assurance that a good king would have nothing to fear, but a bad one must be restrained by the barons and further that it was their duty, as a community representing the community of the realm, to act:

Oh! if princes would but seek the honour of God, they would rule their realms rightly, and without error. If princes had knowledge of God, they would show their justice to all men. Knowing not the Lord, as it were blinded, they seek the praises of men, delighted with vain things. He who knows not how to rule himself, will rule many badly; if anyone is willing to examine the psalms, he will read the same: how Joseph taught himself to teach princes, for which cause the king wished him to be preeminent; and how David in the innocence of his heart and by understanding fed Israel.

From all that has been said above, it will be clear that it is the duty of the magnates of the kingdom to see what things are convenient for the governance of the kingdom, and expedient for the preservation of peace and that the king have natives at his side, whether as councillors or as the greater men of the realm, not strangers nor favourites who supplant others and the good customs. For such discord is the step-mother of peace, and brings in battles, devises treachery. For just as the envy of the devil brought in death, so does hate divide the court.

The king shall keep the natives in their rank, and by this management shall rejoice in ruling. But if he have sought to degrade his own men, have overturned their rank, it is in vain that he will ask, why when so deranged they do not obey him; nay, they would be mad if they were to do so.

Simon led the king and his other prisoners back into London on 27 May and set about getting a grip on the reins of government. William de Nangis explained that Simon, Gilbert and the Bishop of Chichester 'entered upon a mutual agreement and covenant that they would both handle the business of government on an equal basis and would guard the people by faithfully ruling in the manner of a republic to the advantage of the king and kingdom'. The arrangement had a vaguely Roman whiff about it but was complicated by the fact that there was realistically, at least in the short term, no means of government that did not involve Henry as king approving and disseminating decisions. The triumvirate were to appoint a council of nine to advise the king, at least three of whom were to be in constant attendance on the king at any one time. The line-up of the nine could be changed at the discretion of and only with the permission of the three, who were, at least in theory, to serve and be responsible to the community of the barons. The problem with high ideals and noble aims is all too frequently the involvement of mere mortals. Simon's problems began when royal castles taken into custody were passed out between his own sons.

The place of Simon de Montfort in English history was defined by the year that followed the Battle of Lewes and appeared unshakeable until fairly recently. Any Victorian scholar would have placed Simon high on a pedestal as the father of the English parliamentary system and of Western democracy. His bloodthirsty crusading lust and anti-Semitism were largely forgotten. There was nothing that Simon did meekly. He was a fierce soldier, a fierce crusader, a fiercely pious man and a fierce reformer. He combined with these traits a fierce hatred of Jews and heretics of any kind, a fierce conviction of the rightness of his cause and a fierce avarice that was fed by his new-found power. How much of what followed Lewes was genuine, far-sighted reform that places Simon centuries ahead of his peers and how much was desperate, enforced, short-term realism is possibly open to debate. The parliament summoned in June to oversee and approve the new form of government included the Marcher Lords, who were to bring their prisoners taken at Northampton, as well as northern barons loyal to Henry. Simon also, crucially, sent out writs in the king's name instructing each shire court to elect four knights to attend the gathering and to represent their shire. This was not, though, the beginnings of a new political movement. In fact, it was not the beginning of anything.

As previously mentioned, in the time before the Norman Conquest Anglo-Saxon kings had operated the Witenagemot, or Witan, a council of the leading nobles of the land who were regularly consulted on matters of policy and law and which had the power to appoint a king at a time when hereditary descent was not a guarantee. After William the Conqueror defeated King Harold at Hastings, the Witan appointed the fifteen-year-old Edgar the Ætheling (an Anglo-Saxon term for a member of the royal family), grandson of King Edmund Ironside, as the new King of England. It was only William's military might and ruthlessness that put a stop to such a practice. After the conquest, kings routinely held council meetings to seek the advice and approval of their barons. The word 'parliament' was first used to describe such a meeting in official documents in 1236, almost thirty years earlier. Knights had attended for decades, too, with the first mention of them doing so as elected representatives appearing in 1254, and it was not unheard of for representatives of towns of burghs to attend either. The question that must be answered from the slim pickings of the evidence available is: what were Simon's motives in the constitution of those he summoned during his time in power?

To begin with, Simon oversaw the installation of measures to enact the Provisions of Oxford. He could hardly do otherwise having made war on the king in the name of them. He also faced a very real military threat from Queen Eleanor, who was now furiously gathering an armed force with the aid of her brother-in-law Louis to rescue her son and husband. Simon called out the feudal levies in Henry's name and set about securing the Cinque Ports against invasion. Simon led Henry and Prince Edward behind him everywhere he went as he took control of more and more royal castles and amassed ever greater power and wealth, of which his sons acquired the lion's share. Henry was with Simon at Oxford, Gloucester and, by 13 December, Worcester.

As chroniclers reflected on the events of the year, it was already becoming clear that Simon was losing the moral high ground and beginning to claw about to hang onto the power he had won. Matthew Paris lamented:

> The whole of that year, with five months and two weeks besides, trembled with the horrors of war; and as every one strove to defend his castles, they ravaged the whole neighbourhood, laying waste the fields, carrying off the cattle for the defence of the castles, and spared neither churches nor cemeteries. Moreover the houses of the poor rustics were rummaged and plundered, even to the straw of the beds.

The Chronicle of Thomas Wyke recorded that the inhabitants of the Cinque Ports descended into piracy in the Channel of the most vicious kind, complaining that 'they became crueller, in their destruction, than the whirlpool of Scylla or Charybdis, for they despoiled of all their goods and slew, without respect of persons, the merchants who were accustomed to bring us stores'. The effect of this was a shortage of food as merchants were either robbed, murdered or stayed away from England in terror. Wyke left a list of the inflationary impact of these problems as,

> Wine, previously sold at forty shillings, easily fetched ten marks; and wax, which generally did not exceed forty shillings, was worth eight marks and more; and a pound of pepper, formerly scarcely worth sixpence, was sold for three shillings. To be brief, there was such a scarcity of salt, iron, steel, cloth, and all manner of goods, that the people suffered terribly from want, and even divers merchants were forced to beg.

He continued that Simon sent word abroad that England was self-sufficient and needed no trade from overseas, 'an idea which is clearly absurd', not least because Thomas believed trade between nations brought 'divers benefits to each in turn'. In order to appease Simon, though, some took to wearing plain white cloth to demonstrate that they needed no foreign dyes to colour their clothes. Henry de Montfort, Simon's oldest son, attracted particular scorn when he, 'to fill up the cup of his greed, greatly tarnished his honour as a soldier by seizing and applying to his own purposes all the wool of the kingdom' so that 'instead of a good soldier, he was known, for a byword, as "the woolcarder"'. Thomas concludes by complaining that in this year 'the kingdom of England was so weakened that, wounded by irreparable losses, it became a most miserable instead of a flourishing country' and became a laughing stock amongst other nations. Simon's form of rule was not going well.

On 14 December 1264, Simon issued writs to summon Parliament for January in what was to go down in history as a defining moment. The writs, given in Henry's name, stated that 'it is commanded all the sheriffs of England that they cause two knights from the loyal, honest and discreet knights of each shire to come to the king at London as said above'. When Parliament gathered at the Palace of Westminster on 20 January 1265 it included elected knights and elected burgesses from major population centres such as York and the Cinque Ports. The distinction offered between Simon's parliament and previous sessions with elected representatives is that others, including that of 1254, had sought approval for taxation from the representatives whereas Simon sought their opinion and approval on policy matters. It is from this distinction that the development of parliamentary representation, a House of Commons and even the notion of democracy in England has traditionally been traced. Simon may have possessed some noble motives and his desire for reform was undoubted, but it is crucial to understand the position of weakness from which Simon now operated.

Whatever power the earl had won for himself, he was unable to enact a single thing without Henry's authority and could do very little by his own. Even the parliament, which may have been summoned against the king's will, had to be summoned by his writ. Simon's rising had been populist rather than baronial, with many of the barons, as they had fifty years earlier, remaining firmly loyal to the king. Only twenty-three barons are believed to have been summoned to Simon's parliament compared to around 120 representatives of the Church, which was far more sympathetic to Simon's cause than the barons were. It is not known how many knights and burgesses attended, but Simon needed metropolitan support to give his cause the added legitimacy that it was deprived of by limited baronial approval. Simon was also still operating out of London and needed to ensure the City's continued support, particularly as supply problems grew and merchants suffered. He would gain perceived legitimacy by their inclusion, and the dalliance with genuine governmental power gave them a voice whilst distracting them from the issues caused by trade and exacerbated by Simon's own sons.

Henry, now fifty-eight, was still carted around the country behind Simon, though as more and more castles fell under Simon's control he ceased taking Edward with him. Richard was kept within the Tower of London; his son Henry, along with Prince Edward, was placed at Dover Castle, though Matthew Paris was keen to acknowledge that 'whatever place they went to, he [Henry] was always received with honour, and as a king, and the earl showed him every kind of respect'. As Simon began to feel the mounting weight of baronial opposition, particularly from the Marcher Lords, he looked west for another alliance with Llywelyn. Simon took up residence for a while at Hereford Castle and had Prince Edward brought there too, perhaps to display his prisoner to the people and remind them who was in control. Simon attacked and took Haye Castle, which belonged to the Earl of Hereford, and then moved on to Ludlow Castle, the property of Roger Mortimer, before proceeding to Montgomery. There, the Marcher Lords were forced to make peace with Simon and offer hostages as security for their behaviour. Gilbert de Clare, Earl of Gloucester, Simon's foremost baronial supporter, seems to have grown concerned by Simon's seizure of so many castles and by the way he and his sons profited from their power. In bringing Edward to Hereford, Simon had left them a tempting prize that might be won. What followed was daring genius.

Gilbert seems to have made contact with Edward, and the two made plans, doubtless supported by the Marcher Lords, who were being roundly pressed under Simon's thumb. Edward, although a prisoner, was enjoying the kind of loose house arrest a noble would expect as a captive of a fellow nobleman. On 28 May 1265, presumably a bright spring day, Edward obtained permission to exercise some horses with his guards and Gilbert's brother Thomas de Clare outside the walls of Hereford. Keeping up his knightly training and his fitness were important and were not an unusual condition of detainment for a noble. Robert of Gloucester recorded the execution of the prince's scheme:

A steed he began to spur well for the mastery, and with him he had of knights a fair company. And then he took another, and weary them made anon, and then he took the third, the best of each one. As it was before bespoke the which he should trust, he spurred it first softly, as him little lust, When he was a little from the folk, with spur he smote to ground, The sides ran a-blood in a little stound. Then of steeds a good and quick they found. Away went this good knight. When he was out of hand, 'Lordings,' he said, 'have now good day, And greet well my father the king; and I shall, if I may, Both see him well betime and out of ward him do.'

Edward had ridden all but one of the horses into the ground and, on mounting the final one, used the only remaining fresh horse to gallop away from his captors with Thomas de Clare. When realisation hit his guards they urgently sought out fresh horses and made to pursue the prince until they saw, according to Matthew Paris, the banners of Roger Mortimer and Roger de Clifford coming toward them to meet the prince, at which they returned to Hereford. Edward made for Mortimer's castle at Wigmore, and from that safe haven moved to Ludlow. When Edward gave his oath to uphold the Charters, the Marcher Lords, the Earl of Gloucester, the Earl of Warenne and William de Valence all swore fealty to Edward and his father.

News of the breaking-out of Prince Edward seems to have been slow to reach Simon, perhaps because no one at Hereford wanted to admit that they had been duped and had lost such a vital prisoner. The earl sent word to his second son Simon the Younger to come west to help him as the earl himself sought out Llywelyn's assistance. A treaty was ratified on 22 June by Henry's seal, giving Llywelyn permanent recognition as ruler of Montgomery and granting him all of his lands there and any he might take from the Marcher Lords during their suppression in return for a 30,000 mark fine. Edward's faction set about securing all of the passages across the Severn whilst Simon was in Wales and laid siege to Gloucester Castle to take the last bridge. Simon moved with Henry to Monmouth as though planning to attack Gilbert de Clare's lands there, but this gave time for Edward to secure all of the river crossings and cut Simon off from his son and any help in England.

Simon the Younger had been slow to come east and had stopped off at Kenilworth, perhaps to gather more support before moving to his father's aid. His leisurely movement suggests he had failed to understand the urgency of the situation. On Sunday 2 August, Simon managed to force a crossing at a ford dangerously close to Edward's position at Worcester and make for Kempsey. As dusk fell on 3 August he arrived at Evesham, fourteen miles from Kempsey. Simon and Henry lodged at the abbey, the fifty-seven-year-old captive king perhaps exhausted at being hauled about his kingdom. As the sun rose on the morning of 4 August, Simon was pleased to see his son's banners swaying into view with the long-overdue reinforcements. His pleasure was short lived as it became clear it was not Simon the Younger approaching.

Word had reached Worcester of Simon the Younger's arrival at Kenilworth and that he had set up camp outside the castle walls rather than within. Prince Edward seized the initiative and sped almost fifty miles to the town, where he caught Simon the Younger unawares. Although the earl's son managed to get inside the fortress, most of the barons and men-at-arms were captured and taken into custody, as was Simon the Younger's standard. The army moving into sharper view was not that of Simon's son but was following Prince Edward and had caught the earl and his army unprepared. Edward manoeuvred to block one exit from Evesham as Roger Mortimer stood across the other, trapping Simon's men against the River Avon. The earl apparently mused that his godson had learned lessons from Lewes and from his godfather. Interestingly, Edward rode onto the field wearing the red cross on a white background as his badge, as did his men, the first recorded instance of an English army wearing the badge of St George in battle – something Edward was to employ again to great effect many years later in Wales.

As the armies hurriedly prepared for a battle, William de Nangis reported that Simon's oldest son Henry pleaded with his father to flee the field and leave him, Henry, to face Edward. Simon replied,

> Far be this from me, who in my days am already an old man, whose journey through life is hastening to its end, whose parental bloodline is known to be so illustrious as one who was never wont to flee from battle; but you, preferably ought to turn aside from such a dangerous conflict so that you do not perish in the flower and time of your youth but live to be a successor to your father and his famous ancestors in feats of arms, which God grant.

When the fighting began it was brutal and bloody with no quarter given and no hostages sought. Prince Edward was in no mood to tolerate the traitors any longer. The Welsh quickly broke and fled the scene, leaving Simon and his men fighting in a tight circle at the centre of the field. William de Nangis wrote that Simon 'defended himself like an impregnable tower' but 'the enemy erupted with such fury and such hostile hatred against Earl Simon, that they were not satisfied with throwing him dead upon the ground, pierced with many wounds: but at the very summit of his noble deeds they rendered him headless, torn to pieces limb by limb and with parts of his manhood amputated'. Robert of Gloucester recorded that 'his head they smote off and to Wigmore it sent, To dame Maud the Mortimer who right foully it shent; But though that men limbed him, he bled not, men said, And the hair-cloth was to his body nearest wed'.

Amidst the furious carnage Henry de Montfort and Hugh Despenser, the well-respected Justiciar appointed by Simon, died. Simon's third son Guy was wounded and taken prisoner, and Humphrey de Bohun died of his wounds weeks later. Somewhere within the knot of Simon's forces, King Henry was caught up in the fray. The *Chronicle of Melrose* recorded that he had been dressed in 'the armour of some other person' and placed with Simon, perhaps because 'the barons wished that the king should die with them, if it were necessary that they should die in the battle'. As the fighting closed in, Henry was subjected to blows and forced to shout out to save himself: 'Being unable to fight like the others he kept calling out at the top of his voice, "I am Henry, the old king of England"; swearing sometimes, "By the love of God," at other times, "By God's head," and constantly affirming that he was the king; and he cried to the men who were hitting at him, "Do not hit me, I am too old to fight."' One of Edward's men, Roger de Leyburn, managed to stop the attacks and, removing Henry's helmet, confirmed that it was him.

The aftermath of the battle was, as the chroniclers mentioned, ugly and unpleasant in the extreme. Simon's body was mutilated to the dishonour of all. His head was cut off and sent to Wigmore Castle as a prize for Roger Mortimer's wife Maud. His limbs were severed and his testicles cut off before Prince Edward ordered the monks of Evesham Abbey to see to the decent burial of all the fallen, especially those of high station. Matthew Paris reported that Edward himself attended the funeral of Henry de Montfort, 'whom the king his father had held at the font when he was baptised, and who had been brought up with, and beloved by, himself from boyhood'. Simon was despised by many of the barons and an enemy of the king and prince, but to many he became something like a folk hero. Miracles were reported at his tomb over the years and decades that followed; when Edward II, Henry III's grandson, visited Whorlton Castle in 1323 he was entertained by songs about Simon de Montfort. The tomb along with the abbey was destroyed during the Dissolution, and today the spot near where Simon fell is marked with a stone bought from his birthplace at Montfort-Lamaury Castle to commemorate the 700th anniversary of his death in 1965.

Simon's character and his impact on English history are both enigmatic and fascinating. The ultimate failure of his uprising exposes the precariousness of his position but also a certain propensity to make poor decisions either in desperation or over-confidence. Simon had come to England to seek his fortune as a second son with no inheritance. His personal magnetism and charisma cannot be doubted: he became close to the king, secured an earldom to which he had a slightly dubious claim, and married the king's sister to further cement his position. Similarly, his uncompromising and unbending ferocity could earn admiration and antipathy in equal measure. He was not afraid to be at odds with his brother-in-law the king and alienated the people of Gascony during his time as seneschal so much that Henry was begged to remove him. The son of a famous crusading warrior, Simon carved a similar reputation for himself and knew how to use it. His criticisms of Henry reached ever-increasing heights until he took the king captive in battle and attempted to rule himself, only to find that he had no method of doing so that didn't involve the king. His father had been touted as a potential King of England in 1215 before the barons turned to Prince Louis, which may have heightened Simon's sense of destiny and even entitlement. He quickly foiled his own success by failing to garner widespread support from his fellow nobles and, rather than persevering, by making alliances with the Welsh that further inflamed the Marcher Lords and instilled fear and distrust of Simon's judgement in the other barons. The final straw was his enrichment of himself and his sons, which appeared a greedy misuse of power. In his defence, Simon might have argued that without the money and authority this gave him he would struggle even to govern in Henry's name and that he would need a broad powerbase of his own to sustain his reforms, but it simply looked more and more like greed as baronial suspicion and dissatisfaction grew.

The contribution attributed to Simon to the birth and growth of parliamentary representation and democracy has perhaps been overstated and romanticised by hindsight. His fall from grace was so quick that the potential of his initial attempts at reform have been rolled forward into changes that were far distant at the time and probably remote from Simon's thinking. He acted out of necessity as Queen Eleanor gathered an army and baronial support slipped through his fingers. Simon needed to demonstrate that he had widespread support for his regime and he could only find that amongst the prelates and by replacing baronial numbers with knights and burgesses. It is unlikely that Simon plotted anything as ambitious as representative democracy, and his swift demise simply allowed grander intentions to be read back into actions taken of necessity. For centuries, his anti-Semitism and persecution of heretics along with his enrichment of himself and his sons have been glossed over to allow him to represent a tendency in the earliest part of English history possible toward freedom and democracy which he might well not have recognised in his own actions. He was a reformer who sought baronial control of the king through the use of a council. Simon had a vision, but a representative parliamentary democracy was not it.

14

Winning the Peace

From Evesham, Edward rode north as his battered, exhausted father was escorted to Gloucester and then on to Marlborough to recuperate from his ordeal. Just three days after the battle, on 7 August, Henry issued proclamations announcing his full resumption of power and cancelling all writs issued under duress during the time of his captivity. On 8 September a parliament met at Winchester which must have been summoned almost immediately after the battle. The lands of Simon and his supporters were taken into the king's hands along with anything any royalist had seized since the battle in an act of opportunism. This was a sound move since it took the idea of a scrabble for booty which would inevitably lead to ugly fighting and lengthy legal suits off the table, but inevitably Henry got it wrong. With a large new pot of patronage to distribute, Henry began to reach in and throw handfuls in random directions. There seemed to be no plan or measured approach to the rewarding of loyal favourites so that a few received far too much and many got far too little. If Henry sought to demonstrate his personal control again, he was in danger of alienating friends by the way he did it. Still, the parliament was large and well attended by both spiritual and temporal lords with no need for the knights and burgesses to appear. All everyone needed to know was that Henry and Edward were firmly back in control.

On 6 October, London formally submitted to the king, but the rocky relationship between monarch and capital city made the reconciliation somewhat painful. Although many Londoners had remained royalist, the actions of the city as a community had effectively made Simon's revolt possible, and their presence at Lewes had both given Simon the numbers to feel able to face the king and, in their flight, drawn Prince Edward away and possibly cost Henry the battle. Many of the civic leaders were thrown into prison and the king imposed a huge fine of 20,000 marks on the City in January 1266. The payment of this debt took the next thirty-five years to complete, the final payment passing through Edward I's Exchequer in 1301 – it is perhaps telling that Henry's son was unwilling to excuse London the payment of it.

During Henry's captivity a new Pope had finally been appointed. It was none other than Gui Faucoi, the former legate to England who had been working from France to try and help Henry in issuing an interdict and, when the clergy had protested, going even further by excommunicating Simon, Gilbert and the Earl of Norfolk by name and the people of London and the Cinque Ports collectively. On his appointment as Pope Clement IV, the second French Pope in a row, another legate, Ottobuono Fieschi, was appointed to travel to England to restore peace. In the aftermath of Simon's revolt, Edward was tasked with bringing about a military victory and Ottobuono with finding a political settlement as well as punishing the large contingent of the clergy that had backed Simon. On 13 October 1265, the rebels, most of whom had fled abroad, were formerly disinherited by Parliament.

The one thorn that remained embedded in Henry's side was Simon the Younger, who was still at Kenilworth Castle and was refusing, probably out of fear for his life, to surrender to Henry. He was induced to release Richard, Earl of Cornwall, and his son Henry of Almain on securing a promise that Richard would protect certain female relatives and children of the de Montforts, but he would have to be extracted from his father's Midlands fortress in order for the episode of civil war to be brought properly to an end. Prince Edward was restored to his Earldom of Chester, which Simon had taken into custody. Henry's second son Edmund was given Simon's Earldom of Leicester and much of the patrimony that would later constitute the Duchy of Lancaster, which was to play a crucial part in English politics 150 years later.

Henry was at Canterbury on 1 November to meet his wife Eleanor, who was escorted by Ottobuono into England. Prince Edward was, at the same time, at Dover Castle, where the Countess of Leicester was stuck having tried to enter the keep but found it held against her. Edward treated his aunt with honour and respect, assuring her that members of her household would be well treated and, where possible, their lands and properties returned, but on 28 October she left England for the last time, never to return to her brother's realm. Resurrecting her previous vows, Eleanor retired to Montargis Abbey in France and lived as a nun until 1275. On 13 December, orders were sent out to gather the feudal levies to prise Eleanor's second son Simon the Younger out of Kenilworth. Christmas was celebrated in London as Henry and his wife surrounded themselves with an increasing number of knights and soldiers.

In the new year, Simon the Younger saw the mounting odds against him and offered to submit to the arbitration of his uncle Richard, the legate Ottobuono and Philip Basset, offering to come before the king if he received assurances that he would not be killed, maimed or permanently imprisoned. The terms agreed, Simon came before his uncle the king at Northampton. Richard began by offering public thanks to Simon the Younger for protecting him when news of the older Simon's death at Evesham arrived, stating that he would surely have been killed by the furious garrison but for the protection of his nephew. On hearing this, Henry offered the kiss of peace to his nephew and seemed willing to offer him favourable terms, until the Earl of Gloucester and others began to protest. As a compromise, Henry forgave Simon and provided him with a pension of 500 marks a year if he would leave the kingdom for a time, though the door was open for him to return when matters were more settled. On this basis Simon agreed to hand Kenilworth Castle over to the king, but the garrison, outraged at the arrangement, refused to surrender, insisting that they had received their commission from the countess, not her son, and would only give up the fortress at her instruction, not her son's.

Meanwhile, Prince Edward was granted responsibility for the protection of English commerce, given the authority to grant licences to foreign merchants, made castellan of the tactically crucial Dover Castle and made Warden of the Cinque Ports. During May the Earl of Derby, Robert Ferrers, joined a fresh uprising of Montfortian barons who felt hard done by Henry's resumption of power. Henry of Almain led an army as the rebels gathered; they quickly dispersed, though the earl was captured, stripped of his lands and titles and spent several years in custody. The earldom was added to Prince Edmund's haul and gave more weight to what later became the Duchy of Lancaster.

Henry's royal army had assembled outside Kenilworth Castle in April 1266 with over 1,000 people, including women and children, refusing to leave the fortress. The king must have cursed his decision to reinforce the castle and then gift it to his brother-in-law. The artificial lake that encircled the castle was broad on two sides, narrower but still substantial on a third, and fed a moat on the final side with a narrow spit of land providing the only solid approach to the outer walls. The king began by trying to convince those within the walls to give up peacefully, but when one of his messengers returned missing one of his hands, Henry's patience snapped and the siege proper began on 25 June. The trebuchets Henry had ordered brought up proved to have too small a range, especially compared to those within that were designed to fire beyond the lake, and the king was forced to send for bigger siege machinery, with nine engines eventually sitting outside Kenilworth pounding those within. Barges were brought down from Chester to try and assault the walls from the water but were easily repulsed by the defenders and the attempt had to be abandoned.

Ottobuono attended to excommunicate all of those within Kenilworth amid rumours of an invasion by Simon the Younger from Normandy which had hardened the defenders' resolve. Simon was, in fact, causing trouble around the Cinque Ports in spite of the incredibly favourable terms he had secured, but there was no real threat of an organised invasion. The legate appears to have been behind a shift in Henry's tactics as the months wore on. Parliament was summoned to sit at Kenilworth and Henry organised the creation of a council of bishops and barons to negotiate not only peace with those inside Kenilworth but to look at defining the way in which all rebels deprived of their lands might find a way back to their inheritances. At the end of October, the committee presented a set of articles that provided rebels with a road map back to royal forgiveness and the restoration of the property. The Dictum of Kenilworth was published on 31 October 1266 and offered the method to anyone involved in the rebellion if they submitted to the king within forty days.

The penalty to be imposed was set at a proportion of the value of land held if the repentant rebel wished to keep it. Medieval property rules valued land at ten times the annual income it produced; there was to be a sliding scale of payment levels based on an individual's involvement in the revolt. Most would pay five times the annual income of their land – so half of its value – to retain it, though some deemed to be less involved might have this reduced to double the annual income, making it a relatively small penalty. Robert Ferrers, Earl of Derby, was fined seven times the value of his lands for his much more central and serious involvement. It was, in essence, a fair and reasonable deal given that under normal circumstances these men could expect never to see their lands and titles again and might be lucky to escape execution or at least exile. The main problem was that most of the barons weren't directly in control of those lands at the moment as they were in royal hands or had been snatched by royalist neighbours, so they weren't enjoying the income of the land in order to raise the capital needed. Anyone at Northampton who had taken refuge within the churches rather than resist the barons was required to pay half the annual income of their lands. Those who did not possess any lands to buy back were required to surrender a third of whatever goods they did own to buy their pardon. Although the preamble referred to the continuing effect of the Charters and the Provisions of Westminster, there is again the strong odour of a sale of justice here. It is likely that no one baulked at the idea because the other option was ruin, exile and possibly even death. For Henry, it would mean an unexpected windfall and the weakening of the position of barons and knights who had opposed him, leaving them less able to do so again.

Those locked up tightly within Kenilworth were not swayed and refused to surrender still. It is to the credit of Henry's government, perhaps heavily influenced by Ottobuono, that they remained patient and continued to negotiate. The garrison were permitted forty days in which to await help from Simon the Younger, which did not come, and on 14 December, after 172 days under siege, they finally agreed to hand over the castle under the terms, obligations and protections of the Dictum of Kenilworth. Even then, the end of hostilities had not been reached. Around the end of September, a group of the 'disinherited', as those rebels deprived of their lands after Evesham had become known, seized the Isle of Ely, a town built on a mound of land that rose from an area of boggy fenland that was notoriously impenetrable and easy to defend. When council met at Bury St Edmunds in February 1267, the rebels were dug in at Ely. *The Chronicle of Thomas Wyke* recorded that in the last third of 1266 the disinherited had 'built defences which so cunningly closed up the entrances and exits that no one could approach without their consent', stocked the town with weapons and supplies and set about plundering the surrounding countryside so that 'they seized and carried off to the aforesaid island, by deeds of evil daring, and without respect of persons or places, for their own sustenance and that of their dependants, whatever food or furnishings they could find in Norfolk, Suffolk, Cambridge, or in any of the districts round about'. They spent the winter safe and secure stealing all they needed from an increasingly frightened local population.

The leader of the disinherited seems to have been identified as John d'Eyville, and the council, continuing their new mood of reconciliation, tried to negotiate the surrender of the rebels and their removal from Ely. Prince Edward, who was possibly chafing at the bit to find a military rather than diplomatic solution, headed north to secure peace there, but there was a shock when Gilbert de Clare, Earl of Gloucester, suddenly sparked a rising in London, besieging the Tower, where Ottobuono was residing, and demanding that he hand it over. A number of the disinherited were with Gilbert and it seems clear that there was a good deal of sympathy with their cause. The determination at Bury St Edmunds to continue negotiations suggests that the royal faction was not united and contained some degree of sympathy that caused them to seek a settlement that would suit all. Henry had been at Cambridge but quickly moved to London, though he had some difficulty entering the city with which he endured such a troubled relationship. For his part, Ottobuono had acted as though nothing had happened, nonchalantly leaving the Tower on one occasion to travel to St Paul's and preach the crusade before returning, unmolested. Henry's beloved Painted Chamber, though, was ransacked by soldiers lodged at Southwark, who broke in, stole the king's wine and smashed all of the glass and broke up everything they could lay their hands on.

The bottom line was that Gilbert was not truly in revolt against the king. What he sought was a better deal for the disinherited, and Henry was willing to listen. Richard, Earl of Cornwall, led the negotiations in which there seems to have been little resistance to a deal on either aside. When improved terms were agreed, Gilbert immediately stood down and was accepted back into Henry's favour. For those on the Isle of Ely, though, their period of grace had ended. Thomas Wyke recorded that Prince Edward resolved to drive them off the island by force when they would not be reasoned with. The rebels used the rising in London and the sudden movement south of the king to step up their raiding, believing themselves even more free than before to do so. Edward was returning south and Thomas Wyke recorded the way in which he attacked Ely by cunning, defending his methods by explaining that 'against such dastardly robbers as these, to employ cunning must not be considered a sin, but rather a virtue, since in dealing with enemies of the State victory is a consideration paramount to good faith'. The prince made contact with Nicholas de Segrave, a baron on Ely tasked with the maintenance and monitoring of the defences. What Nicholas was offered is not recorded but he was induced to effectively ensure that a blind eye was turned to what Edward was about to do.

Installing himself and his men at the monastery at Ramsey, Edward drew in as many of the locals as he could 'by promises and bribes' in order to arm himself with people who knew the treacherous terrain of the fenland, and they 'fashioned hidden paths through places formerly impassable, making bridges by means of bundles of reeds wrought together; and the bounty of Nature supplied the defects of their skill'. Two years of dry weather made the task all the easier for Edward, as the boggy ground was drier and firmer than usual. Nicholas performed his part of the bargain and Edward and his men erupted into the town of Ely completely unexpectedly. They were only divided from the rebels by a stream, into which they began to throw their spare bundles of reeds to make it passable. The disinherited sent all of the crossbowmen and archers they could find to the bank of the stream to delay Edward's force while they donned their armour and found their weapons. Edward's own archers and crossbowmen faced off against them and the prince himself warned the rebels of the fate that awaited them when he 'publicly proclaimed that if anyone attacked any of his men or by any act of rebellion hindered him in carrying out his enterprise, such an one would suffer death by hanging or execution, should success – and of that there was no doubt – crown his efforts'. The choice was simple: fire one bolt or arrow, raise one sword, and face execution without hope of reprieve. The threat worked, and 'all, struck by sudden fear, laying aside their haughty fierceness, with bowed heads meekly surrendered, and – though they had refused to hear of it previously – submitted themselves to the ever-gracious clemency of the Prince'. Edward gave them two days to gather their belongings and vacate the Isle of Ely, which the shamed rebels duly did. The citizens reportedly rejoiced in the freedom their prince had won for them.

In September 1267, Henry, Edward and Ottobuono were at Shrewsbury to conclude a truce with Llywelyn, who had, perhaps unsurprisingly, used the unrest in England to further his own aims, making gains across Mid Wales and Cheshire. Llywelyn wanted recognition as the prince of all Wales and Henry, after long and inconclusive discussions, left the negotiation to Ottobuono. Four days later, the truce was sealed. Llywelyn got his recognition as Prince of Wales in return for giving homage to Henry as his liege lord. The peace with Wales that was agreed at Shrewsbury was to endure for the rest of Henry's reign. The disinherited had been offered their olive branch and route to salvation and those who refused it had been roundly crushed and embarrassed by Edward, who by now was surely the strong arm of his father's regime if and when one was needed. The Second Barons' War was over, bar the messy settlements that had to be concluded. The uprising had not been quite as serious in nature as that John had suffered and was led by one figurehead with only narrow baronial support, yet it had achieved the custody of the king and a year of rule by someone other than the monarch, secured by force that was a kind of template for Oliver Cromwell four hundred years later.

The real question was whether anyone had really won. At almost sixty years of age and after half a century on the throne, Henry was still dogged by disgruntlement all around his kingdom. He had spent a year as a puppet dragged about his own kingdom to dance at the will of one of his earls. The barons had gained nothing. The Provisions of Oxford were still in tatters, the Charters and Provisions of Winchester, which Henry had continually supported, were still in place, and Simon's cause of reform was broken. The baronial party had gained nothing from the venture which had, in fact, cost them potentially large sums of money to obtain pardons for. Possibly the only winners were Ottobuono and Edward. The legate had contributed to a peaceful resolution capable of enduring and would go on to serve as Pope Adrian V in 1276, his appointment coming just thirty-eight days before his death. Sir Maurice Powicke suggested that Ottobuono might well have been remembered as one of the greatest popes in the history of the Catholic Church if he had lived to perform the role. Prince Edward had won a very different, but complimentary, reputation as a general and soldier. Part of the reason barons had always been willing to rise against Henry was the king's military incompetence which made it easy for them. Edward had shown that the Crown now had a strong sword arm ready to enforce its will if offers of peace were ignored. It was a powerful mix.

The year was rounded off with the king's issuing of the Statutes of Marlborough, a set of twenty-nine articles that remained in force as law in England for centuries – four still sitting on the statute books today. The statutes effectively confirmed and enshrined the Provisions of Westminster, as the preamble explained:

Whereas the Realm of England of late had been disquieted with manifold Troubles and Dissensions; for Reformation whereof Statutes and Laws be right necessary, whereby the Peace and Tranquillity of the People must be observed; wherein the King, intending to devise convenient Remedy, hath made these Acts, Ordinances, and Statutes underwritten.

What followed was an enshrinement of the principle of the rule of law every bit as important as Magna Carta and given by the king to be enacted as binding law. It provided for matters as apparently trivial and irrelevant to the recent troubles as preventing a landowner from allowing his tenants to suffer any detriment caused by a failure in the upkeep of his lands, to weighty principles like the insistence that, although law may become hard to enforce during times of civil unrest, the moment that unrest ended the rule of law must be observed. The only way to obtain satisfaction or compensation for anything that had happened during or outside unrest was through the king's courts. The importance of the Statutes of Marlborough, named for the town in which Parliament sat to hear them, lies not only in their longevity, which itself suggests startlingly impressive legislation, but in the final reassertion, after more than fifty years of argument, of the sovereignty of the king. His rule and his courts were supreme, but the victory of that period of turmoil lay in the admission in the Charters and the Statutes that this law applied to the king as well as every single one of his subjects.

The newly found peace was reflected in 1268, as it had been half a century earlier, by a swathe of men taking the Cross and looking outside of England to the duty Ottobuono had been preaching to them of supporting papal plans to retake the Holy Lands. Ottobuono oversaw a convocation of the English Church at which plans for reform and restructure were enacted. Soon after this was complete, he was at Northampton to confer the cross upon both of King Henry's sons, Edward and Edmund, as well as Gilbert de Clare, Earl of Gloucester, and a number of other nobles.

In August, Ottobuono left England. There is little of the usual vitriol in the account of Matthew Paris: he left 'with a large amount of treasure', suggesting that there was a widely recognised feeling that this legate had earned his prize and served England well. Pope Clement IV died in November and although Ottobuono had to wait another eight years, he eventually achieved recognition in Rome, too.

During 1269 the settlement continued to bear the fruits of peace. The new Westminster Abbey was sufficiently complete for Henry to oversee the translation of the body of St Edward the Confessor into a new golden shrine that Henry had commissioned and paid for to house the mortal remains of his favourite saint. The abbey was not finally completed until the early sixteenth century, with Richard II having a large input during the later years of the fourteenth century, but Henry was able to see the bones of the saint in whose honour he had rebuilt the entire abbey settled into their new home. Henry also had planned his own tomb to lie next to his hero and, although it had taken twenty-five years and untold gold to reach this point, there can be no doubt that Henry, in his piety and hero-worship of Saint Edward, believed it was worth the time, expense and effort as he stood within the tallest Gothic nave in England.

Henry could also stand before the high altar and admire the floor that he had commissioned the previous year. It was a unique piece of art that can still be seen today. Henry brought Italian artists to England to lay a mosaic pavement using a technique called 'cut work', widely known as 'Cosmati work' after an Italian family who specialised in it. A base of Purbeck marble was laid and onto it were placed differently shaped stones – triangles, squares and circles – along with coloured glass to form an abstract design. Unlike the regular size and shape and geometric pattern of traditional Italian mosaic work, Westminster Abbey's Cosmati pavement incorporated irregular pieces of black onyx, yellow limestone, purple porphyry, and green serpentine, along with glass in red, blue and green. In another departure from Italian tradition, the pavement contains an inscription in brass lettering which is now illegible but was noted and translated by John Flete in the fifteenth century. The inscription reads:

In the year of Christ one thousand two hundred and twelve plus sixty minus four, the third King Henry, the city, Odoricus and the abbot put these porphyry stones together.

If the reader wisely considers all that is laid down, he will find here the end of the primum mobile; a hedge (lives for) three years, add dogs and horses and men, stags and ravens, eagles, enormous whales, the world: each one following triples the years of the one before.

The spherical globe here shows the archetypal macrocosm.

The inscription judges that the world will last for 19,683 years by tripling the lifespan of the listed creatures. The odd way in which the year is noted suggests that it was added after Henry's death; one thousand two hundred and twelve plus sixty gives the year 1272, when Henry died, and taking off four leaves 1268 when the pavement was laid. A monk of Westminster named Richard Sporley explained that the macrocosm referred to 'the great world in which we live' and that the microcosm was mankind. The spherical globe, Robert wrote, referred to 'the round stone, having in itself the colours of the four elements, fire, air, water and earth' and appears to offer early confirmation of the belief that the world was spherical. Henry, therefore, laid out the world and everything in it, as well as its doom, at the feet of God before the high altar within the ultimate act of his piety.

In April 1270, Henry was granted a twentieth in taxation toward the funding of the crusade and appears to have had little difficulty in securing it. The Pope released the sixty-two-year-old king from the crusading vow he had made in 1249 on the condition that Prince Edward should go in his place, and on 19 August Edward left from Dover for the Holy Land. He and his father would not see each other again. King Louis IX of France was already in the Holy Land, where sickness was ravaging the Christian army. Louis' third son (the second still living) John, Count of Nevers, succumbed – and soon afterwards, on 25 August, Louis himself died. Louis was, like Henry, a famously pious man and would later become a saint, something Henry might grudgingly admit he would love to have happen to him after his own death.

Louis was succeeded by his son Philip III of France. During Louis' forty-four years on the throne a difficult and fractious relationship between the Angevin and Capetian kings had been reduced to a personal friendship cemented by mutual admiration between men who considered themselves brothers and whose sons were first cousins by virtue of their mothers. It was a golden age in Anglo-French relations during the medieval period that was not repeated. Within a century, Henry's great-grandson Edward III would initiate the Hundred Years War with France.

During February of 1271, Henry wrote to his son Edward in the Holy Land to tell him that he was ill beyond any hope of recovery, but the aging king rallied by 8 April when he attended the wedding of his second son Edmund to the eleven-year-old heiress Aveline, daughter of the Earl of Albemarle and the Countess of Devon. She would pass away just a few years later without issue, and the inheritance never came to Edmund, who later married Blanch of Artois, daughter of the Count of Artois. After three years without a Pope, Tebaldo Visconti was finally elected as Gregory X whilst in the Holy Land with Prince Edward.

The rest of the year saw tragedy for King Henry. Henry of Almain, the king's nephew who had been so crucial to his cause, was also in the Holy Land with his cousin Edward. Matthew Paris reported that Henry, now aged forty-one, asked Edward for permission to return home, wishing to see England and his father Richard, Earl of Cornwall, again. Whilst at Tuscany on the journey home, Henry was hearing Mass at St Lawrence's Church in Viterbo on 13 March 1271 when he was assassinated by Simon the Younger and Guy de Montfort in revenge for the deaths of their father and brother at Evesham six years earlier. The deed became so infamous that, almost half a century later, Dante Alighieri cited the incident in his *Divine Comedy* as the reason that Guy was condemned to the seventh circle of Hell, where violent men are immersed in a river of boiling blood and fire for eternity. During Dante's tour, the centaur Nessus points Guy out amongst other famous killers such as Alexander the Great and Attila the Hun, demonstrating the anathema the action drew. Henry's body was returned to England and buried at Hailes Abbey in Gloucestershire, but the news broke his father and the sixty-three-year-old Richard was afflicted with paralysis. There was more bad news to come. On 1 August 1271, Prince Edward's firstborn son John died at the age of five. The king was reported to be devastated.

On 2 April 1272, Richard, Earl of Cornwall and King of the Romans, died at Berkhampstead Castle, crushed by the death of his oldest legitimate son. Henry of Almain had been the only child Richard had shared with his first wife Isabel Marshal to survive infancy, and the father and son appear to have had the closest of relationships that came closer to friendship and comradery than noble father and son. Richard left a son, Edmund, by his second wife Sanchia of Provence, but his bond with Henry seems to have been something special and his son's death affected him greatly. Richard remains the only Englishman to ever be elected King of the Germans, King of the Romans or Holy Roman Emperor. He was the richest man in England, a crusader and a well-respected man. Whenever there was trouble between Henry and his barons, it was made worse if Richard was out of the country, and it was most often to Richard that both sides turned for assistance and to mediate their causes.

Richard was perhaps the perfect brother for a King of England. He was never afraid to tell his older brother when he was wrong and to oppose him when he needed to, but when swords were drawn he would never flinch to stand at Henry's side. There is not a single shred of evidence to suggest that Richard ever entertained any notion of taking his brother's crown, no matter how bad things got for Henry. He was a pillar of his brother's government and like his relationship with his son that with his brother appears to have more than a small measure of genuine friendship keeping it warm in even the coldest moments. Had Richard remained in Germany for any amount of time or abandoned his brother's cause, it is hard to know how bad things might have become for Henry, but it is certain that they would have been far, far worse than they were. Richard's body was buried at Hailes Abbey, his own foundation and for which he had purchased an authenticated and exorbitantly expensive phial of Christ's blood and where his son had been laid to rest. His heart was buried at Oxford. Henry's was broken.

In May, the king wrote to Philip III of France to ask that he be excused travelling to pay homage for Gascony as he was too ill. Whether this was genuine, a ploy to avoid the potentially embarrassing act, or a reaction to the stream of personal blows is unclear. By August, the king was well enough to be in Norwich to put down riots before moving to Winchester, but his health was now beginning to fail. In November he moved to Westminster, and Matthew Paris recorded that the king 'confessed his sins with humility, beating his breast with grief, remitted ill-will to all, and promised an amended state of life'. He received absolution and the Body of Christ before offering prayers to God. Henry ordered that all his debts be paid and that any residue of his personal property be sold and the money distributed amongst the poor. Given that his demise was not quick, it seems likely that his wife of thirty-six years, Eleanor, to whom he appears to have been utterly devoted, would have been with him. There may have been a loss of will in Henry as the shining gilt of his recent achievements was tarnished by personal loss and a sense of outliving those he shouldn't. He had recently seen his friend Louis, his nephew Henry, his grandson John and his younger brother Richard lost and buried.

On 16 November 1272, at the age of sixty-five and after fifty-six years as King of England, Henry, the third of that name since the Conquest, offered his soul to God and surrendered his mortal body in the hope of eternal life. Four days later, on 20 November, the feast day of St Edmund the Martyr, another Anglo-Saxon saint-king and favourite of Henry's, the king was buried beside St Edward the Confessor in Westminster Abbey. His tomb had been carefully placed on the very spot from which St Edward's body had been removed and where it had rested for two hundred years, demonstrating the extent of Henry's obsessive devotion. In spite of everything, he left a kingdom at peace and secure. Perhaps the most telling testament to Henry's rule was that there was absolutely no question about the succession, even though Prince Edward was thousands of miles away in the Holy Land. Edward heard of the deaths of his son, his uncle and his father from Charles of Anjou, the brother of Louis IX, whilst returning to England in January. It had been arranged before Edward's departure that in the event of his father's death and the ending of government in Henry's name that this necessarily entailed, government in Edward's name would begin instantly and would not rely upon his coronation.

Still, the news appears to have understandably rocked Edward. As Charles passed on news of the trio of losses, he was surprised that Edward was more upset by the news of his father's death than by that of his son. When Charles asked why that was, Edward, perhaps cold-heartedly or perhaps just made honest by his grief, replied that a man could have more sons, but would only ever have one father. It showed the tight and genuine bond between father and son, similar to that enjoyed by Richard and Henry of Almain, and is testament to the loss the new king felt. Whether Edward chose to test his own position is unclear, but he did not return to England and undergo his coronation until 19 August 1274, almost two years after his father's death, at the age of thirty-five. King Edward I went on over the thirty-five years of his reign to remould much of England. Called by some the English Justinian, Edward transformed Parliament into the legislative hub of his nation, codifying everything and enshrining as much as he could in law that bound everyone, including, at least in theory, him. Others remember him as the conqueror of Wales, ruthlessly subduing a region long at odds with the English Crown and its barons and building a belt of immense fortresses to choke any attempt at resistance. For some, he was the Hammer of the Scots, attempting to repeat his success in Wales north of the border in bloody fashion. Although he didn't quite achieve it, he left enough of a mark for the epithet to have stuck.

At the end of this story, he was perhaps simply a beloved son of a doting father. Eleanor survived her husband by nineteen years. Their oldest daughter, Margaret, died in 1275 still queen consort of Scotland, though her husband Alexander III was only survived by their daughter, Margaret of Norway, whose premature death whilst travelling to Scotland opened the door to her uncle Edward's ambitions. Beatrice, the couple's second daughter, also died in 1275 as Duchess of Brittany, a title upheld by her son and grandson, though her grandson John's death without an heir sparked the Breton War of Succession between 1341 and 1364. Henry's second son, Edmund, became known as Crouchback, meaning cross-back, for the crusading cross that he was entitled to wear. Edmund lived until 1296 and served his brother loyally. He became Earl of Lancaster and it is from him that the Duchy of Lancaster grew into richest patrimony in England and eventually provided three kings of England.

So, how should we judge King Henry III?

15

A Forgotten King

King Henry III slips beneath the historical radar of famous kings with eternal achievements to recommend them to posterity. He represents no change of dynasty, no seismic event that shaped England. Many might struggle to place him in a timeline, define his reign, or make a judgement as to whether he was a good king or a bad one. Without chroniclers, most notably the prolific and opinionated Matthew Paris, we would know very little about this period. The project to work through the Fine Rolls has been invaluable, but governmental paperwork only ever tells part of the story – the dry business of the day. Monkish writing offers a more colourful, albeit undeniably coloured, view of events in which everything ought to be turned into a moral tale for the edification of the reader. Henry III was, perhaps, a boring king, and so languishes, forgotten, somewhere low down on the list of more memorable men and women. Yet this, surely, is the greatest signal of the success that he should be credited with.

There were issues from the moment that Henry took the throne as a nine-year-old boy, who seems, from the accounts of chroniclers, to have been utterly bewildered by his sudden propulsion into the forefront of a war he knew very little of. These issues were to have a profound impact on Henry's long reign, but he can hardly attract any form of blame for them. He inherited a kingdom at war, in which the Crown held the minority of land in the country against a foreign prince seeking to make himself king with the support of much of the baronage. Henry retained his kingdom because he was able to abdicate all responsibility to a man like Sir William Marshal. And there was no other man like Marshal. It cannot be denied that without the greatest knight of his age England would have become a Capetian state in a repeat of the Norman acquisition, with all of the problems that had brought to the indigenous population. However, the unforeseen and unavoidable consequence of Marshal's unlikely and glittering successes, which deserve far more attention than they receive, was the long-term weakening of kingship in England. In 1217, Magna Carta became a tool of the Crown rather than a weapon of rebels, and it is to that reversal that the Great Charter owes its immortal status. Henry's minority, though, under Marshal, Guala, Pandulf, Hubert de Burgh and Peter des Roches, necessarily set a tone that predicated problems for the future. A new tone was set, in the absence of a king in possession of his authority, for the relationship between the king and his barons. Cooperation was no longer wished for: it was demanded and expected. Once the path had been trodden, retracing steps would prove very difficult.

What the barons had wanted from their imposition of Magna Carta was a hand in government, the restraining of the king where they saw fit, and the authority to correct the errors that they saw in him. By virtue of the long minority of Henry III, they got this. Marshal's nature was inclusive and consultative, and although Hubert and Peter would vie for control over the following years, it was clear that neither they nor anyone else, including Henry, could fully exercise the authority of the Crown. The barons had what they wanted, taking the sting from their rebellion, and they enjoyed it for over a decade. The question was always going to be how a king could take back the authority due to him in thirteenth-century feudal society. A hugely capable figure such as his grandfather Henry II might have managed it. Henry's great-grandson Edward III fostered a notion of brotherhood that almost disguised his authority. It might have been possible, but Henry grew into a man who lacked any extreme quality which might have helped him. His rule became a game of prodding, poking and probing to try and take back small pieces of power and achieve obscure, theoretical and often pyrrhic victories over his nobles. The alternative, though, was someone like his father, who would have driven the country back into civil war out of petulance and inflexibility.

Henry did oversee a serious civil war towards the end of his reign, the Second Barons' War, but even this must be seen in context. From the Conquest onward, England fell into a cycle, at roughly fifty-year intervals, of the most serious kinds of rebellions and civil wars that can be plotted. After 1066, there was a relatively long period without such an episode until the Anarchy of 1135 broke out, when rival Norman claimants battled for the throne. There was then a serious rebellion in 1173 against Henry II, the first Angevin and Plantagenet king, by his own wife and three of his sons as his sons sought more power than their father was willing to give away. By 1215 the country was at war again as the barons invited a French prince to take the place of King John. By 1264, the country was about due another outbreak, though the axis of rebellion had shifted from rival family members to baronial pressure directed upward in the feudal structure for more power to be passed down to them (but no further). The cycle continued with Edward II's deposition in 1327, Richard II's removal from the throne in 1399, and the outbreak of the Wars of the Roses around 1455. The 1490s saw pretenders and tax riots, 1536 the Pilgrimage of Grace, and there was the Spanish Armada in 1588, the Gunpowder Plot in 1605 and the Civil War in 1642. Henry's longevity simply meant that he was exposed to a serious risk of major civil unrest.

The other major factor at play was Henry's father's decision to sell the country to the Pope. Henry was in the odd position of being a vassal-king. He was a crowned and anointed King of England, but he had a feudal master. This created a swath of problems to contend with. If Henry failed to adhere to his feudal duty to the Pope, he would be opening the floodgates for his own nobles to follow his example. By performing his feudal duty, Henry was making himself unpopular as the Pope demanded more and more cash from a kingdom struggling to make ends meet (or at least, so it claimed – whether any Pope believed this is doubtful and whether it is true is hard to determine). Rome very clearly seems to have viewed its acquisition as something of a piggybank to be raided whenever cash was needed for crusades or even war with the Holy Roman Emperor. Henry's predicament was neatly summed up when his brother-in-law Frederick II complained that he published the papal bull of excommunication against him on the Pope's orders; balancing family loyalty and feudal obligations was not easy. Henry was able to enjoy benefits of this problem though. Popes always viewed him as a special case, protected his interests and prevented his excommunication. Whenever Henry was in a bind he could rely on a Pope to release the knots, though allowing the abdication of responsibility forced on him during his minority to continue was perhaps more a hindrance than a help as magnates saw their concerns swept under the carpet of papal absolution. Henry could use his relationship with the Pope as both sword and shield, but it perhaps prevented him putting down his sword and shield and resolving long-standing problems properly.

The beginning of Henry's rule set an example for future minorities from which no lessons ever seemed to be learned or could be learned. Richard II and Henry VI would endure long minorities and emerge less-than-competent kings who would plunge the country into civil war. Henry III at least died still seated upon his throne. The task of preparing a child for ultimate authority was perhaps no easy one, and Henry's was the first reign to need to find a way since Anglo-Saxon times. Imbuing him with the authority to rule an entire nation including its barons who had watched him grow without creating a spoilt monster was clearly enough to tax England several times in the medieval period with no satisfactory resolution. Henry III seems, at least, to have lacked the extremes of entitlement the dragged Richard II from his throne and of utter incompetence which saw Henry VI obliviously drag the nation into the Wars of the Roses. So what can we say about the man that emerged?

It is beyond doubt that Henry was a committed and devoted family man. He married late but had no recorded mistresses before or during his marriage and therefore no known illegitimate children. Eleanor travelled with her husband seemingly whenever possible, and he left

A Forgotten King

her in France whenever he saw too much danger for her in England. Henry enjoyed a crucially close relationship with his brother and sisters, until he was left with little choice other than to exile Eleanor, which he noticeably sent Edward to do. Edmund appears less clearly from the records, but Henry and Edward seem to have enjoyed the closest of father-son bonds. Edward wept when his father left on campaign, Henry was distraught at the news that Edward had briefly sided with Simon de Montfort, and Edward grieved more for his father than his son. Henry's willingness to raise an army to rescue his daughter Margaret from imprisonment in a Scottish castle has all the hallmarks of chivalric rescue, and the way Margaret and Alexander were supported by Henry and welcomed into England reveals a truly doting father whose commitment to his family is to his credit and to be admired.

Henry's failings were equally obvious. Although able to find cash for his building projects, Henry was perennially broke. It is true that the papacy was bleeding England and that the Church and the barons were not keen to give money to the Crown from their newly adopted positions of empowerment, but when Henry did have funds he was accused by his peers of wasting it and, to make matters worse, wasting it all too often on foreign favourites who gave nothing back to England. A part of Henry's problem here was in the new bargain that Magna Carta represented between the king and his barons under which they expected complaints to be heard and corrected in return for grants of taxation. No king had been required to justify his expenditure in such a way before. A king demanded taxation: that was it. John had pushed this to a whole new extreme, which was part of what led to Magna Carta in 1215, and it was perhaps fear and suspicion of this that made the barons all the more wary of Henry's demands and critical of his use of the money he did have. Nevertheless, fiscal management was not one of Henry's strong points.

Military matters always evaded Henry, too, in a way grasped thoroughly by men like Marshal, Simon de Montfort and even his brother Richard, Earl of Cornwall. With the exception of one successful campaign into Gascony, his endeavours ended in varying degrees of mediocrity and failure that were embarrassing to him and his nobles. Their resistance to calls to follow him over the Channel is testament to widespread belief in his lack of capability. Knowing

249

how his father had felt about the retrieval of Angevin lands and the stain left on his father's reputation by their loss, Henry may have felt obliged to make the attempts rather than been driven. Foreign policy must also have been dominated by the shadow of John's defeat at Bouvine, when the odds had been in his favour but the loss catastrophic. Lincoln had gone against the odds, too, showing the dangerous unpredictability of battle. His eventual peace with Louis IX on terms not far from a complete backing down suggest that he realised the futility of his efforts both because France was growing stronger and Henry lacked the will or the capacity to defeat them. Henry was much happier when the matter was put to bed once and for all, finally feeling the weight of his father's expectation lifted from him. Lacking his grandfather or uncle's innate flair for war or his father's boundless energy, Henry seems to have preferred the certainty of peace to the perils of war. By the end of his reign, the Capetians had been transformed from deadly, invading enemies to close allies.

Henry's reign was crucially important to England. He ruled for fifty-six years, longer than anyone would for another six centuries, and the landscape of England was transformed throughout those years. So why is Henry III such a forgotten figure of English history? The times in which Henry lived were, through no fault of his, some of the most tumultuous and challenging England has ever known. There were complex and heavy pressures, both internal and external. The papacy was increasingly confident and tried to reach deeper into the politics and pockets of Christians across Europe. With successive highly competent and ambitious popes in Innocent III, Honorius III and Gregory IX the papacy became a political force in pursuit of the crusading dream, interested in building something close to a centralised Christian state feudally bound to Rome. France had been surging forward under Philip Augustus and expanded into territory previously belonging to their Angevin neighbours. Once they had put down roots, they would always be difficult to supplant. Wales was constantly seeking to exert freedom from the English Crown, frequently exploiting trouble anywhere else to advance the aims of princes there, causing Henry additional problems or forcing him to divert resources from other endeavours.

At home, the rebalancing of the baronial relationship with the Crown which began in 1173, and of which Magna Carta in 1215 was another step, was organic and hard to manage. The barons felt less obligations and demanded more rights, disrupting unity in the realm and causing a period of inward focus whilst events in the rest of the world rumbled on. Much of the view of Henry III as untrustworthy comes from the actions of barons with their own agenda, frequently diametrically opposed to that of a king trying to assert his feudal rights, and from monkish writers like Matthew Paris who felt Henry should have protected the Church more than he was able, tied as he was by his own feudal obligations to the Pope. The constant retreat to foreign ministers caused outrage amongst the barons, but only because it diminished their positions as they sought to diminish the king's. Foreign appointments were far less likely to push back against royal and papal authority. Poitevin and Savoyard ministers offered a reliable and dependable antidote to the creeping demands of the barons and their retreat to xenophobia was a mask for this fact.

Another reason Henry is forgotten is that he is easy to lose amidst the towering, monumental figures of his reign. Sir William Marshal, the greatest knight, Peter des Roches, the warrior-bishop, Hubert de Burgh, the last great Justiciar, Simon de Montfort, the supposed father of Parliament, and even Prince Edward would have been memorable in any time, and simply pushed Henry to the sidelines of his own kingship in terms of the historical memory. Henry always seemed to lack an overall plan or scheme – in contrast to his son, who as Edward I would reshape the British Isles – and almost lurched from one crisis to another, but with the list of internal and external pressures this is perhaps not surprising. Simon de Montfort, considered a highly capable man in all the ways that Henry was not, held onto power for less than a year. Henry died as king after fifty-six years. He must, surely, have done something right. Henry's knack seems to have been to probe at the re-establishment of his powers without ever going too far. He wriggled under baronial demands where his father had kicked and marched to war. Henry was always able to bend in a way that evaded his father but perhaps saved the Crown.

Henry also represented a transition and a watershed. With his death, much of the old Angevin legacy left England and the Plantagenet period really began. In quick succession, Louis IX, Richard, the Holy Roman Emperor and Henry died. During

Henry's reign the idea of Englishness emerged cautiously into the light. As ties with the Norman and Angevin Continental lands faded, a national identity that was new, and decidedly English, was born. This was developed by Edward I and perhaps completed by Edward III, who finally grasped and enshrined a notion of English nationhood. During the Wars of the Roses, when deciding the relative strengths of claims to the throne, Henry III was the starting point from whom descent was mapped. This is because, whilst we might consider Henry boring, he also embodied stability and certainty in an uncertain world. The disconnect that is hard to reconcile between the pious builder and the shifty politician become comprehensible if we consider Henry adopting holding positions whilst his feudal lord gave guidance rather than lies, and if the selfish motives of the barons and chroniclers are taken into account. He harked back in an old-fashioned way that might have seemed odd to his contemporaries, what with his obsession with Edward the Confessor and the Saxon names he gave his sons. To later, troubled times that might have begun to seem enduring and secure.

William the Conqueror slaughtered thousands across the north of England. William Rufus was roundly condemned for his dissolute personal beliefs. Henry I was implicated in personally killing a man. The Anarchy caused chaos throughout Stephen's reign. Henry II was cursed for his involvement in the death of Thomas Becket. Richard killed prisoners in the Holy Land. John was a vicious man and reportedly involved in the murder of his nephew. Edward I is infamous in Welsh and Scottish history despite his legal reforms. The list goes on, but Henry III is one of the few kings in English medieval history to whom a personal crime cannot be attributed. His reputation is soaked in mediocrity because he bridges a gap between the failures of his father and the successes and reforms of his son, clearing the mess of the former to lay the foundations for the latter.

Whilst a diagnosis is tricky enough in the present and all but impossible from the past, it has struck me that there were incidents throughout Henry's reign that may point to what we might consider high-functioning autism or Asperger's Syndrome. Matthew Paris gives the king a good rote memory, able to reel off lists of electors and saints for example. He seems to have struggled to make social alliances and lurched from one decision to its reversal and back again at the instruction of whoever was before him at the time. He misjudged people's reactions to his actions and said things without considering the consequences. The incidents relating to gifts that the king received on Edward's birth and his return to London might support this theory, as he flatly told people their gifts weren't enough based on some internal assessment of what they should have given. Although impossible to prove at such a distance, it is a theory worthy of consideration.

So why is Henry so forgotten? I have seen it suggested that his reign is simply too vast and too complicated, so I can only hope that I have done him justice in these pages. I have found it hard to reach any conclusion other than that his lack of reputation is deeply unjust and a huge, gaping hole in our understanding of medieval England. King John is remembered as the father of Magna Carta but it was during Henry's reign that it was truly birthed. The Magna Carta of 1215 would have been forgotten as a failed attempt at peace if it weren't for William Marshal's clever reinvention of the sword as a shield. It was under Henry's careful, if not necessarily intentional, management that it was to become the foundation of constitutions around the world. The carefully balanced relationship between the king and his subjects, the correct exercise of authority, and the giving of money in return were to define much of Western government for centuries to follow. Henry used Magna Carta as both a sword and a shield as he used papal authority, but the barons were equally able to wield it and it is in this equitable relationship that the success of Magna Carta can truly be found. That success is entirely due to Henry's determination that it should succeed. He represented stability in choppy waters; he was a bridge between chaos and calm that was trodden by a nation. It is perhaps unfair that the bridge has been allowed to crumble and be forgotten.

The son of Magna Carta deserves to be remembered as a father of nations.

Appendices

Appendix I: The Great Charter of 1225

The 1225 edition of Magna Carta is the final version issued and the first done by Henry's own will. Clauses marked with a + are additions to the original document of 1215.

Henry by the grace of God, king of England, lord of Ireland, duke of Normandy, Aquitaine, and count of Anjou, to the archbishops, bishops, abbots, priors, earls, barons, sheriffs, stewards, servants and to all his bailiffs and faithful subjects who shall look at the present charter, greeting. Know that we, out of reverence for God and for the salvation of our soul and the souls of our ancestors and successors, for the exaltation of holy church and the reform of our realm, have of our own spontaneous goodwill given and granted to the archbishops, bishops, abbots, priors, earls, barons and all of our realm these liberties written below to be held in our kingdom of England for ever,

1. In the first place we have granted to God, and by this our present charter confirmed for us and our heirs for ever, that the English church shall be free and shall have all its rights undiminished and its liberties unimpaired. We have also granted to all free men of our kingdom, for ourselves and our heirs for ever, all the liberties written below to be had and held by them and their heirs of us and our heirs for ever.

2. If any of our earls or barons or others holding of us in chief by knight service dies, and at his death his heir be of full age and owe relief he shall have his inheritance on payment of the old relief, namely the heir or heirs of an earl £100 for a whole earl's barony, the heir or heirs of a baron £100 for a whole barony, the heir or heirs of a knight 100s, at most, for a whole knight's fee; and he who owes less shall give less according to the ancient usage of fiefs.

3. If, however, the heir of any such be under age, his lord shall not have wardship of him, nor of his land, before he has received his homage; and after being a ward such an heir shall have his inheritance when he comes of age, that is of twenty-one years, without paying relief and without making fine, so, however, that if he is made a knight while still under age, the land nevertheless shall remain in the wardship of his lords for the full term.

4. The guardian of the land of such an heir who is under age shall take from the land of the heir no more than reasonable revenues, reasonable customary dues and reasonable services, and that without destruction and waste of men or goods; and if we commit the wardship of the land of any such to a sheriff, or to any other who is answerable to us for the revenues of that land, and he destroys or wastes what he has wardship of, we will take compensation from him and the land shall be committed to two lawful and discreet men of that fief, who shall be answerable for the revenues to us or to him to whom we have assigned them; and if we give or sell to anyone the wardship of any such land and he causes destruction or waste therein, he shall lose that wardship and it shall be transferred to two lawful and discreet men of that fief, who shall similarly be answerable to us as is aforesaid.

5. Moreover, so long as he has the wardship of the land, the guardian shall keep in repair the houses, parks, preserves, ponds, mills and other things pertaining to the land out of the revenues from it; and he shall restore to the heir when he comes of age his land fully stocked with ploughs and all other things in at least the measure he received. All these things shall be observed in the case of wardships of vacant archbishoprics, bishoprics, abbeys, priories, churches and dignities that pertain to us except that wardships of this kind may not be sold.

6. Heirs shall be married without disparagement.

7. A widow shall have her marriage portion and inheritance forthwith and without any difficulty after the death of her husband, nor shall she pay anything to have her dower or her marriage portion or the inheritance which she and her husband held on the day of her husband's death; and she may remain in the chief house of her husband for forty days after his death, within which time her dower shall be assigned to her, unless it has already been assigned to her or unless the house is a castle; and if she leaves the castle, a suitable house shall be immediately provided for her in which she can stay honourably until her dower is assigned to her in accordance with what is aforesaid, and she shall have meanwhile her reasonable estover of common. There shall be assigned to her for her dower a third of all her husband's land which was his in his lifetime, unless a smaller share was given her at the church door.

No widow shall be forced to marry so long as she wishes to live without a husband, provided that she gives security not to marry without our consent if she holds of us, or without the consent of her lord if she holds of another.

.8. We or our bailiffs will not seize for any debt any land or rent, so long as the available chattels of the debtor are sufficient to repay the debt and the debtor himself is prepared to have it paid therefrom; nor will those who have gone surety for the debtor be distrained so long as the principal debtor is himself able to pay the debt; and if the principal debtor fails to pay the debt, having nothing wherewith to pay it or is able but unwilling to pay, then shall the sureties answer for the debt; and they shall, if they wish, have the lands and rents of the debtor until they are reimbursed for the debt which they have paid for him, unless the principal debtor can show that he has discharged his obligation in the matter to the said sureties.

9. The city of London shall have all its ancient liberties and free customs. Further-more, we will and grant that all other cities, boroughs, towns, the barons of the Cinque Ports, and all ports shall have all their liberties and free customs.

10. No one shall be compelled to do greater service for a knight's fee or for any other free holding than is due from it.

11. Common pleas shall not follow our court, but shall be held in some fixed place.

12. Recognitions of novel disseisin and of mort d'ancestor shall not be held else-where than in the counties to which they relate, and in this manner—we, or, if we should be out of the realm, our chief justiciar, will send justices through each county once a year, who with knights of the counties shall hold the said assizes in the counties, and those which cannot on that visit be determined in the county to which they relate by the said justices sent to hold the said assizes shall be determined by them elsewhere on their circuit, and those which cannot be determined by them because of difficulty over certain articles shall be referred to our justices of the bench and determined there.

13. Assizes of darrein presentment shall always be held before the justices of the bench and determined there.

14. A free man shall not be amerced for a trivial offence except in accordance with the degree of the offence and for a grave offence in accordance with its gravity, yet saving his way of living; and a merchant in the same way, saving his stock-in-trade; and a villein other than one of our own shall be amerced in the same way, saving his means of livelihood; if he has fallen into our mercy: and none of the aforesaid amercements shall be imposed except by the oath of good and law-worthy men of the neighbourhood. Earls and barons shall not be amerced except by their peers, and only in

accordance with the degree of the offence. No ecclesiastical person shall be amerced according to the amount of his ecclesiastical benefice but in accordance with his lay holding and in accordance with the degree of the offence.

15. No vill or individual shall be compelled to make bridges at river banks, except one who from of old is legally bound to do so.

16. No river bank shall henceforth be made a preserve, except those which were preserves in the time of king Henry, our grandfather, in the same places and for the same periods as they used to be in his day.

17. No sheriff, constable, coroners, or others of our bailiffs shall hold pleas of our crown.

18. If anyone holding a lay fief of us dies and our sheriff or bailiff shows our letters patent of summons for a debt that the deceased owed us, it shall be lawful for our sheriff or bailiff to attach and make a list of chattels of the deceased found upon the lay fief to the value of that debt under the supervision of law-worthy men, provided that none of the chattels shall be removed until the debt which is manifest has been paid to us in full; and the residue shall be left to the executors for carrying out the will of the deceased. And if nothing is owing to us from him, all the chattels shall accrue to the deceased, saving to his wife and his children their reasonable shares.

19. No constable or his bailiff shall take the corn or other chattels of anyone who is not of the vill where the castle is situated unless he pays on the spot in cash for them or can delay payment by arrangement with the seller; if the seller is of that vill he shall pay within forty days.

20. No constable shall compel any knight to give money instead of castle-guard he is willing to do it himself or through another good man, if for some good reason he cannot do it himself; and if we lead or send him on military service, he shall be excused guard in respect of the fief for which he did service in the army in proportion to the time that because of us he has been on service.

21. No sheriff, or bailiff of ours, or other person shall take anyone's horses or carts for transport work unless he pays for them at the old-established rates, namely at ten pence a day for a cart with two horses and fourteen pence a day for a cart with three horses. No demesne cart of any ecclesiastical person or knight or of any lady shall be taken by the aforesaid bailiffs. Neither we nor our bailiffs nor others will take, for castles or other works of ours, timber which is not ours, except with the agreement of him whose timber it is.

22. We will not hold for more than a year and a day the lands of those convicted of felony, and then the lands shall be handed over to the lords of the fiefs.

23. Henceforth all fish-weirs shall be cleared completely from the Thames and the Medway and throughout all England, except along the sea coast.

24. The writ called Praecipe shall not in future be issued to anyone in respect of any holding whereby a free man may lose his court.

25. Let there be one measure for wine throughout our kingdom, and one measure for ale, and one measure for corn, namely "the London quarter"; and one width for cloths whether dyed, russet or halberget, namely two ells within the selvedges. Let it be the same with weights as with measures.

26. Nothing shall be given in future for the writ of inquisition by him who seeks an inquisition of life or limbs: instead, it shall be granted free of charge and not refused.

27. If anyone holds of us by fee-farm, by socage, or by burgage, and holds land of another by knight service, we will not, by reason of that fee-farm, socage or burgage, have the wardship of his heir or of land of his that is of the fief of the other; nor will we have custody of the fee-farm, socage, or burgage, unless such fee-farm owes knight service. We will not have custody of anyone's heir or land which he holds of another by knight service by reason of any petty serjeanty which he holds of us by the service of rendering to us knives or arrows or the like.

28. No bailiff shall in future put anyone to manifest trial or to oath upon his own bare word without reliable witnesses produced for this purpose.

29. No free man shall in future be arrested or imprisoned or disseised of his freehold, liberties or free customs, or outlawed or exiled or victimised in any other way, neither will we attack him or send anyone to attack him, except by the lawful judgment of his peers or by the law of the land. To no one will we sell, to no one will we refuse or delay right or justice.

30. All merchants, unless they have been publicly prohibited beforehand, shall be able to go out of and come into England safely and securely and stay and travel throughout England, as well by land as by water, for buying and selling by the ancient and right customs free from all evil tolls, except in time of war and if they are of the land that is at war with us. And if such are found in our land at the beginning of a war, they shall be attached without injury to their persons or goods, until we, or our chief justiciar, know how merchants of our land are treated who were found in the land at war with us when war broke out; and if ours are safe there, the others shall be safe in our land.

31. If anyone who holds of some escheat such as the honour of Wallingford, Boulogne, Nottingham, Lancaster, or of other escheats which are in our hands and are baronies dies, his heir

shall give no other relief and do no other service to us than he would have done to the baron if that had been in the baron's hands; and we will hold it in the same manner in which the baron held it. Nor will we by reason of such a barony or escheat have any escheat or wardship of any men of ours unless he who held the barony or escheat held in chief of us elsewhere.

32. No free man shall henceforth give or sell to anyone more of his land than will leave enough for the full service due from the fief to be rendered to the lord of the fief.

33. All patrons of abbeys who have charters of advowson of the kings of England or ancient tenure or possession shall have the custody of them during vacancies, as they ought to have and as is made clear above.

34. No one shall be arrested or imprisoned upon the appeal of a woman for the death of anyone except her husband.

35. No county shall in future be held more often than once a month and where a greater interval has been customary let it be greater. Nor shall any sheriff or bailiff make his tourn through the hundred save twice a year (and then only in the due and accustomed place), that is to say, once after Easter and again after Michaelmas. And view of frankpledge shall be held then at the Michaelmas term without interference, that is to say, so that each has his liberties which he had and was accustomed to have in the time of king Henry our grandfather or which he has since acquired. View of frankpledge shall be held in this manner, namely, that our peace be kept, that a tithing be kept full as it used to be, and that the sheriff shall not look for opportunities for exactions but be satisfied with what a sheriff used to get from holding his view in the time of king Henry our grandfather.

36. It shall not in future be lawful for anyone to give land of his to any religious house in such a way that he gets it back again as a tenant of that house. Nor shall it be lawful for any religious house to receive anyone's land to hand it back to him as a tenant. And if in future anyone does give land of his in this way to any religious house and he is convicted of it, his gift shall be utterly quashed and the land shall be forfeit to the lord of the fief concerned.

37. Scutage shall be taken in future as it used to be taken in the time of king Henry our grandfather. And let there be saved to archbishops, bishops, abbots, priors, Templars, Hospitallers, earls, barons and all other persons, ecclesiastical and secular, the liberties and free customs they had previously.

All these aforesaid customs and liberties which we have granted to be observed in our kingdom as far as it pertains to us towards our men, all of our kingdom, clerks as well as laymen, shall observe as far as it pertains to them towards their men. In return for this grant and gift of these liberties and of the other liberties contained in our charter on the liberties of the forest, the archbishops, bishops, abbots, priors, earls, barons, knights, freeholders and all of our realm have given us a fifteenth part of all their movables. We have also granted to them for us and our heirs that neither we nor our heirs will procure anything whereby the liberties contained in this charter shall be infringed or weakened; and if any thing contrary to this is procured from anyone, it shall avail nothing and be held for nought. These being witness: the lord S. archbishop of Canterbury, E. of London, J. of Bath, P. of Winchester, H. of Lincoln, R. of Salisbury, B. of Rochester, W. of Worcester, J. of Ely, H. of Hereford, R. ofChichester and W. of Exeter, bishops; the abbot of St Albans, the abbot of Bury St Edmunds, the abbot of Battle, the abbot of St Augustine's, Canterbury, the abbot ofEvesham, the abbot of Westminster, the abbot of Peterborough, the abbot of Reading, the abbot of Abingdon, the abbot of Malmesbury, the abbot of Winchcombe, the abbot of Hyde, the abbot ofChertsey, the abbot ofSherborne, the abbot of Cerne, the abbot ofAbbotsbury, the abbot of Milton, the abbot ofSelby, the abbot of Whitby, the abbot of Cirencester, H. de Burgh the justiciar, R. earl of Chester and Lincoln, W. earl of Salisbury, W. earl of Warenne, G. de Clare earl of Gloucester and Hertford, W. de Ferrers earl of Derby, W. de Mandeville earl of Essex, H. le Bigod earl of Norfolk, W. count of Aumale, H. earl of Hereford, John the constable of Chester, Robert de Ros, Robert fitz Walter, Robert de Vipont, William Brewer, Richard de Munfichet, Peter fitz Herbert, Matthew fitz Herbert, William de Aubeney, Robert Grelley, Reginald de Braose, John of Monmouth, John fitz Alan, Hugh de Mortimer, Walter de Beauchamp, William of St John, Peter de Maulay, Brian de Lisle, Thomas of Moulton, Richard de Argentein, Geoffrey de Neville, William Mauduit, John de Balun.

Given at Westminster on the eleventh day of February in the ninth year of our reign.

Appendix II: The Charter of the Forest

The Charter of the Forest was born out of a set of provisions originally within the 1215 Magna Carta. In 1217, they were moved into their own document to reflect the importance and complexity of the issues involved. The Charter of the Forest arguably had a greater impact on a wider population's day-to-day existence than Magna Carta, which was essentially a set of baronial grievances and a shopping list of demands to improve their own lot. Wider provisions were all but accidental. The Charter of the Forest genuinely affected people living from hand to mouth off the land of Henry's kingdom. The version below is the text approved and reissued by King Edward I in 1297.

Edward by the Grace of God, King of England, Lord of Ireland, and Duke of Guyan, to all to whom these presents shall come, sends greeting: we have seen the charter of the Lord Henry our father, sometime King of England, concerning the Forest in these words.

Henry, by the Grace of God, King of England, Lord of Ireland, Duke of Normandy and Guyan and Earl of Anjou, to all archbishops, bishops, abbots, priors, earls, barons, justicers, foresters, sheriffs, provosts, officers, and to all his bailiffs, and faithful subjects which shall see this present charter, greeting.

Know ye, that we, unto the honour of Almighty God, and for the salvation of our soul and the souls of our ancestors and successors, to the advancement of Holy Church, and amendment of our realm, of our mere and free will have given and granted, to all archbishops, bishops, earls, barons and to all of this our realm, these liberties, following, to be kept in our kingdom of England forever.

1. First, we will that all forests, which King Henry [II] our Grandfather afforested, shall be viewed by good and lawful men; and if he has made forest of any other wood more than of his own demesne, whereby the owner of the wood has been hurt, forthwith it shall be disafforested; and if he has made forest of his own wood, then it shall remain forest, saving the Common of Herbage, and of other things in the same forest, to them which before were accustomed to have the same.

2. Men that dwell outside of the forest, from henceforth shall not come before the justicers of our forest, by common summons, unless they be impleaded there, or be sureties for some others that were attached for the forest.

3. All woods which have been made forest by King Richard our uncle, or by King John our Father, until our first coronation, shall be forthwith disafforested unless it be our demesne wood.

4. All archbishops, bishops, abbots, priors, earls, barons, knights, and other our freeholders which have their woods in forests, shall have their woods as they had them at the first coronation of King Henry [II] our grandfather. So that they shall be quite forever of all purprestures, wastes, and asserts, made in those woods after that time, until the beginning of the second year of our coronation. And those that from henceforth do make purpresture without our licence, or waste, or assert in the same, shall answer unto us for the same wastes, purprestures, and asserts.

5. Our rangers shall go through the forest to make range, as it has been accustomed at the time of the first coronation of King Henry our grandfather, and not otherwise.

6. The enquiry or view for lawing of dogs within our forest shall be made from henceforth when the range is made, that is to say, from

three year to three year; and then it shall be done by the view and testimony of lawful men, and not otherwise; and he whose dog is not lawed, and so found, shall pay for his amercement 3 shillings: and from henceforth no ox shall be taken for lawing of dogs. And such lawing shall be done by the Assize commonly used, that is to say, that three claws of the fore foot shall be cut off [by the skin]. But from henceforth such lawing of dogs shall not be, but in places where it has been accustomed from the time of the first coronation of the foresaid King Henry our Grandfather.

7. No forester or bedel from henceforth shall made scotal, or gather garb, or oats, or any corn, lamb, or pig, nor shall made any gathering, but by the sight and upon the view of the twelve rangers, when they make their range. So many foresters shall be assigned to the keeping of the forests, as reasonably shall seem sufficient for the keeping of the same.

.8. No swanimote from henceforth shall be kept within this our realm, but thrice in the year; namely, the beginning of the fifteen days afore Michaelmas, when that our gest-takers, or walkers of our woods, come together to take agestment in our demesne woods; and about the feast of St Martin [in the winter] when that our gest-takers shall receive our pawnage; and to these two swanimotes shall come together our foresters, verders, gest-takers, and none other, by distress; and the third swanimote shall be kept in the beginning of the fifteen days before the feast of St John Baptist [when our gest-takers do meet to hunt our deer;] and at this Swanimote shall meet our foresters, verders, and none other, by distress. Moreover, every forty days through the year our foresters and verders meet to see the attachments of the forest, as well as for Greenhue, as for hunting, by the presentment of the same foresters, and before then attached. And the said Swanimotes shall not be kept but within the counties in which they have used to be kept.

9. Every freeman may agest his own wood within our forest at his pleasure, and shall take his pawnage. Also we do grant, that every freeman may drive his swine freely without impediment through our demesne woods, for to agest them in their own woods, or else where they will. And if the swine of any freeman lie one night within our forest, there shall be no occasion taken thereof, whereby he may lose anything of his own.

10. No man from henceforth shall lose either life or member for the killing of our deer; but if any man be taken and convited for the taking of our venison, he shall make a grievous fie, if he has anything whereof; and if he has nothing to lose, he shall be imprisoned a year and a day; and after the year and day expired, if he can find sufficient sureties, he shall be delivered; and if not, he shall abjure the realm of England.

11. Whatsoever archbishop, bishops, earl or baron, coming to us at our commandment, passing by our forest, it shall be lawful for him to take and kill one or two of our deer, by view of our forester, if he be present; or else he shall cause to blow a horn for him, that he seem not to steal our deer. And likewise they shall do returning from use, as it is aforesaid.

12. Every freeman from henceforth, without danger shall make in his own wood, or on his land, or on his water, which he has within our forest, mills, springs, pools, marlpits, dykes, or earable ground, without enclosing that earable ground, so that it be not to the annoyance of any of his neighbours.

13. Every freeman shall have, within his own woods, ayries of hawks, sparrow-hawks, falcons, eagles and herons: and shall have also the honey that is found within his woods.

14. No forester from henceforth, which is not forester in fee, paying to us farm for his bailiwick, shall take any chimmage or toll within bailiwick; but a forester in fee, paying us farm for his bailiwick, shall take chimmage; that is to say, for carriage by cart the half-year 2 pence, and for another half-year 2 pence, for an horse that beareth loads, every half-year, an half-penny, and by another half-year half a penny; and but of those only that come as merchants through his bailiwick by licence to buy bushes, timber, bark, coal and to sell it again at their pleasure; but for none other carriage by cart chimmage shall be taken; nor chimmage shall not be taken, but in such places only where it used to be. Those which bear upon their backs brushment, bark, or coal to sell, though it be their living, shall pay no chimmage to our foresters, except they take it within our demesne woods.

15. All that be outlawed for the forest only, since the time of King Henry our grandfather, until our first coronation, shall come to our peace without let: and shall find to us, sureties, that from henceforth they shall not trespass unto us within our forest.

16. No constable, catellan, or bailiff shall hold plea of forest, neither for greenhue nor hunting; but every forester in fee shall make attachments for pleas of the forest, as well for greenhue as hunting, and shall present them to the verders of the provinces; and when they be enrolled and enclosed under the seals of the verders, they shall be presented to our chief justicers of our forest, when they shall come into those parts to hold the pleas of the forest, and before them they shall be determined. And these liberties of the forest we have granted to all men; saving to archbishops, bishops, abbots, priors, earls, barons, knights, and to other persons, as well spiritual and temporal, templars, hospitallers, their liberties and free customs, as well within the forest as without, in warrens and other places, which they have had.

And all these customs and liberties aforesaid, which we have granted to be holden within this our realm, on our part towards our men, all men of this our realm, as well spiritual as temporal, shall observe on their part towards their men. And for this our gift and grant of these liberties, and of the other liberties contained in our Great Charter of other liberties, the archbishops, bishops, abbots, priors, earls, barons, knights, freeholders and other our subjects have given unto us the fifteenth part of all their moveables.

We, ratifying and approving the gifts and grants aforesaid, do grant and confirm the same for us and our heirs, and by the tenor of these presents, do renew the same: willing and granting for us and our heirs, that the charter aforesaid in all and singular its articles forever shall be firmly and inviolably observed; even although any article in the same charter contained, yet hitherto peradventure has not been kept. In witness whereof we have caused these our letters patents to be made.

Witness Edward our son at Westminster the 12th day of October in the 25th year of our reign.

Appendix III: The Provisions of Oxford 1258

The articles presented to Henry at Oxford in 1258 were an attempt to stifle royal autonomy in response to patronage of unpopular foreign favourites, just as Magna Carta had sought to rein in the worst excesses of King John's personality in 1215. It was a radical programme that Henry initially accepted but later sought papal approval to set aside.

It has been provided that from each county there shall be elected four discreet and lawful knights who, on every day that the county is held [i.e. the county court], shall assemble to hear all complaints touching any wrongs and injuries inflicted on any persons by sheriffs, bailiffs, or any other men, and to make the attachments that pertain to the said complaints until the first arrival of the chief justiciar in those parts: so that they shall take from the plaintiff adequate pledges for his prosecution, and from the defendant for his coming and standing trial before the said justiciar on his first arrival; and that the four knights aforesaid shall have all the said complaints enrolled, together with their attachments, in proper order and sequence – namely, for each hundred separately and by itself – so that the said justiciar, on his first arrival, can hear and settle the aforesaid complaints singly from each hundred. And they shall inform the sheriff that they are summoning all his hundredmen and bailiffs before the said justiciar on his next arrival, for a day and a place which he will make known to them: so that every hundredman shall cause all plaintiffs and defendants of his bailiwick to come in succession, according to what the aforesaid justiciar shall bring to trial from the aforesaid hundred; also as many men and such men — both knights and other free and lawful men — as may be required for best proving the truth of the matter, in such a way that all are not troubled at one and the same time; rather let as many come as can be tried and concluded in one day.

Also it is provided that no knight of the aforesaid counties, by virtue of an assurance that he is not to be placed on juries or assizes, shall be excused by a charter of the lord king or be exempt from this provision thus made for the common good of the whole kingdom.

Those chosen from the Lord King's side:

The lord bishop of London; the lord bishop elect of Winchester; the lord Henry, son of the king of Germany; the lord John, earl de Warenne; the lord Guy de Lusignan; the lord William de Valence; the lord John, earl of Warwick; the lord John Mansel; Brother John of Darlington; the abbot of Westminster; the lord Henry of Hengham.

Those chosen from the side of the earls and barons:

The lord bishop of Worcester; the lord Simon, earl of Leicester; the lord Richard, earl of Gloucester; the lord Humphrey, earl of Hereford; the lord Roger Marshal; the lord Roger de Mortimer; the lord John Fitz-Geoffrey; the lord Hugh Bigod; the lord Richard de Gray; the lord William Bardulf; the lord Peter de Montfort; the lord Hugh Despenser. And if it should happen that of necessity any one of these cannot be present, the rest of them shall elect whom they please in place of the absentee, namely, another person needful for carrying on that business.

Thus the community of England swore at Oxford:

We make known to all people that we have sworn on the holy gospels and are held together by this oath, and promise in good faith, that each one of us and all of us together will help each other, both ourselves and those belonging to us against all people, doing right and taking nothing that we cannot take without doing wrong, saving faith to the king and crown. And we promise on the same oath that none of us will ever take anything of land or movables whereby this oath can be disturbed or in any way impaired. And if any one so acts contrary to this, we will hold him as a mortal enemy.

This is the oath of the twenty four:

Each one swore on the holy gospels that he for the glory of God and in loyalty to the king and for the benefit of the kingdom will obtain and treat with the aforesaid sworn persons upon the reform and improvement of the condition of the kingdom. Sand that he will not fail for gift or promise, for love or hatred, for fear of any one, for gain or loss, loyalty to act according to the tenor of the letter that the king has given on this and his son likewise.

Thus swore the chief justiciar of England:

He swears he will well and loyally according to his power do what belongs to the justiciars office of dispensing justice to all men and for the profit of the king and the kingdom, in accordance with the provision made and to be made by the twenty four, and by the king's council and the magnates of the land, who will swear to help and support him in these things.

Thus swore the chancellor of England:

That he will not seal any writ except a writ of course without the order of the king and of the councillors who are present. Nor will he seal a gift of great wardship or of a large sum of money or of escheats without the assent of the full council or of the greater part of it. And that he will not seal anything that is contrary to what has been and will be ordained by the twenty four or by the greater part of them. And that he will not take any reward otherwise than is agreed for others. And he will be given a companion in the way that the council will provide.

This is the oath taken by the wardens of the castles:

That they will keep the king's castles loyally and in good faith for the use of the king and his heirs. And that they will give them up to the king or his heirs and to no other and through his council and in no other way, that is to say, through men of standing in the land elected to the council or through the greater part of them. And this form above written is to last full twelve years. And henceforth they shall not be prevented by this establishment and this oath from being able to give them up freely to the king or his heirs.

These are the men sworn of the king's council:

The Archbishop of Canterbury, The bishop of Worcester, the earl of Leicester; the earl of Gloucester, the earl Marshal, Peter of Savoy, the count of Aumale, the earl of Warwick, the earl of Hereford, John Mansel, John Fitz-Geoffrey, Peter de Montfort, Richard de Gray, Roger Mortimer, James Audley.

The twelve on the king's side have chosen from the twelve on the side of the community the earl Roger Marshal and Hugh Bigod. And the party of the community has chosen from the twelve who are on the side of the king the earl of Warwick and John Mansel.

And these four have power to elect the council of the king; and when they have made the election, they shall designate those to the twenty-four. And that shall hold on which the majority of these four agree.

These are the twelve who have been elected by the barons, on behalf of the whole community of the land, to consider common needs along with the king's council at the three annual parliaments:

The lord bishop of London, the earl of Winchester, the earl of Hereford, Philip Basset, John de Balliol, John de Verdun, John de Grey, Roger de Sumery, Roger de Mohaut, Hugh Despencer, Thomas de Gresley, Giles d'Argentein.

These are the twenty-four appointed by the community to consider aid for the king:

The bishop of Worcester, the bishop of London, the bishop of Salisbury, the earl of Leicester, the earl of Gloucester, the earl Marshal, Peter of Savoy, the earl of Hereford, the count of Aumale, the earl of Winchester, the earl of Oxford, John Fitz-Geoffrey, John de Grey, John de Balliol, Roger Mortimer, Roger de Sumery, Roger de Mohaut, Peter de Montfort, Thomas de Gresley, Fulk of Kerdiston, Giles d'Argentein, John Kyriel, Philip of Basset, Giles of Erdington.

And if any one of these cannot or will not be present, those who are present shall have power to elect another in his place.

Concerning the state of Holy Church:

It should be remembered that the state of Holy Church is to be amended by the twenty-four chosen to reform the state of the kingdom of England — at what time and place they think best, according to the powers that they hold by writ of the king of England.

Concerning the chief justice:

Furthermore that a chief justice — or two — shall be appointed; also what power he shall have; and that he shall be for only one year, so that at the end of the year he shall render account of his term before the king and the royal council and before the man who is to follow him.

Concerning the treasurer and the exchequer:

The same with regard to the treasurer; so that he shall render account at the end of the year. And according to the ordinance of the said twenty-four, other good men are to be appointed to the exchequer, whither all the issues of the land are to come, and not elsewhere. And let that be amended which seems in need of amendment.

Concerning the chancellor:

The same with regard to the chancellor; so that he shall render account of his term at the end of the year, and that merely by the king's will he shall seal nothing out of course, but shall do so by the council that surrounds the king.

Concerning the power of the justice and of the bailiffs:

The chief justice has power to redress the misdeeds of all other justices, of bailiffs, of earls, of barons, and of all other people, according to the rightful law of the land. And writs are to be pleaded according to the law of the land in the proper places. And the justices shall accept nothing unless it is a present of bread and wine and like things: namely, such meat and drink as have been customarily brought for the day to the tables of the chief men. And this same regulation shall be understood for all the king's councillors and all his bailiffs. And no bailiff, by virtue of his office or of some plea, shall take any fee, either by his own hand or in any manner through another person. And if he is convicted, let him be punished; likewise the man who gives. And the king, if it is suitable, shall give fees to his justices and to his people who serve him, so that they shall have no need of taking anything from others.

Concerning the sheriffs:

As sheriffs there shall be appointed loyal persons, good men who are landholders; so that in each county there shall be as sheriff a feudal tenant of the same county, who shall well, loyally, and justly treat the people of the county. And he shall take no fee; that he shall be sheriff for no more than a year in all; that during the year he shall render his accounts at the exchequer and be responsible for his term; that the king, from the royal income, shall make allowance to him in proportion to his receipts, so that he may rightly keep the county; and that he shall take no fees, neither he nor his bailiffs. And if they are convicted, let them be punished.

It should be remembered that, with regard to the Jewry and the wardens of the Jewry, such reforms are to be established as shall carry out the oath in this respect.

Concerning the escheators:

Good escheators are to be appointed. And they shall take nothing from goods of deceased persons whose lands ought to be in the king's hands; but that, if a debt is owing to him, the escheators shall have free administration of the goods until they have carried out the king's wishes — and this according to the provision in the charter of liberties. Also inquiry shall be made concerning the misdeeds committed there by escheators, and that redress shall be made for such. Nor shall tallage or anything else be taken, except as it should be according to the charter of liberties.

The charter of liberties is to be strictly observed.

Concerning the exchange of London:

It should be remembered to establish reforms touching the exchange of London; also touching the city of London and all the other cities of the king, which have been brought to shame and ruin by tallages and other oppressions.

Concerning the household of the king and queen:

It should be remembered to reform the household of the king and queen.

Concerning the parliaments, as to how many shall be held annually and in what manner:

It should be remembered that the twenty-four have ordained that there are to be three parliaments a year: the first on the octave of St. Michael, the second on the morrow of Candlemas, and the third on the first day of June, that is to say, three weeks before St. John [this means 6th October, 3rd February and 3rd June]. To these three parliaments the chosen councillors of the king shall come, even if they are not summoned, in order to examine the state of the kingdom and to consider the common needs of the kingdom and likewise of the king; and by the king's command also at other times, whenever it is necessary. So too it should be remembered that the community is to elect twelve good men, who shall come to the three parliaments and at other times, when there is need and when the king and his council summon them to consider the affairs of the king and the kingdom. And the community shall hold as established whatever these twelve shall do — and this is to reduce the cost to the community. Fifteen are to be named by these four men — that is to say, by the earl Marshal, the earl of Warwick, Hugh le Bigot, and John Mansel — who have been elected by the twenty-four to name the aforesaid fifteen, who are to form the king's council. And they are to be confirmed by the aforesaid twenty-four, or by the majority of those men. And they shall have the power of advising the king in good faith concerning the government of the kingdom and concerning all matters that pertain to the king or the kingdom; and of amending and redressing everything that they shall consider in need of amendment or redress. And [they shall have authority] over the chief justice and over all other people. And if they cannot all be present, that shall be firm and established which the majority of them shall enact.

Appendix IV: The Provisions of Westminster 1259

The Provisions of Westminster were a counter-offer to the Provisions of Oxford produced the previous year. Prince Edward led the movement that reacted to the alleged failure of the baronial party to uphold their side of the agreement at Oxford and took the chance to weaken the control it tried to place in the king. This set of provisions was largely accepted and observed by Henry.

In the year 1259 from the Incarnation of the Lord, the forty-third of the reign of King Henry, son of King John, at a meeting of the lord king and his magnates at Westminster on Michaelmas fortnight, the provisions hereinunder written, by the common counsel and consent of the said king and his magnates, were enacted and published by the same king and his magnates in this form.

1. With regard to the performance of suit to the courts of the magnates and of other lords who have such courts, it is provided and established by general agreement that no one who is enfeoffed by charter shall henceforth be distrained to perform suit to his lord's court, unless he is specifically obliged by the tenor of his charter to perform the suit; with the sole exception of those whose ancestors were accustomed to perform suit of this kind, or who, before the first crossing of the said lord king into Brittany — after the time of which crossing twenty-nine and a half years had elapsed down to the time that this constitution was made.

2. If anyone distrains1 his tenant contrary to this provision let quick justice be done about it in the king's court as is subsequently provided.

3. If it happens that an inheritance is divided between several parceners, the other parceners shall help with the cost of doing the suit reasonably. And if tenants are enfeoffed with the same inheritance the lord many no longer demand more than one suit as is aforesaid.

4. If any lords distrain their tenants contrary to this provision, than at the complaint of the tenant let them be attached to come to the king's court at an early date to answer them; on which day they shall have one excuse for nonappearance if they are in the realm and the beasts in this connection are to be released immediately to the plaintiff and so remain until the action between them is terminated. And these who have levied the distress do not appear on the date that was given them by way of essoin or on the first date if they were not essoined, then shall the sheriff of the district be ordered to cause them to appear on another date, and if they do not appear the sheriff shall be ordered to distrain them by all that they possess in his bailiwick, and he be answerable to the king for the issue therefrom and that he produce them in person in court on another day. And then on that day if they do not appear the plaintiff shall go away without day and the beast shall stay released, so that the lords henceforth shall not be able to distrain them on that account until they have their deraignment [i.e. their suit or case] by and action in the king's court, saving to the lords their rights in respect of the suits whatever they dare to institute legal proceedings about them. And the lords are to come to the court of the king to answer. And the plaintiffs can have

their plaints; then by judgement of the court they shall recover the damages they have had by reason of this distress.

5. On the other hand let lords distrain their suit by the same speedy justice tenants who withhold from their lords suits which they owe and which they have done since the aforesaid term, and recover their damages just as their tenants do from them. As to suits which were withheld before the aforesaid term the common law shall run as usual.

6. With regard to the sheriff's tourn, it is provided that, unless their presence is specially demanded, archbishops, bishops, abbots, priors, earls, and barons, or other men of religion, or women, shall not of necessity come thither. But tourns are to be held in the way they were held in the time of the predecessors of our lord king who now is. And if any have lands in several hundreds they are not to be distrained or to attend tourns except where they live. And the tourns shall be held according to the form of the king's Great Charter, and as they were customarily held in the time of the kings John and Richard.

7. It is also provided that neither on the eyres of the justices nor in the counties nor in the courts of barons nor in a liberty or elsewhere shall fines henceforth be taken from anybody for miskenning, or on condition that people are not molested.

.8. Furthermore it is provided that in a plea of dower that is before the bench one should give four days in the year at least, namely one day each term. And if one can give more, one should give more.

9. Like is essoins of darein presentment and or quarteimpedit of churches that are vacant one should give a day every fortnight or every three weeks according to whether the district is a long way off or near. And if anyone who is impleaded by quare impedit does not come on the first day and does not have himself essoined, on another day if he does not come let him there be distrained by all his lands and his chattels by the great distress, as said above.

10. Moreover, with regard to charters of exemption and liberty, that those securing them are not to be put on assizes, juries, or recognitions, it is provided that, if their oath is so essential that without it justice cannot be administered as in the grand assize or in a perambulation or where they are witnesses, by name either in charters in writing, in attaints or in other case which cannot be decided without the oaths of knights, in such cases they shall be forced to swear, saving to them their aforesaid liberty and exemption in other respects.

11. No one except the king is in future to levy a distress outside his own fee or on the king's highway where everybody can come and go.

12. In addition, if it happens that the lord after his tenant's death takes his lands into his hand becuase the heir is under age and then

when the heir comes of age will not surrender his land without being sued, that the heir get back his land into his hand by writ of mort d'ancestor together with the damaged he has sustained on account of the detention after his full age. And likewise if the heir is of age when his ancestor dies and in as the heir apparent who is regarded and accepted, that the chief lord may not evict him, or take anything or remove anything, except take a simple seisinonly. And if the chief lord keeps him out, so that he is allowed to obtain a writ of mort d'ancestor or of cosinage, he may recover his land and his damages as by writ of novel disseisin.

13. On wardship of socage it is so provided that if land which is held in socage is held in wardship by his kinsmen because of the heir who is under age, the guardian cannot do waste, sale or any destruction of the land that is in his wardship, but shall safely keep it for the benefit of the heir so that when he comes of age the guardian shall answer to him loyally for the issues and the profits of the thing, saving to him his reasonable outlay. Nor can he sell or give the marriage except to the advantage of the minor.

14. In addition it is provided that the escheators, those appointed to hold inquests, justices assigned to take assizes and justices assigned to hear and determine pleas of trespass, or any other bailiff, have no power to amerce for failure to obey a common summons, except the chief justice and the justices in eyre for all pleas.

15. It is likewise provided that no man of religion can buy any land without the agreement of the lord, namely that lord who is nearest except for the mesne lord.

16. It is likewise provided on essoins that no one henceforth is to be distrained to take an oath in warranty of the essoin either in county court or elsewhere. Hereafter no one but the king shall hold in his court a plea concerning false judgment rendered in a court of his tenant; for pleas of this sort especially pertain to the crown and dignity of the king.

17. It is provided that if anyone is distrained and his beasts are kept against gage and surety, the sheriff when complaint has been made can freely release the beasts in accordance with the law of the land, if they are taken outside a liberty, without contradiction and without hindrance from him who took them. And if they are within a liberty and the bailiff will not release them the sheriff shall release them for default on the part of the bailiff of the liberty.

18. Without the king's writ, no one may henceforth distrain his free tenants to respond concerning their free tenements or anything that pertains to their free tenements. Nor may he cause his free tenants against their will to take oaths; so that no one may do this without the king's precept.

19. It is provided that no bailiff who ought to render account is to take himself off away from his lord. And if he will not render his account

and has no land or tenement whereby he can be distrained he is to be attached in person, so that the sheriff in whose bailiwick he is found shall make him come to render account if he is in arrears.

20. It is provided that no farmers during the period of their farm shall do sale or exile of woods, houses, men or other things belonging to the tenement which they have at farm, unless they have special permission in writing to make the sale. And if they do it and are convicted, they shall render the damages for it.

21. Hereafter itinerant justices shall not amerce vills on their eyres because particular twelve-year-old persons do not come before sheriffs and coroners for inquests concerning a man's death or other matters pertaining to the crown; so long as, nevertheless, enough men come from those vills for satisfactorily carrying out such inquests.

22. No coroner or sheriff or other bailiff from now on shall amerce townships because they do not come to inquests. But when they find a default, let it be put in the coroner's roll and presented before the justices in eyre who have power to amerce townships and no one else.

23. No judgment of murder shall henceforth be rendered before the justices in a case that is adjudged merely one of accident; but murder shall be proper in the case of a man feloniously slain, and not otherwise.

24. No justice or sheriff or other bailiff is from now on to amerce townships for hue and cry raised and not followed up if it is not raised for reasonable cause, such as for the death of a man, robbery, wounding or similar case with pertains specially to the crown.

25. Furthermore is any one is vouched to warranty in a plea of land in the eyre of the justices he is not from now on to be amerced for not being present, inasmuch as no free man ought to be amerced for default except on the first day of the coming of the justices. But if he who is vouched to warranty is then within the same county, then it is for the sheriff to cause him to come on the third day or the fourth according to whether he is far away or near, as is the practice in the eyre of the justices. And if he is living in another county he shall have a reasonable summons of 15 days in accordance with the common law.

26. Furthermore than justices are provided to go through the land. And there is to be one of the 12 or others of the community to see that justice is done to plaintiffs and to all others. And so they are to see that order is sent to the counties that establishments made for the benefit if the realm, those that are made and those that will, are to be kept.

27. Likewise that the provisions that have been made since the beginning of these establishments are to be upheld and maintained.

28. Furthermore the rolls of these establishments are to be read and affirmed. And the charters of liberties and of the forests are to be kept and maintained. It is likewise provided that no one is to come and attend parliament with horses or with arms, or armed, unless he is specifically ordered by the king or by his councillor by writ for the common business of the land.

29. Where itinerant justices were lately on circuit, good men and sage are to be appointed to hear and inquire into all complaints that could have been terminated without writ during the last seven years; similarly that if anyone has not made plaint before the seven years and has not had justice he is to recover to get it. And they are to have the power to inquire concerning the sheriffs and their bailiffs, how they have behaved towards the district since their establishment.

30. They are to enquire also concerning the bailiffs of the rich men of the land and concerning the rich men themselves.

31. Itinerant justices are to have the same power as sheriffs in their eyre; in addition they are to have their own power throughout their eyre. And there are to be provided from the less important people of the council two or three who are to be constantly in attendance on the king between parliaments. And they are to be changed at each parliament and others appointed. And their action is to be viewed at each parliament. And if there is anything in it to be amended, it is to be amended by those of the council. And if any important business arises between parliament that cannot be settled by the aforesaid two or three, or can not well be delayed until the next parliament, all those of the council are to the summoned by writ to settle this business. And there is to be put in the writ the occasion of the summons, if this is not secret. And if any of the others of the council, or of the aforesaid two or three, comes to king's council as long as the business lasts both as to their own business and as to the king's business for which they are summoned.

32. It is to be remembered that two good men are to be provided to sell the wardships that are now of right in the king's hand.

33. Furthermore that two good men are to be provided to ordain equally with the council of the exchequer concerning sheriffs and counties.

34. Furthermore people are to be provided to go with the king to France. And who shall stay in the land with the Justiciar.

35. And that an answer is to be given to the envoys from Wales. And it is to be provided how the writs of the provisions and of the establishments shall issue from the chancery without delay. And likewise about the envoys who shall go to Rome.

36. For selling the wardships the Justiciar, the treasurer, Mr Thomas of Wymondham, Sir Roger of Thirkleby and Sir Henry of Bath

are to be appointed immediately. And that these same are to ordain and provide on what items the queen ought to get gold.

37. It is provided that these same are to come to the exchequer and view the sums of all kinds of tallages that have been imposed since the king's accession. And that they are to estimate how much each one can raise. And these same are to provide how one ought to proceed in pleas about customs and about services. And these same are to provide how one ought to proceed in escheats and in wardships.

38. It is to be provided which people ought to go to correct trespasses and wrongs done, which can be determined without writ.

39. The Justiciar is to provide this with the others. And which are to be at the bench with the justices, and which at the exchequer.

40. It is provided that four knights are to be appointed in each country to observe the wrongs which sheriffs do; that if it happen that they do wrongs, these four are to admonish the sheriffs to have them corrected. And if they will not correct them, let them enter the wrongs done onto a roll, and show them to the chief justices at the end of the year when he asks for them; or earlier if he asks for them, if so be that the plaintiffs to who the wrongs have been done are willing to prosecute. And that these aforesaid four knights are not to have any authority to interfere with the performance by the sheriffs of their office.

41. If a clerk is accused of the death of a man, of robbery, or larceny or other crime that concerns the crown, then it is by command of the king delivered on bail to 12 good men that they have him before the justices or released by pledges without command of the king if the aforesaid 12 or the pledges have his person before the justices on the first day, they are not in future to be amerced, even though the clerk will not answer or stand his trial in the king's court, insomuch as they were not pledged or going surety for anything other than to produce the clerk's person in court.

42. The justiciar, the treasurer Sir Henry of Bath, Sir Roger of Thirkleby and the barons of the exchequer are to provide this year instantly which good men, upright and sage, are to be sheriffs this year. And they are to be vavasours in the shire they are sheriffs of. On the other hand, next year at the last county court before Michaelmas there are to be chosen in full county court four good men, upright and who will be advantageous to the king and to the shire in this office. And they are to be at the exchequer at Michaelmas. And the barons are to pick out the most sufficient in their estimation.

43. Furthermore good men are to be chosen by the Justiciar and the treasurer to provide during this advent and the festival days, against the next parliament, what is to be amended at the great exchequer and at the exchequer of the Jews. And by the same reasonable sustenance is to be provided for those who are at either exchequer.

44. It is provided that Sir Thomas de Gresley, justice of the forest, is to take Nicholas of Ramsey and three knights from each county and they are to enquire into the condition of the forests, of vert and venison, and of sales and destructions, and by whom they are done. And they are to enquire about malpractices in connection with forest pleas and by whom they were established and from what time; and when he has done this he is to make it known to the king and his council.

45. It is to be done the same way with the forests beyond the Trent; that the chief justice provide four knights and enquire about all the forests beyond Trent in the way aforesaid.

46. The archbishop, the bishop of Worcester, the earl marshal, the earl of Warwick are to be with the Justiciar to deal with the important business of the kingdom as long as the king is out of England. And all those of the council and the community's twelve who stay in England are to be summoned if needs be. Sir Philip Basset and Sir Roger Mortimer are to be constantly with the Justiciar.

47. It is provided that the Justiciar is to provide that the castellans are to have reasonable sustenance for keeping the king's castles and maintaining them. It is provided to put two good men from the community for from the community's twelve or from others with the justices at the bench. And that they are to see that justice is done. And in the same way two good men from the community or from the community's twelve or from others are to be put at the exchequer.

These are the provisions and the establishments made at Westminster at the Michaelmas parliament by the king and his council and the twelve chosen by the common counsel before the community of England which then were at Westminster in the forty third year of the reign of Henry the son of king John.

Appendix V: The Dictum of Kenilworth 1265

When the Second Barons' War was almost over, a garrison held out at Kenilworth Castle, defying the king for six months. As Parliament met nearby, the influence of the papal legate Ottobuono can perhaps be seen in the conciliatory nature of the Dictum, which effectively maps out for rebels the road back to royal favour and to the recovery of their land and possessions. It importantly established a legal mechanism for peace that could be relied upon by all sides.

In the name of the Holy and Undivided Trinity, amen. To the honour and glory of Almighty God, the Father, the Son, and the Holy Ghost, of the glorious and most excellent Mother of God the Virgin Mary, and of all saints by whose merits and intercessions we are governed on Earth. To the honour of the Holy Catholic and Apostolic Roman Church, which is the mother and ruler of all the faithful; to the honour of the Most Holy Father and out lord Clement, ruler of that universal Church; to the honour and good prosperous and peaceable estate of the most Christian prince, lord Henry, illustrious king of the whole realm of England, and of the English Church. We, Walter, bishop of Exeter, Walter, bishop of Bath and Wells, Nicholas, bishop of Worcester, and Richard, bishop of St David's, Gilbert de Clare, earl of Gloucester and Hertford, and Humphrey de Bohun, earl of Hereford, Philip Basset, John Balliol, Robert Walerand, Alan de la Zuche, Roger de Somery, and Warin de Bassingbourne have been given full power from the lord king, from other nobles, counsellors of the realm, and from the leading men of England according to the terms enrolled in letters published and sanctioned by the seals of the king and others, to provide for the state of the realm especially in the matter of the disinherited, favouring no person in this matter, but having God alone before our eyes, doing all things as in the sight of Almighty God and in order, rightly preferring the Head to the Members.

1. We declare and provide that the most serene prince, lord Henry, illustrious king of England, shall have, fully receive, and freely exercise his dominion, authority, and royal power without impediment or contradiction of anyone, whereby the royal dignity may be offended contrary to approved rights, laws, and long established customs, and that full obedience and humble attention be given to the same lord king, to his lawful mandates and pre-cepts, by one and all, greater and lesser men of the king-dom. And one and all shall, through writs, seek justice and be answerable for justice at the court of the lord king as was the custom before the time of the disorder.

2. Furthermore, we ask the same lord king, and with reverence urge him in his piety, that he appoint, for doing and rendering justice, such men as, seeking not their own interests but those of God and right, shall justly settle the affairs of subjects according to the praiseworthy laws and customs of the kingdom and thereby strengthen the throne and royal majesty with justice.

3. Likewise we ask and urge the lord king that he fully protect and observe the liberties of the Church, and the charters of liberties and of the forest, which he is expressly bound to keep and hold by his own oath.

4. Also the lord king shall provide that the grants which, up to the present, he has made freely and not under compulsion shall be observed; and he will establish firmly other necessary measures which are devised by his men at his pleasure. Furthermore, the English Church shall be fully restored to its liberties and customs which it had and should have had before the time of such dis-orders, and shall be permitted to exercise them.

.5. We declare and provide that the lord king shall completely excuse and pardon each and all of those who, from the beginning and up to the present time, because of the present disorders of the realm, have offended against or done any injury to him or the royal crown and who return to his peace within forty days after the publication of this our ordinance. The lord king shall in no way for any cause or reason, because of these past injuries or offences, bear any vengeance against these offenders nor shall he inflict any penalty or revenge against them in life, limb, imprisonment, exile, or fine. Excluded are those mentioned below in this our present ordinance.

6. We also declare and provide that all places, rights, goods, and all other things pertaining to the royal crown shall be restored to that crown, and to the lord king, by those who detain them in their possession unless they can show that hold them by reasonable warrant from the lord king or from his ancestors.

7. Also, we declare and provide that all bonds, deeds, and instruments which the lord king, his eldest son the Lord Edward, or other faithful subjects have hitherto made or drawn up by reason of the Provisions of Oxford or because of the disorder present in the realm, at the instance of the late Simon de Montfort, earl of Leicester, and his accomplices, are absolutely nullified and destroyed and shall be held completely annulled and valueless. The injurious and damnable acts of the said Simon and his accomplices, together with the agreements about land made by them when he exercised power, are nullified and have no force.

8. Humbly begging both the lord legate and the lord king that the lord legate shall absolutely forbid, under distraint of the Church, that Simon, earl of Leicester, be considered to be holy or justs as he died excommunicate according to the belief of the Holy Church. And that the vain and fatuous miracles told of him by others shall not at any time pass any lips. And that the lord king shall agree strictly to forbid this under pain of corporal punishment.

9. We reverently and humbly beseech our venerable father Lord Ottobono, cardinal deacon of St. Adrian and apostolic legate of the Holy See, that, since he knows it expedient for the king, he should announce that benefit of absolution may be given both to the lord king and to other men of the realm both great and small, who have made little effort to observe the sworn charters, to the observation of which all are bound by the sentence of excommunication pronounced against all who do not observe the said charters.

10. Likewise we beseech and urge, saving the approved customs of the realm, that no man of any condition shall take corn or any manner of victual, or any other goods under guise of borrowing or provision of future payment, without licence of those who own the things or goods.

11. We commend London and urge and beseech the lord king that he provide, by his council, for the reform of the state of the city in the matter of lands, rents, power, and liberties, and that provision of this kind be made immediately.

12. Concerning the condition and business of the disinherited, amongst other things which we have ordained and established, wishing to proceed in the way of God and the path of equity, we have been led to provide, by assent of the venerable father Ottobono cardinal deacon of St. Adrian and apostolic legate of the Holy See and by assent of the noble Henry of Almain, having similar power, that there be no disherison but rather ransom, as follows. Those who fought at the start of the war and are still in arms ; those who violently and maliciously held Northampton against the king ; those who fought against and assailed the king at Lewes; those captured at Kenilworth after having sacked Winchester; those who have in other ways opposed the king and have not been pardoned; those who fought at Evesham; those who were in the battle at Chesterfield; those who freely and of their own will sent their followers against the king or his son; the bailiffs and officers of the earl of Leicester who robbed their neighbours and caused murder, arson, and other evils to be committed shall pay five times the annual value of their lands. If they pay this redemption they shall recover their lands. Furthermore, if any one shall be forced to sell land, only he who holds it by gift of the lord king may buy it, if he offer as much as any other buyer and on the same terms. Similarly, if he who wishes to redeem his lands be forced to place the land to farm no one shall have greater right to farm the land than he who holds it of the gift of the lord king, and he shall have it on these terms that he be willing to give as much as any-one else to hold it at farm. He who gives satisfaction for all his land shall have full possession ; if satisfaction be given for a half or a third part he shall immediately have a half or a third part. If the person redeeming his lands has not fulfilled his obligations at the last appointed term, half the remaining land shall remain with those to whom the land has been granted by the lord king. The person redeeming the land shall be free, within the said term, to see all or part of the land in the manner above mentioned, and similarly he may place the land to farm.

13. If anyone has woods and wishes to sell them for his ransom, he who holds them by gift of the lord king shall appoint a trustworthy representative who shall receive the money while the disinherited tenant, who sells the woods, shall name a representative whom he trusts. These two receivers shall, in their presence, pay the money which they have received for the woods to those to whom the ransom is due.

14. Be it noted that earl Ferrers shall be punished by a ransom of seven times the annual value of his lands. Knights and squires who were robbers and collaborated with the leading robbers in skirmishes and plundering raids, if they have no lands but have goods shall pay as ransom one half of their goods. Further-more they shall find a trustworthy surety that they will henceforth preserve the peace of the king and of the realm. Those who have no possessions shall swear on the Holy Gospel of God, and find a trustworthy surety that henceforth they will preserve the peace of the king and of the realm. Furthermore, they shall suffer fitting and satisfactory penance under judgement of the Church. Excepted are the banished whom the king alone may remit.

15. The lords of heirs under age and in ward shall pay ransom for them to the grantee. When the heirs attain their majority they shall pay the ransom to their lords according to the terms under which others pay in two or three years. The lords of such lands shall have custody of the heirs with rights of marriage until the majority of the heirs. If, however, the lords of the lands refuse to pay the ransom to those to whom the lands were given by the lord king, these shall have custody of the heirs with rights of marriage with-out disparagement until the full age of the heirs who should then pay ransom to the grantee as others have paid and on the same terms.

16. Wardships which belong to the lord king shall remain with those to whom they have been given by the lord king. When the heirs shall come of full age they shall pay ransom at the same terms as others and no waste shall be made by those who have custody. If such waste be made justice shall be enforced against them as is contained in Magna Carta.

17. All persons in the castle shall be in the common way and form of peace, except Henry de Hastings and those who mutilated the king's messenger. These shall be punished by a ransom of seven times the annual value of their lands or they shall place themselves at the king's mercy.

18. The king shall by just award pronounce his pleasure concerning any one who supported the lord king before the battle of Lewes and was disinherited after the battle because he was unwilling to support the king's son and come to his aid.

19. Woods shall not be sold or wasted in any way by those who hold them now except after failure to make payment at the last term. Those to whom the lands have been given by the lord king shall have necessaries for the maintenance or restoration of dwellings. If they act otherwise they shall be severely punished.

20. If there be anyone about whom it is feared that he wishes to cause or wage war the legate and the lord king shall provide for themselves such security as they shall deem expedient, sending him

out of the realm for a fixed time or otherwise as they shall see fit. Nevertheless if it so happens that such a person be hindered from paying his ransom he shall not on this account be dis-inherited.

21. If there be anyone (who is dissatisfied) with this ordinance let him submit to the judgement of the court of the lord king before the feast of St. Hilary [13 January 1267]. If any man be out of the kingdom he shall have the respite granted to those across the sea according to the law and custom of the land, provided he remain in peace, otherwise he shall not be in this form of peace.

22. As the king is bound to many who have aided him and have faithfully stood by him, for whom he has provided no lands, and some have more than they should have, the king shall provide for them from the ransoms which are collected, lest this be a cause of further unrest.

23. Furthermore let the legate, the king, and Henry of Almain stipulate that there be chosen twelve who will diligently and faithfully execute these things and let the lord king and his heirs cause them to be firmly observed and maintained. Let them examine and fulfil the ordinances made by the twelve selected, in the manner of the regulations which have already been enacted. Otherwise they shall make true and reasonable estimates accord-ing to what the twelve executors shall provide.

24. Those holding lands at farm, who were against the lord king, shall lose the farms; those who keep the farms, saving the rights of the lords of e lands, shall pay an annual rent and at the end of the term the lands shall revert to the true lord.

25. Concerning castles which were built by charter, and by consent of the lord king, without the consent of the disinherited. We ordain that the lord of the land pay the cost, which was imposed before the proclamation by consent of the king or make reasonable exchange of land.

26. Laymen who openly supported the interests of the earl and his supporters, gaining followers by lies and false tales, rousing them to the side of the earl and his accomplices and withdrawing them from supporting the lord king and his son, shall be punished by the payment of twice the annual value of their lands.

27. Those who were coerced or driven by fear to battle but who neither fought nor did evil; weaklings who because of force or fear sent their military following against the king or his son; those who were coerced or driven by fear to be robbers and made plundering raids with the leading robbers but who, when possible, ceased plundering and returned to their homes, remaining there at peace, shall pay a ransom of one year's value of their lands.

28. Those who knowingly bought the goods of others shall restore the value of the things which they bought. They are at the mercy

of the lord king for they did this unjustly, as the lord king forbade this six months ago.

29. Those who, at the command of the earl of Leicester, entered Northampton but neither fought nor did harm, if they fled to the church when they saw the king coming and this is proved by lawful men; those who did not hold lands of the earl of Leicester but obeyed his command shall pay a half year's value of their lands. Those who held lands of the earl are in the mercy of the king.

30. Powerless people and others who did no harm shall immediately recover their lands and receive their damages in the court of the lord king. Let the accuser so be punished so that henceforth the king will not easily believe them and let them be punished as were those who unjustly caused the king's faithful subjects to be disinherited, nevertheless without danger of mutilation or disherison. Those who are maliciously accused shall immediately have their lands and recover their damages in the king's court, as mentioned above.

31. Women shall have their heritages and dowers of their first husbands. They shall have the lands of their husbands49 in the manner in which the king has ordained, and the lands shall be ransomed.

32. The ransom of those who opposed the king shall be paid. No ransom shall be paid by those who were not against the king, instead they shall immediately recover their lands and recover damages as mentioned above.

33. Mention has been made of those maliciously accused, and receivers shall be punished as mentioned above. Submission has been made to the king, either by the other lords through you or let it prevail in its own right through a friendly or imposed peace.

34. We say nothing of Simon de Montfort, the countess, and the sons of the earl, as the lord king has placed their case in the hands of the king of France.

35. All those who have been received in peace by those so appointed shall remain in the condition in which they were so received. All who have been ransomed shall not be bound to answer for damages and for trespasses committed by them against those whom they fought at the time of the unrest. Mutual damages and trespasses are excused, saving, nevertheless, the right of action of each man who was not involved in the unrest and saving, as far as he is concerned, that which pertains to the Church.

36. Furthermore, as it is considered to be most dangerous that castles be in the control of those who acted evilly against the king, we award and ordain concerning the castles of Eardisley [Herefordshire], Bytham [Lincs.], and Chartley [Staffs.] that a reasonable exchange be given for them.

37. Henceforward all shall keep a firm peace and none shall commit murder, arson, robbery, or any other violation of the peace. He who shall do this and shall be convicted shall have judgement and law according to the custom of the realm.

38. Furthermore all of those whom it concerns shall swear on the Holy Gospels that they will not, on account of the disorders, take revenge nor procure, consent to, nor support such action. If anyone takes revenge he shall be punished by the court of the lord king and let those who have harmed the Church make satisfaction to it.

39. Furthermore, he who does not consent to this decision shall be a public enemy of the king, of his sons and of the community. Laymen and clergy, allowed by canon and lay law, may prosecute him as an enemy of the peace of the church and of the realm.

40. Those who are imprisoned or in custody, having found a sufficient and reasonable surety, shall be liberated by pledge or by another competent and reasonable surety according to the ordinance of the legate and of the king.

Given and published in the castle at Kenilworth, on the second day before the kalends of November [31 October], in the year of grace 1266, the fifty-first year of the reign of the lord Henry, king of England.

Bibliography

Devon, F., *Issues of the Exchequer* (1837)
Gasquet, A., *Henry the Third and the Church* (1910)
Giles, J. A., *Matthew Paris's English History* (1854)
Halliwell, J. O., *Letters of the Kings of England* (1848)
Hardy, T. D., *Rymer's Foedera* (1869)
Hutton, W. H., *Simon de Montfort and His Cause* (1907)
Lawrence, M. P., *The Life of St Edmund* (1996)
Luard, H. R., *On the Relations Between England and Rome* (1877)
Norgate, K., *The Minority of Henry the Third* (1912)
Norwich, J. J., *The Popes* (2012)
Morris, M., *Edward I* (2008)
Powick, M., *The Thirteenth Century* (1962)
Wickham Legg, L. G., *English Coronation Records* (1901)
Wright, W. A., *The Metrical Chronicle of Robert of Gloucester* (1887)

Index